CONFLICT
Recognizing Human Dignity as a Solution to Humanity's Greatest Challenges

FREEDOM AND RESPONSIBILITY

INSTITUTE

Copyright © 2024 Freedom and Responsibility Institute™ LLC

All rights reserved.

eBook ISBN: 979-8-9917066-0-5
Paperback ISBN: 979-8-9917066-1-2
Hardback ISBN: 979-8-9917066-2-9

DEDICATION

This book is dedicated to all – past and present – who have shown us the possibilities of human dignity, and to future generations who will continue to pave the way for an international culture rooted in respect for the inherent value and dignity of each human being.

PREFACE

Beyond natural disasters or disease, conflict has been a persistent cause of human suffering throughout history. Yet not all conflicts are destructive. Healthy conflict has driven humanity to innovate, solve problems, and advance throughout millennia. However, the conflict we address in this book is of a different kind – the kind that degrades humanity by placing ideologies through political power and material interests above the dignity and intrinsic worth of the human person.

From the Chinese dynasties or the Pharaohs in Egypt, civilizations have been marred by slavery, division, and power struggles. Looking into the recent global tragedies of the World Wars, history offers stark examples of what happens when the dignity of individuals is cast aside in the pursuit of dominance or ideology. In each of these cases, *human-degrading conflict* has not only brought immense suffering but has also set back societal progress, undermining the very values that could have enhanced the quality of life on earth.

To understand *human-degrading conflict* and explore lasting solutions, we must first recognize the shared principles that uphold basic human needs and dignity. These principles, when universally embraced, can serve as the foundation for a world where conflict no longer leads to unnecessary suffering. By centering human dignity in our worldview, we open the door to conflict resolution that preserves humanity.

As we explore this subject, it is vital to understand how individual perspectives shape our worldviews and the course of history. A person's mindset – whether grounded in empathy and respect for others or driven by fear and self-interest – leads to one of two outcomes: the solidification of fixed viewpoints, or the cultivation of a worldview grounded in respect for human dignity and for life itself. We can only move beyond the cycles of violence that have plagued humanity for centuries by fostering the latter.

We have all seen first-hand perspectives shape decisions, whether in small-scale interactions or in large geopolitical events. For instance, the use of enslaved peoples in the Atlantic slave trade demonstrates how entire groups can fall into acceptance of human-degrading conflict if it benefits them, or how the horrors of the holocaust can become normal for people under the influence of power, or even how the more recent dehumanizing policies of apartheid in South Africa subjugated millions based solely on race. These conflicts remind us that without a commitment to human dignity, we are doomed to repeat the same mistakes, with painful and devastating results.

This lesson is particularly critical as we stand at the threshold of unprecedented technological advancement. The rapid pace of technological innovation – Artificial Intelligence (AI), automation, and biotechnology – presents new opportunities but also new risks. If these technologies are developed and deployed without considering the dignity of the human person, we risk perpetuating the same human-degrading conflicts we have seen throughout history, only with far greater consequences. Learning from the past is essential if we are to guide technology in ways that uphold human values rather than undermine them.

This book is not simply an exploration of past failures but a call to action. It offers a framework for understanding how we can create a future where human dignity is central to decision-making – where our differences can be addressed through reason, empathy, and mutual respect, rather than through force. The lessons of history are clear: when dignity is sacrificed, conflict inevitably spirals into violence and chaos. But when dignity is preserved, conflict can lead to growth, understanding, and a better future for all.

By reading this book, you are not merely learning about conflict; you are becoming part of the solution. A future where dignity prevails even amidst conflict is not just possible, but absolutely essential for humanity's survival and progress. Together, we can ensure that the next chapter of history is one where human dignity stands at the forefront of every decision, every conflict, and every resolution.

In this book, we not only explore the causes of human-degrading conflict but also offer a framework rooted in the mission of the Freedom and Responsibility Institute – to advance an international culture of human dignity by promoting the responsible use of freedom.

TABLE OF CONTENTS

CONFLICT

RECOGNIZING HUMAN DIGNITY AS A SOLUTION TO HUMANITY'S GREATEST CHALLENGES

PREFACE iv
RATIONALE TO RESEARCHING HUMAN CONFLICT viii

PART ONE: CONFLICT IN THE CONTEXT OF HISTORY 1

I. HUMAN ORIGIN *(7 TO 2.5 MILLION YEARS AGO)* 2
   I.i AN EMPIRICAL APPROACH TO HUMAN CONFLICT 5
   I.ii MILLIONS OF YEARS AGO… TO THE "PRESENT TIME" 8
   I.iii CLOSING THOUGHTS 10

II. PREHISTORY: *(2.5 MILLION YEARS AGO TO 3300 BCE)* 12
   II.i A SUMMARY OF EARLY HUMAN MIGRATION 14
   II.ii THE AGRICULTURAL REVOLUTION 18
   II.iii THE EVOLUTION OF SPIRITUALITY 21
   II.iv THE LANGUAGE BARRIER 23
   II.v CLOSING THOUGHTS 24

III. RECENT HISTORY *(3300 BCE TO PRESENT TIME)* 26
   III.i THE BRONZE AGE CIVILIZATIONS 27
   III.ii CLASSICAL ANTIQUITY AND THE IRON AGE 40
   III.iii THE MIDDLE AGES 72
   III.iv THE INDUSTRIAL AND MODERN ERAS 116
   III.v CLOSING THOUGHTS: THE CYCLE OF CONFLICT 152

PART TWO: HOW CONFLICT AFFECTS US TODAY 159

IV. PERCEPTIONS, PERSPECTIVES, & PSYCHOLOGY 160
   IV.i PERCEPTION IS NOT ALWAYS REALITY 162
   IV.ii PERSPECTIVE IS UNDERSTANDING 164
   IV.iii PSYCHOLOGY: THE GOODNESS PARADOX 168
   IV.iv THE SOURCE OF DIGNITY 172
   IV.v CLOSING THOUGHTS 175

V. POWER AS AN ADDICTION 177
V.i THE DEVELOPMENT OF UNCHECKED POWER 178
V.ii THE FIRST STEP TO OVERCOMING ADDICTION 180
V.iii MINIMIZING OTHERS' BELIEFS TO FEEL COMFORTABLE WITH OUR OWN 182
V.iv CLOSING THOUGHTS 183

VI. GLOBAL CHALLENGES: THREATS TO OUR SURVIVAL 184
VI.i ENVIRONMENTAL CHANGES 185
VI.ii WORLD-ENDING WAR 189
VI.iii BUREAUCRATIC ORGANIZATIONS 192
VI.iv NATURE'S INSTINCT TO EVOLVE 194
VI.v CLOSING THOUGHTS 196

PART THREE: A GLOBALLY UNIFIED HUMANITY 199

VII. BASIC REQUIREMENTS FOR UNITY 200
VII.i ACHIEVING STEADFAST INTERNATIONALISM AMID GLOBALISM'S RISE 202
VII.ii IDEOLOGICAL NARRATIVES AND EDUCATION 205
VII.iii POLITICAL SYSTEMS 207
VII.iv ECONOMIC SYSTEMS 209
VII.v TECHNOLOGY AND COMMUNICATION 211
VII.vi CLOSING THOUGHTS 213

VIII. LEVERAGING TECHNOLOGY TO AID HUMAN DIGNITY 214
VIII.i THE EVOLVED USE OF TECHNOLOGY 215
VIII.ii PHYSICAL TECHNOLOGY 217
VIII.iii DIGITAL TECHNOLOGY 219
VIII.iv HUMAN DIGNITY 222

CONCLUSION 224

RATIONALE TO RESEARCHING HUMAN CONFLICT

The study of human conflict is not an academic exercise alone, it is an essential step in promoting dignity. When dignity is threatened or violated, *human-degrading conflict* often arises. The Freedom and Responsibility Institute, through its commitment to advancing an international culture of dignity, believes that by understanding the roots of conflict, we can safeguard dignity for all. Our commitment to human dignity deepens as we explore the intersections of freedom and responsibility. This research reflects more than theoretical curiosity; it represents a mission to preserve human dignity and life itself, even in the most challenging circumstances.

Throughout history, high-stakes decisions have repeatedly shown how easily human dignity can be overlooked. When objectives take precedence, ethical dilemmas emerge, often leading to decisions that undermine dignity on both sides of a conflict. These challenges are prevalent in a variety of sectors, whether in political, corporate, or social sectors. Whether driven by ambition or self-interest, decision-making processes that benefit an organization or individual can inadvertently devalue others, eroding dignity and weakening relationships.

But how do we protect the dignity of individuals while addressing corporate or even geopolitical demands? And how can we prevent the dehumanization of others in conflict resolution in the hopes of achieving conflict resolution?

Ambition or self-interest can lead even sound-minded individuals to make decisions that, while beneficial for themselves or their organization, diminish the humanity of others. This research seeks to uncover how – through the exploration of our history – to better identify antiquated processes and perspectives that, while serving organizational or personal interests, end up undermining human dignity. By identifying these patterns, we can work to adopt new approaches that prioritize human value.

We live in a world where conflicts that degrade dignity are widespread, often stemming from a lack of recognition and respect for this fundamental value. If we address the core needs and dignity of individuals, many human-degrading conflicts could be prevented. With greater access to information about global conflict, it is essential to understand the origins of human behavior and how it shapes our modern geopolitical landscape, particularly when viewed through the lens of human dignity.

Recent conflicts on the global stage have often been justified by narratives that dehumanize adversaries or obscure the human cost. Such dignity-eroding conflicts span from large-scale international disputes, to politics, to everyday interactions in individual relationships. The research conducted in this book advocates for an approach rooted in dignity – a value that, if universally respected, can help nations and individuals reconcile their differences without resorting to destructive actions.

As these conflicts continue to evolve, one of the most pressing challenges of our time is the rapid advancement of technology, which threatens to outpace our understanding of its impact on humanity. If technological innovations are not oriented toward the dignity of the human person, they risk reshaping humanity in ways that undermine us. By prioritizing human dignity in our actions, we establish the moral foundation necessary for guiding the ethical use and development of technology. If this transformation is approached responsibly, technology can be shaped to uphold human values rather than diminish them.

We must elevate human dignity above our differences and desires. On every level – from individual relationships to global treaties – our perspectives on dignity shape how we understand and respond to conflict. As humanity becomes increasingly interconnected, the survival of our global society depends on the universal recognition of each person's inherent dignity.

This research does not view modern human-degrading conflict as merely a failure of personal character or international diplomacy. It reveals a deeper evolutionary struggle with ethical questions of justice, freedom, and the very essence of our humanity. At its heart, it challenges us to confront how fully we recognize and uphold human dignity, and whether we truly value the humanity of each individual in every decision we make.

By placing human dignity at the foundation of conflict resolution, we believe our differences can be resolved not through force, but through reason, empathy, and mutual respect.

PART ONE

CONFLICT IN THE CONTEXT OF HISTORY

I

HUMAN ORIGIN
(FROM 7 TO 2.5 MILLION YEARS AGO)

In order to understand the present, we must first understand the past – how we came to be and why we behave the way we do. By exploring the origins of humanity from a scientific viewpoint, the first three chapters of this book (Part One) will seek to lay the foundation for why human conflict is such an enduring aspect of human existence. As we analyze historical events, it is important to reflect on two critical insights that we believe shape the nature of conflict:

1. **Humanity's Inherent Desire for Good:** Without bias, when information is clear and the needs of all parties are recognized with empathy, there is a general tendency to act ethically and fairly on an individual level.

2. **Conformity's Role in Conflict:** The *Social Identity Theory* suggests that humans categorize themselves into "in-groups" and categorize others as part of "out-groups."[1] Often subconscious, it helps the mind organize thoughts by aligning with in-group norms. While enhancing social cohesion, it can reinforce stereotypes and deepen divisions. This categorization helps individuals feel a sense of belonging and self-worth; however, it also leads to in-group favoritism and out-group bias, making it easier to think less of those who are different.

---

[1] Tajfel, H., & Turner, J. C. (1979). An integrative theory of intergroup conflict. In W. G. Austin & S. Worchel (Eds.), *The social psychology of intergroup relations* (pp. 33-47). Brooks/Cole.

I. HUMAN ORIGIN

The first part of this book will serve as a broad overview of history, identifying key trends of human conflict while supporting the empirical basis for positioning human dignity as a foundation for humanity's survival. While certain themes and events will be revisited, this repetition is meant to emphasize enduring patterns in human behavior that contribute to conflict.

To better understand how these forces shape human-degrading conflict, we will examine the interconnected nature of human behavior, development, and society that drives both conflict and progress. The three main factors to identify sources of conflict are:

1. **Ideological Developments** (psychology, philosophy & religion): Evolving worldviews, moral systems, and belief structures have justified – and restrained – conflict throughout history, shaping human behavior and societal values.
2. **Technological Advancements**: From the invention of bronze weapons to modern AI, technological shifts have fueled competition and warfare, but they have also enabled human rights via communication, collaboration, and peacebuilding.
3. **Political Power Dynamics**: Politics, in its broadest sense, includes not only statecraft but also the creation of power structures and systems of governance. These systems have been used to suppress or elevate human rights, and power struggles often become central to conflict.

A final factor we will consider is nature itself, which influences the survival of a species through the **environmental challenges** we face. While environmental challenges – such as droughts, floods, pandemics, and climate shifts – have undeniably shaped human history, they often function as catalysts, rather than primary causes, of human-degrading conflict. Historically, societies have interpreted these events through ideological lenses, viewing natural disasters as divine retribution or as opportunities for moral reform. In the last few centuries, the accelerated pace of climate shifts has been attributed to technological advancements that came at a high cost to nature. In the short term, these crises can exacerbate existing political and social tensions, leading to intensified competition for scarce resources or shifts in power dynamics. For example, prolonged droughts have historically driven mass migrations or sparked wars over water access. In the long term, environmental pressures can alter political structures or drive technological innovation, reshaping societies entirely.

However, it is not the environmental challenge itself that determines the outcome, but the human response to it. Unlike **ideological developments, political power dynamics**, or **technological advancements** – which can actively shape or create conflict in the same generation – environmental impacts today are external forces beyond short-term human control.

In all cases, when responses prioritize equitable resource distribution and inclusive decision-making, human rights can be preserved. Conversely, responses marked by exclusion or ignorance can amplify conflict. While nature sets the stage, it is human choices that determine whether dignity is upheld or diminished. By examining these intertwined factors and the human response to them, we begin to understand the evolution and impact of *human-degrading conflict*.

We will attempt to use an objective approach to identify these subjective factors with **"(+)" to highlight their positive impact on human rights**, and **"(-)" to highlight their impact on human-degrading conflict**, and a brief description to help us analyze how they influenced conflict. If you do not need full historical context, focus on the bold items in Part One of the book to extract the factors from history that we will use later to advocate for human dignity as a solution to human-degrading conflict. The table below further defines the criteria for applying these three factors to historical events:

Influential Factor of Conflict	Advocates human rights "(+)"	human-degrading conflict "(-)"	Examples
Ideological Developments (Use of behavior and values to shape beliefs)	1. Promotes human rights, equality, and dignity 2. Encourages cooperation or ethical behavior	1. Leads to discrimination, exclusion, or dehumanization 2. Justifies oppressive behavior or hierarchies	(+) Human rights movements (-) Ideologies promoting slavery or inequality
Political Power Dynamics (Structure of influence over nature and humanity)	1. Promotes fairness, economic stability, diplomatic resolution 2. Supports civil rights 3. Cultural openness	1. Encourages authoritarian rule, oppression, or conflict 2. Prioritizes state/leader power over individual welfare 3. Instills a sense of superiority or dominance over others	(+) Governing bodies whose policies create equal opportunity (-) Governing bodies whose policies create inequality
Technological Advancements (Use of natural resources to drive innovation and application)	1. Enhances human welfare, safety, or dignity 2. Facilitates cooperation 3. Enables better communication 4. Increases equity	1. Contributes to inequality, exploitation, or warfare 2. Enables dominance or control over others 3. Reduces overall equality	(+) Development of agriculture (-) Weapons of mass destruction

I. HUMAN ORIGIN

I.i AN EMPIRICAL APPROACH TO HUMAN CONFLICT

Charles Darwin's theory of evolution, developed in the 1800s, was the first theory of the time to use an empirical approach to inform us that a species will evolve into a form that fits the demands of their environment. The theory itself had been proposed in different fashions before, but Darwin's empirical approach changed the scientific process by setting a precedent for how theories should be developed, tested, and presented by extracting objective data from subjective information. His work not only provided a change in thinking in evolutionary biology but also solidified the empirical foundation of modern science, emphasizing that data and observation are crucial for validating any hypothesis.

Darwin's ideas were controversial at the time to religious leaders, but his theory created a demand for deeper research into human origins because of his methodical collection of evidence from a wide range of sources – geology, zoology, paleontology, and embryology – which gave his theory of evolution by natural selection a scientific rigor that earlier ideas lacked. As Darwin himself predicted, "In the distant future... Light will be thrown on the origin of man and his history."[2] His insight shaped not only our understanding of biology and natural selection but informed the underlying influences of human behavior as well, which laid the groundwork for later theories and sciences that explored evolutionary roots of behavior using the same empirical approach that Darwin used.

By understanding the underlying factors of human behavior using an empirical approach, we can better understand the evolution of humanity with respect to conflict and seek a solution toward ensuring conflict resolution prevails over human-degrading conflict.

Since Darwin's foreshadowing works and empirical approach, science's technological advancements have increased human dignity (+) by shedding light onto many interesting facts that reinforce Darwin's theory of evolution and help shape how we fit into the big picture of life.

For example, we have learned that the Earth is approximately 4.54 billion years old, based on radiometric dating of the oldest rocks and meteorites.[3] It is believed that life first emerged between 3.8 to 4 billion years ago, shortly after the planet's surface cooled enough to sustain

---

[2] Charles Darwin, (1859). On the Origin of Species. first edition, 488.
[3] Dalrymple, G. B. (1991). *The Age of the Earth*. Stanford University Press.

liquid water.[4] We have learned that the first forms of life were single-celled organisms, such as prokaryotes, which dominated for billions of years before the emergence of eukaryotic cells around 2 billion years ago.[5] The transition from single-celled to multicellular organisms began around 1.5 billion years ago, a gradual process driven by environmental pressures, genetic variation, and cellular cooperation, which ultimately led to the development of complex life forms.[6] These events were vital to the forming of humanity, and we must include them for context because they naturally inform our evolutionary nature.

Just as Darwin's theory empowered scholars to study and understand how the natural world came to be, we now stand on the cusp of a new era in which scholars must seek deeper understandings of how the rise of Artificial General Intelligence (AGI) will be informed. Darwin reminded us that in the near distant future, light will be thrown on the nature of a technology which surpasses the intellectual capabilities of man. Will we, as sentient and complex living cells, respect one another as we inform AGI on how to ethically think? If so, it is our ethical responsibility to act now in an empirical method to ensure universal understanding of human rights and life itself, so that we can properly inform the research and development of new technology, like AGI.

Throughout human history, humans have engaged in conflict as a means of survival, competing for resources, territory, and influence. This drive to survive and thrive, rooted in our evolutionary past, continues to shape our behaviors and decisions in the present, even as our conflicts have grown more complex.

Today, thanks to technological advancements which promote human welfare, safety, and dignity (+), many parts of the world spend less time focusing on acquiring basic needs, and more time focused on encouraging civil rights, cooperation, and promoting ethical behavior (+) through political power dynamics and ideological developments.

In Abraham Maslow's *hierarchy of needs*,[7] we have basic physical and psychological building blocks that enable us to be the best version of ourselves. While Darwin's theory helps us understand the physical evolution of humans, Maslow's *hierarchy of needs* provides insight into

---

[4] Knoll, A. H. (2003). *Life on a Young Planet: The First Three Billion Years of Evolution on Earth*. Princeton University Press.
[5] Margulis, L. (1981). *Symbiosis in Cell Evolution: Life and Its Environment on the Early Earth*. W.H. Freeman.
[6] Grosberg, R. K., & Strathmann, R. R. (2007). *The Evolution of Multicellularity: A Minor Major Transition?* Annual Review of Ecology, Evolution, and Systematics, 38, 621-654.
[7] Maslow, A.H. (1954). Motivation and Personality. Harper & Row, NY.

the psychological evolution that followed biological evolution. Once basic survival was secured, humans evolved from the competition for resources to conflicts over higher-order needs – status, ideas, recognition, and self-actualization.

To better understand how these evolutionary psychological forces shape conflict, imagine for a moment that you were an outside observer, like an alien, studying humanity from an empirical point of view. From this vantage point, you would see that humanity's actions often reflect the principles of natural selection, where the strongest dominate the weak, shaping historical narratives to create a future that favors the values and principles of the strong. In witnessing individual cultures or religions, you would see that despite efforts to establish common ground, cultures and religions hold different perspectives, both between and within themselves, each shaped by their own *hierarchy of needs*. You would recognize that in humanity's documentation of their history, human influence is often shaped by ideology, which in turn has often been shaped by differing forms of conflict – either conflict resolution or human-degrading conflict. Those who win in conflict tend to write history, while those whose voices are marginalized or suppressed often fade away. The "influence" that has won over history has, historically, been defined by that which "wins" in conflict.

From our own human perspective, we witness that human-degrading conflict often arises from the perspectives whose actions and interests take precedent over the dignity of the human person. In other words, ideologies often take precedence over the dignity of the human person, justified as part of one's survival. When this happens, human-degrading conflict – like wars, slavery, or even the civil suppression of individual freedoms – have often been justified in the name of preserving power.

Despite these moments in history, forward-thinking individuals – such as Confucius, Buddha, Aristotle, Mencius, Goethe, Eleanor Roosevelt, and Martin Luther King Jr. – have consistently championed human dignity, paving the way for societies to evolve beyond human-degrading ideas. In Part One of this book, we will use an empirical approach to explore how evolutionary and early societal dynamics have contributed to human-degrading conflict – and more importantly, we will reflect on how we can minimize future conflicts by placing human dignity at the forefront of our decisions.

I.ii FROM MILLIONS OF YEARS AGO... TO THE "PRESENT TIME"

Understanding our inherent draw to conflict is vital to knowing how to reduce future conflict. This section will use the expertise of evolutionary scientists to help establish the history of our origins. As we walk through the scientific works that prove our origins, they will establish that conflict is quite literally in our DNA.

From 7 to 2.5 million years ago – DNA Divergence: The first divergence of human DNA sequences from chimpanzees began around seven million years ago. Roughly 2.5 million years ago, Humans became their own species.[8,9] A million years after human divergence from chimpanzees, bonobo divergence from chimpanzees occurred.

Despite the vast differences in our evolution, human DNA is nearly 99% similar to that of chimpanzees and bonobos. **Since humans share a common ancestor with the bonobos (the chimpanzee), this genetic similarity helps explain why humans exhibit a blend of behaviors – both the aggression and dominance of chimpanzees (-), and the cooperation, empathy, and peaceful conflict resolution seen in bonobos (+).**

Even though human DNA split from chimpanzee DNA prior to the bonobo DNA split, it could point toward a "dual potential" within each of us, which originated in a subdued manner within chimpanzee DNA, and is now present in both humans and bonobos. **The dual potential highlighted in the stark contrast between chimpanzee and bonobo behavior points to a potential source of positive and negative ideological developments witnessed throughout human history. On one end, we have the growth of universal human rights, fostering global empathy and equitable societal structures (+); on the other side, we have witnessed the rise of exclusionary nationalism or dogmatic adherence to beliefs, leading to forms of oppression or dehumanization (-).** All that to say, chimpanzee and bonobo behavior sheds light on how to address conflict today, providing us with a framework for consciously choosing empathy and cooperation over aggression.

---

[8] Sudmant, P. H., Kidd, J. M., Li, H., Kelley, J. L., Veeramah, K. R., Woerner, A. E., D., T., Santpere, G., Cagan, A., Theunert, C., Casals, F., Laayouni, H., Munch, K., Hobolth, A., Halager, A. E., Malig, M., Prüfer, K., Pybus, M., Johnstone, L., ... Eichler, E. E. (2013). *Great ape genetic diversity and population history*. Nature, 499(7459), 471-475. https://www.nature.com/articles/nature12228

[9] Prüfer, K., Munch, K., Hellmann, I., Akagi, K., Miller, J. R., Walenz, B., Koren, S., Sutton, G., Kodira, C., Winer, R., Knight, J. R., Mullikin, J. C., Meader, S. J., Ponting, C. P., Lunter, G., Higashino, S., Hobolth, A., Dutheil, J., Karakoç, E., ... Pääbo, S. (2012). *The bonobo genome compared with the chimpanzee and human genomes*. Nature, 486(7404), 527-531. https://www.nature.com/articles/nature11128

I. HUMAN ORIGIN

Bonobos, studied extensively in the Democratic Republic of Congo, have more tolerant intergroup relations.[10] Understanding our DNA heritage allows us to witness why we display certain contrasting characteristics. Chimpanzees, for instance, exhibit aggression, violence, dominance hierarchies, and in-group favoritism. Bonobos, on the other hand, emphasize cooperation, empowerment for all, conflict resolution through physical affection, empathy, and sharing. These inherited traits offer humans the unique opportunity to reflect on our inherent characteristics, providing the potential to choose between cooperation, like the bonobo, or conflict-driven behaviors seen in chimpanzees. We inherently possess both capacities, even if unconsciously, in this dual potential.

From 2.5 to 1.5 million years ago – Geographical Influence: As evolution continued, environmental factors played a vital role in shaping how each species exhibited their inherent traits. Geographically, the modern-day Democratic Republic of Congo was the original homeland of the chimpanzee and bonobo species. The chimpanzees lived on the north side of the Congo river, while the bonobos lived within the meandering curve of the river on the south side.[11] The south provided a favorable and lush environment for the Bonobos to reinforce the more cooperative characteristics that we see in them today, while the environment to the north reinforced more defensive behavior in the chimpanzees due to their lack of protection from the river.

If geography indeed shaped the mindsets of chimpanzees and bonobos, it was a contributing factor to ideological developments of bonobos, which exhibit inherent peaceful cooperation (+). Likewise, it was a contributing factor to the chimpanzees' ideological developments, which exhibited aggression, defensiveness, and violence (-). As one of the first insights into evolutionary geopolitical conflict, this example adds depth to how geography can shape behavior. By understanding the origins of these contrasting traits, we not only gain insight into our own behavior but also uncover the possible roots of human dignity, providing us with a framework for choosing empathy and cooperation over aggression.

---

[10] Brooks, J., Epping, A., Lee, S. H., Niksarli, A., Pope, A., Clay, Z., Kret, M. E., Taglialatela, J., & Yamamoto, S. (2024). Increased alertness and moderate ingroup cohesion in bonobos' response to outgroup cues. PLOS ONE, 19(8). https://journals.plos.org/plosone/article?id=10.1371/journal.pone.0307975

[11] Prüfer et al., *The bonobo genome compared with the chimpanzee and human genomes*, 2012.

I.iii CLOSING THOUGHTS

Our human origins provide a dual potential for our nature, as demonstrated in the different behaviors exhibited in the chimpanzees and bonobos. Chapter II will explore what has shaped these dual potentials within human nature. The primary contributing factors of ideological developments, technological advancements, and political power dynamics will increasingly become more relatable to our way of life, offering valuable insights into managing conflict by prioritizing basic human rights above systemic flaws.

Understanding how the beginning of humanity – and its shift from individual tribal nature to more complex group dynamics – will provide clarity to why the world experiences complex, often times miscalculated, human-degrading conflict today. We will trace the journey of human conflict as it grew from local disputes to confrontations between newly settled civilizations in prehistory. By examining the forces shaping conflicts throughout human history, we will gain insights into the journey that brings us closer to recognizing dignity on a larger scale – a recognition that may offer solutions to today's complex challenges.

I. HUMAN ORIGIN

II

PREHISTORY:
(FROM 2.5 MILLION YEARS AGO TO 3300 BCE) FROM MIGRATORY COMMUNITIES TO SETTLED CIVILIZATIONS

This chapter works to uncover how humanity lived for nearly 2.5 million years, roughly 98% of our existence. When humans first emerged in East Africa, the world was largely uninhabited, offering vast expanses of open land. **During this time, conflicts were typically resolved on an individual or small-group level, often involving face-to-face interaction or simple migration away from sources of conflict to new, unclaimed territories. Many of these interactions and movements were based heavily on ideological developments, which sought out survival (+).** It was not until about 15,000 years ago that humans finally settled across the entirety of earth's diverse landscapes, claiming new territories as they expanded.[12]

Prior to 15,000 years ago, humans may have largely avoided the complex cross-cultural conflicts we see today thanks to migratory trends; further, they primarily only knew individual and small-group conflict resolution. The complex technological advancements and political power dynamics we see today – often required for cross-cultural conflicts – had yet to exist; rather, ideological developments continued to be the primary influence of conflict.

Hence, as the earth became more densely populated, the

---

[12] Kuzoian, A. (Producer), & Lallanilla, M. (2015, May 27). *Animated map shows how humans migrated across the globe*. Business Insider. Retrieved from https://www.businessinsider.com/prehistoric-human-migration-from-africa-animated-map-2015-5

II. FROM MIGRATORY COMMUNITIES TO SETTLED CIVILIZATIONS

opportunity for migration (to avoid conflict) diminished, and human groups were forced to negotiate, compete, or fight over resources, land, and influence. **Humanity's spread across the earth marked the beginning of more complex group conflicts, which required cooperation and diplomacy on a scale never before seen, spurring increased technological advancement to optimize resources (+) and political power dynamics to manage the forced conflict resolution (+).** As settlements began to compete for resources, such as water and fertile soil, group identity and loyalty became critical as early humans had to navigate interactions with neighboring communities.

This growing complexity led to the eventual need for diplomacy and understanding as humans began to realize that long-term survival meant not just inhabiting land or gathering resources to attain basic needs, but also managing relationships with other groups.

When we see a different group, it is often easier for us to stereotype the individuals within that group because of a natural bias known as out-group homogeneity effect.[13] The out-group homogeneity effect states that the instinct toward conformity can lead individuals to participate in human-degrading actions towards those outside of the group, especially when powerful members influence the group dynamic (insight #2). **Despite an intrinsic desire to help others, the introduction of the out-group homogeneity effect (-) introduces the need for political power dynamics to address problems through either diplomacy or human-degrading conflict.** This idea is the precursor to the political power dynamics and international relations we see today, where geographical borders and resource distribution drive much of the conflict and diplomacy between nations.

Chapter III will cover recent human history (within the last 5,000 years) with respect to intracultural conflict in more depth. **The intent of this chapter is to cover how we, as a human race, developed in a way that now – unlike the first few thousand millennia of human history – requires such in-depth understanding of proper use of technology and diplomacy in order to achieve peaceful cooperation.**

---

[13] Park, B., & Judd, C. M. (1990). Measures and models of perceived group variability. *Journal of Personality and Social Psychology*, 59(2), 173–191.

CONFLICT

II.i A SUMMARY OF EARLY HUMAN MIGRATION

To find the answers we seek in this chapter, we must go back two million years to understand how the *Homo* species became the human species. Much of the research was performed through the Smithsonian Museum of Natural History, in addition to the Leakey Foundation and American Museum of Natural History.[14, 15]

From 2.4 to 1.5 million years ago – Homo Habilis: Once the Homo species began to split from chimpanzees, as noted in the last chapter, we eventually became the *Homo habilis* species. Considered one of the first members of the Homo genus, Homo habilis is often associated with the development of simple stone tools (Oldowan tools). **Oldowan tools mark the beginning of the Paleolithic period of the stone age, identifying the beginning of humanity's innovative technological advancements, which were used at times to gather resources (+), and at other times to dominate other species (-). Prior to the stone age, nature's methods for harm relied on biological evolution rather than human-made tools or technologies, marking a significant change in the way in which nature utilized its resources.**

The use of such tools is attributed to evolutionary traits, such as the fact that Homo habilis had a larger brain size compared to earlier Hominins like Australopithecus, which may have provided some early capacity for rudimentary speech.[16] **Speech, while beneficial for survival, could have allowed for widespread communication and understanding for using such technological advancements for exploitation or even warfare (-).**

From 1.9 million to 300,000 years ago – Homo Erectus: Following Homo habilis, *Homo erectus* emerged. This was the first hominoid species to leave Africa. A distinct split occurred in evolutionary paths as some of the Homo erectus species left Africa. The species that left Africa went on to populate parts of modern-day Europe, leading to the emergence of *Homo heidelbergensis* roughly 700,000 years ago. Homo heidelbergensis were the first early human species to build shelters. They eventually evolved into *Homo*

---

[14] Smithsonian Museum of Natural History. (n.d.). *Human origins: Homo sapiens*. Retrieved from https://humanorigins.si.edu

[15] Leakey, R. E., & Lewin, R. (1992). *Origins Reconsidered: In Search of What Makes Us Human*. New York: Doubleday.

[16] Klein, R. G. (2009). *The Human Career: Human Biological and Cultural Origins*. University of Chicago Press.

II. FROM MIGRATORY COMMUNITIES TO SETTLED CIVILIZATIONS

neanderthalensis around 400,000 years ago. The Homo erectus that remained in Africa eventually evolved into *Homo sapiens* 300,000 years ago, which were our first anatomically human ancestors. The oldest fossils have been found near modern-day Morocco, which are believed to be 300,000 years old.

This large geographical split in our evolutionary history foreshadows the first potential large-scale conflict that spawned due to geographical separation. **The geographical split is important to note, especially within the context of this book, because it reinforces how we have evolved with distinct ideological, political, and technological developments. These distinct evolutions may still directly contribute to the human-degrading conflict we see today (-).** In attempts to understand these distinctions, we may be able to isolate the features of such conflict and exclude them from future societal development. We will discuss this more in Part Three.

300,000 years ago – European Neanderthals: In Europe, we see the rise of the Neanderthals displaying the first modern traits of humans through art and tools. **As a technologically advanced species, they even used fire and created sharp objects to shape things in nature (+). On a personal level, they developed ideological developments in which they took time to bury their dead (sometimes with grave goods, suggesting symbolic thought), and cared for injured or elderly individuals (+), displaying a unique trait in nature only to the Homo species.** As Neanderthals migrated throughout modern Europe and West Asia, they thrived at the top of nature's food chain.

From 300,000 to 70,000 years ago – African Homo Sapiens: Meanwhile in Africa, Homo sapiens thrived at the top of their food chain. **Neanderthals and Homo sapiens lived separate lifestyles. During this period, Homo sapiens developed more complex tools and behaviors, including early forms of art, symbolic thinking, and early forms of language. Evidence of this can be seen in artifacts like beads, cave art, and carved objects found in Africa, suggesting technological advancement and ideological development (+).**

From 115,000 to 70,000 years ago – Environmental Change: The last Ice Age began roughly 115,000 years ago, forcing mass

migrations. By around 70,000 years ago, the coldest, driest period of the Ice Age occurred, spurring further migration. Homo sapiens officially migrated out of Africa 65,000 years ago through the Arabian Peninsula.[17,18] During this time, Homo sapiens interacted with Neanderthals, leading to a period of interbreeding and coexistence for a few thousand years.[19] Evidence suggests that both species coexisted in sites like the Skhul and Qafzeh caves in Israel, the Vindija Cave in Croatia, and the Denisova Cave among the Altai Mountains in Siberia, until Neanderthal extinction 40,000 years ago.[20] Denisovans, who went extinct around 15,000 BCE, were a separate hominin branch thanks to the interbreeding of Homo sapiens and Neanderthals.

From 70,000 to 50,000 years ago − Cognitive Revolution: Homo sapiens underwent a significant Cognitive Revolution, which led to newfound abstract thought and symbolic communication. **This led to ideological developments which laid the groundwork for artistic expression and spirituality which promoted human dignity (+).** Paired with advancements in societal organization, **the advancements in the cognitive revolution also demonstrated a newfound knowledge of political power dynamics which could be used to promote stability among society (+).** As migrations continued, Homo sapiens made it all the way to Australia, populating it over 50,000 years ago by sailing across several straits in the Wallacea region of Southeast Asia. At the same time, another group of Homo sapiens left Africa for the Middle East, Central Asia, and toward Europe and Asia. **Migrations stretching large distances across water suggest significant technological advancements contributing to human welfare (+).**

Once Homo sapiens entered Europe, they became the dominant species in the lands they migrated to, since neanderthals had yet to experience a cognitive revolution.[21] Through the Homo Sapiens' ability to communicate through complex language, use advanced tools (and weapons), and organize socially, the Neanderthals quickly became inferior in capability. **The Neanderthals likely experienced oppression (-) from the Homo Sapiens, which was likely the most**

---

[17] Harcourt, A. H. (2012). *Human Biogeography.* University of California Press.
[18] McDougall, I., Brown, F. H., & Fleagle, J. G. (2005). Stratigraphic placement and age of modern humans from Kibish, Ethiopia. *Nature*, 433(7027), 733-736.
[19] Green, R. E., et al. (2010). A draft sequence of the Neandertal genome. *Science*, 328(5979), 710-722.
[20] Prüfer, K., Racimo, F., Patterson, N., et al. (2014). "The Complete Genome Sequence of a Neanderthal from the Altai Mountains." *Nature*, 505(7481), 43-49.
[21] Stringer, C. (2012). *The Origin of Our Species.* Penguin Books.

II. FROM MIGRATORY COMMUNITIES TO SETTLED CIVILIZATIONS

influential aspect that drove Neanderthal extinction around 40,000 years ago. Although their extinction is not fully understood, it is likely that competition for goods and resources, climate change from the Ice Age, and diseases from Homo sapiens migrating from Africa were all factors.

From 40,000 to 15,000 years ago – Populating the World: After the extinction of the Neanderthals, Homo Sapiens were the last remaining hominin species. Roughly 25,000 years ago, the world entered the last glacial maximum of the Ice Age. Spurring more migration in which Japan, Korea and Northeastern Russia became populated roughly 20,000 years ago. The Americas did not become populated until about 15,000 years ago, when the homo sapiens first migrated into the Americas via Beringia, the land bridge that connected Siberia in Asia to Alaska.

Between 15,000 and 8,000 years ago – Sea Level Rises: As the Ice Age began to end, ice melt caused the sea levels to rise roughly 400 feet. Prior to the melt, migrations via land were much easier. **The environmental changes caused by sea level rises were unbearable for many civilizations that lived along coastal waters.**

Rising water submerged land bridges and created islands. The British Isles, previously connected to mainland Europe by the Doggerland Landbridge, was formed. Sahul, a massive landmass included Tasmania, New Guinea, and Australia was turned into three islands by the Ice Age. Less than one hundred kilometers to the north, the landmass of Sunda was divided by sea into Indonesia and mainland Asia. Today, scientists call the Lombok Strait, or the Wallace Line – a section of deep sea (800 feet deep) – the primary divider between Asia and Australia before the last ice age. It remains a bio-geographical barrier for species. **These shifts dramatically changed geography, migration patterns, and continue to shape how we see the world today.**[22]

---

[22] Roberts, N., et al. (2014). The End of the Last Glacial Maximum and the Role of Sea-Level Rise in the Formation of Islands. *Geography Review*, 28(2), 15-25.

CONFLICT

II.ii THE AGRICULTURAL REVOLUTION AND THE RISE OF COMPETITION THROUGH TECHNOLOGY AND ISOLATION

11,700 years ago – The rise of Agriculture: When the last ice age ended, migratory patterns also slowed, giving rise to the Agricultural Revolution. This marked a significant shift from nomadic hunter-gatherer societies to settled farming communities. **The environmental changes sparked a leap in technological advancement, which increased equity and cooperation among individuals (+). It was a precursor to many changes in the way humanity would deal with ideological developments and political power dynamics in the coming millennia.**

The revolution allowed humans to cultivate crops, domesticate animals, and produce surplus food, which led to population growth and the rise of early cities and villages. Settling in one place allowed for more stable, organized societies with the ability to innovate and develop new technologies. Not all regions of the world adopted agricultural practices until much later, but the most technologically advanced societies adopted them quickly.[23] As Homo sapiens began to settle into permanent communities to cultivate crops and domesticate animals, the relationship between humans and their surroundings fundamentally shifted. For the first time, humans were able to produce surplus food, leading to population growth and signs of civilization.

As agricultural societies became tied to specific pieces of land, out-group isolation grew, triggering conflicting political power dynamics that introduced biases of superiority within groups (-). Unlike the migratory hunter-gatherers of previous millennia, these settled communities had a vested interest in defending their resources and had significantly less interaction with other groups. **Isolation fostered distinct technological advancements within different regions, which in turn fueled competition as groups sought to protect and expand their wealth and territories. The need for fertile land for agriculture combined with the economic benefit of controlling trade routes spurred conflicts between neighboring communities (-).**

The ability to produce surplus food led to ideological developments to help promote equality and cooperation within

---

[23] Bellwood, P. (2005). *First Farmers: The Origins of Agricultural Societies.* Malden, MA: Blackwell Publishing.

II. FROM MIGRATORY COMMUNITIES TO SETTLED CIVILIZATIONS

society (+). **As political power dynamics took a hold of the surplus of resources, societies began to specialize labor by gender and created social hierarchies, to include slavery (-).** Large accumulations of wealth through cooperation created the need for taxation in order to fund publicly shared interests. **Through trust and cooperation (+) came new opportunities for corruption and human-degrading conflict (-) as communities grew.**

As technology developed, it reinforced the divisions between groups, leading to competition for resources and pride in technological superiority. **Rather than fostering cooperation, some technological advancements contributed directly to inequality, exploitation of resources, and dominance over entire peoples (-). This clearly created new forms of human-degrading conflict as political power dynamics quickly shifted from a theory of cooperation to a reality of power control. Groups clashed over trade routes, fertile lands, and valuable resources without concern of the welfare of the people inhabiting them.**

The development of agriculture set the stage for the rise of early civilizations such as Mesopotamia, Egypt, and the Indus Valley, where territorial expansion, resource control, and political power dynamics were now the norm. **These early empires used technological advancement to wage wars for control over trade, labor, wealth, power, and eventually ideas (-).**

Although archaeological evidence has mostly been lost over time, remnants such as Göbekli Tepe are reminders of humanity's complex collaborations during the agricultural revolution. Considered one of the oldest known monumental structures, Göbekli Tepe was built during the Pre-Pottery Neolithic period (circa 9600 BCE) and stands today in modern day Türkiye.[24] This site predates Stonehenge and the pyramids of Egypt by several thousand years and challenges traditional views of early human society and the development of civilization. Göbekli Tepe is notable for its massive T-shaped limestone pillars, intricately carved with images of animals and abstract symbols. The site is believed to have been a ceremonial or religious center rather than a settlement, suggesting complex social and spiritual practices. **The recent discovery of Göbekli Tepe in 1990 provided new insights into early human social organization, indicating that large-scale collaborative projects and sophisticated symbolic expression (+) through ideological developments were possible in hunter-**

---

[24] Schmidt, K. (2010). *Göbekli Tepe: The World's First Temple?* In *Scientific American* (Vol. 302, No. 6, pp. 54-60).

gatherer societies going into the agricultural revolution.

Thus, the Agricultural Revolution, while providing stability and technological growth, also laid the groundwork for more complex and large-scale human interactions. Settlements transformed into societies with social hierarchies, political power struggles, and a growing need to control land, labor, and resources. **The evolution from simple migratory communities to complex civilizations introduced a new idea of geopolitical conflict, where human dignity was often overlooked in favor of economic and political gain (-).**

Unlike the early hominis or even chimpanzees or bonobos, human civilizations entered uncharted evolutionary territory with respect to their needs. Humans were no longer fighting for mere survival, but for something seemingly bigger: ideas. These isolated ideas and technological advancements changed how human civilizations approached conflict resolution.[25]

Similar to the extinction of a species highlighted between the Neanderthals and Homo sapiens in the last section, group isolation once again foreshadowed future conflict; however, this time it would be on a much larger scale due to advancement of technology and ideas. The shift from tribalism to more complex societies with political, economic, and social hierarchies is what laid the evolutionary groundwork for the modern system of nation-states.

The very issues that began during the Agricultural Revolution – territorial disputes, resource control, and social inequality – are still at the heart of many of today's geopolitical conflicts. **As we witness humanity begin to climb the ladder of Maslow's *hierarchy of needs*, thanks to the advancements made in the agricultural revolution (+), we begin to see that higher-level ideological developments consequentially create complex levels of human-degrading conflict (-) if not managed with human dignity as an inherent quality of all people.** Understanding the roots of these issues helps us not only trace the history of human conflict but also recognize the need for global cooperation and the protection of human rights in an increasingly interconnected world.

---

[25] Diamond, J. (1999). *Guns, Germs, and Steel: The Fates of Human Societies.* W.W. Norton & Company.

II.iii THE EVOLUTION OF SPIRITUALITY AS AN IDEOLOGICAL DEVELOPMENT

As the Cognitive Revolution equipped humanity with advanced language and abstract thinking, people became more mutually aware of their spiritual nature. Although the exact origins of spiritual beliefs remain unknown, evidence suggests that such practices date back tens of thousands of years, long before the advent of written history. **What we do know is that spiritual beliefs have been a fundamental part of ideological development within human societies since the earliest recorded civilizations, playing an essential role in advocating for human rights and human dignity (+).**

Before going into the timeline of spiritual evolution, it is important to note a few shared themes present across many religions & belief systems in history in order to understand how it plays a role in human conflict. First, spiritual beliefs tend to have a background of divine creation, a moral code advocating for compassion, and the idea of universal equality. In this way, human dignity is reinforced as these beliefs attempt to explain the inherent worth of each human being. Second, many beliefs emphasize free will and spiritual freedom – to choose how to act, worship, and treat others. They often outline the blessings and consequences of one's behavior, promoting responsible action, justice, and the welfare of others. While religion, when practiced within a culture, has historically been a source of moral guidance and societal unity, human-degrading conflict often arises when religious beliefs cross cultural boundaries or out-groups, leading to competition for religious and political power.

So, where did our spiritual beliefs actually begin? **Evidence shows that both Homo sapiens and Neanderthals performed ritualistic burials almost 100,000 years ago to respect their dead, suggesting the early ideological development of spiritual beliefs (+).**[26] Prior to this, humans and Neanderthals likely buried their dead, but not in a ritualistic way. The inclusion of grave goods suggests a developing sense of spirituality in Homo sapiens, particularly during the Cognitive Revolution.

After the extinction of the Neanderthals 40,000 years ago, we see the rise of cave art and carved figures that are tied to spiritual figures such as the Venus figurines,[27] which symbolized fertility and the promotion of human life. These early spiritual symbols were not

---

[26] Pettitt, P. (2011). The Palaeolithic origins of human burial. *Routledge*.
[27] Clottes, J. (2008). Cave art. *Phaidon Press*.

necessarily tied to a specific deity but represented humanity's growing capacity for abstract and symbolic thought.

With the advent of the agricultural revolution around 11,700 BCE, we begin to see animistic beliefs, where spirits were believed to inhabit animals, plants, and other natural elements that provided life and sustenance. These animistic traditions emerged in regions such as the Near East, China, and Mesoamerica.[28] This marked a shift toward community-based spirituality.

The Near East, now known as the Middle East, encompassed modern day Türkiye, Syria, Lebanon, Israel, Palestine, Jordan, Iraq, Iran (western regions), Egypt (particularly the Sinai Peninsula), and Parts of the Arabian Peninsula (northern regions). This region became known as the crossroads of ancient civilizations.

Fast forwarding to between 3500 and 3000 BCE, large civilizations begin to take shape. In Sumer (Mesopotamia) and ancient Egypt, polytheism arose as people attributed various aspects of their environment – like agriculture, fertility, and military protection – to different deities.[29] **As we approach the bronze age, we witness religious leaders acting as intermediaries, performing rituals and sacrifices to ensure prosperity. We see these ideological developments promote cooperation (+); however, as belief systems begin to gain influence within communities, we begin to see the deification of political leaders, creating political power dynamics that led to authoritarian rule and oppression of common people (-).** As these polytheistic beliefs spread throughout their civilization, they began to influence other cultures as well,[30] often leading to inequality in the early ages.

Although the evolution of the spiritual beliefs described is really just beginning, it already provides insights to the significant changes to the ways in which humans rapidly transition from learning to cooperate with tangible items to needing to learn to respect and grow together with intangible belief systems. This is the point at which we will pick up this discussion later, in Chapter III.

---

[28] Cauvin, J. (2000). *The birth of the gods and the origins of agriculture. Cambridge University Press.*
[29] Bottero, J. (2004). *Religion in ancient Mesopotamia.* University of Chicago Press.
[30] Jacobsen, T. (1976). *The Treasures of Darkness: A History of Mesopotamian Religion.* New Haven, CT: Yale University Press.

II. FROM MIGRATORY COMMUNITIES TO SETTLED CIVILIZATIONS

II.iv THE LANGUAGE BARRIER

A final topic that needs to be covered during the period of prehistory is language and communication. One of the most significant aspects of human history is our ability to communicate. While there is no written record of language from prehistory, we know it existed due to genetic evidence, anatomical developments in the vocal tract, and cognitive advancements seen during the Cognitive Revolution. Early hominins likely had some form of communication, but the evolution of complex languages took thousands of years.[31] Communication served as both a limitation and a catalyst for human evolution, and it was not until the Cognitive Revolution that language truly became a key driver of societal and spiritual growth.

We will explore language more in Chapter III, but it is important to recognize that our ability to understand one another is still evolving. As the language barrier diminishes thanks to technology, effective communication is increasingly contingent on our acknowledgment of each individual's inherent dignity. **When we walk through the Bronze Age in Chapter III, we will witness rapid technological advances and ideological developments which overlook the crucial aspect of human connection through respectful communication (+).** How have we learned from this?

Today, we stand at a threshold where language barriers are diminishing, presenting a unique opportunity for universal enrichment. Yet, as much as it is an opportunity, we must also meet the challenge of maintaining cultural dignity and practices as we integrate through global communication. While translation technology enables easier cross-cultural exchanges, it is important to remember that cultural nuances and context within languages vary greatly, making direct translations difficult. Communication today – in all its forms – remains a universal challenge, whether seeking a common language among diverse groups, learning a new software language, or finding the right word to express a novel idea. Language continues to shape how we interact with the world and with one another.

As we delve into more recent history in the next chapter, we will draw from a range of historical sources to capture the most accurate perspectives, especially regarding the evolution of language and communication.

---

[31] Roberts, A. (2011). *The incredible human journey: The story of how we colonised the planet.* Bloomsbury Publishing.

II.v CLOSING THOUGHTS

As humanity's great migrations are recorded in history, the relationship between culture and geography became a significant area of study. This study, known as geopolitics, explores how political power is shaped by geography and helps us understand global factions and how people organize their lives around natural and political boundaries. Swedish political scientist first used the term geopolitics Johan Rudolf Kjellén in the early 20th century.[32] For the first few million years of human existence, political issues related to geography were rare; for most of early human history, migration to unpopulated areas was often the simplest solution to conflict.

As we transition to Chapter III, we will see civilizations increasingly affected by geopolitics. These new challenges introduce a deeper level of conflict as competing civilizations use political power dynamics to prioritize their own survival and ideologies, often at the expense of the inherent human dignity of individuals who make up our global society (-). How have we responded to such conflicts throughout history? And as technology advances – offering greater means to meet individuals' needs, wants, and desires – will we respond differently in the future?

Technological advancement continues to drive competition for ideas, resources, and power, fueling the choice between human-degrading conflict and steadfast conflict resolution. By recognizing dignity, can we envision a future where technology – through AI, automation, and biotechnology – supports humanity as a whole by stressing the need to uphold individual human dignity?

---

[32] Kjellén, J. R. (1924). *The State as a Living Organism*. Stockholm: Geber.

II. FROM MIGRATORY COMMUNITIES TO SETTLED CIVILIZATIONS

III

RECENT HISTORY *(3300 BCE TO PRESENT TIME)*
THE EMERGENCE OF INTERCULTURAL CONFLICT

This chapter covers less than 2% of the time that humans have inhabited the Earth, yet it may be the most pivotal period for understanding the kind of conflict that this book addresses. **During this time – from the start of the Bronze Age in 3300 BCE to today – we have seen the rise of increasingly organized and large-scale human-degrading conflict, often times through political leaders who take advantage of a people by conforming them to an idea which takes precedent over basic human rights.** While humanity has made strides toward peace through treaties, agreements, and pledges that aim to protect human rights, **we have often fallen short of peace because of the conformity of individuals around political dynamics grounded in power (-).**

In this chapter, we will witness humanity seeking power over peace, time and time again, leading to unnecessary suffering. Failure to find peaceful cooperation has frequently resulted from the pride and power-hunger of individuals under the influence of the out-group homogeneity effect.

While this chapter may feel like you are reading a long, dry history book at times, it is necessary to put into context the three factors of conflict that have impacted humanity consistently throughout history. Doing so will inform us on how to avoid human-degrading conflict in the future. We will now shift from understanding humanity as a migratory species (Chapter II) to seeing it as a settled species in the process of developing civilizations across the globe (Chapter III).

III.i THE BRONZE AGE CIVILIZATIONS
(3300 TO 1200 BCE)

The Bronze Age marked humanity's first organized attempts at complex societies, where technological advancements, particularly in metallurgy and agriculture, enabled stable settlements and the growth of cities (+), often founded on mutual beliefs and concepts (+) through inherited ideological developments. These developments allowed for specialized labor, social hierarchies, and the first recorded laws – attempts at early governance that aimed, however limited, at balancing power. **Human rights were rarely a consideration when it came to political power dynamics (-), given that the divisions between classes and the rise of powerful ruling elites often led to hierarchical conflicts and subjugation of the majority. During this era, ideological developments gave way for promising religious structures which began to play a role not just in explaining the world to the average person (+), but in justifying the social order and conflicts that arose from it (+/-)**.

3300 to 1900 BCE – Indus Valley: We begin to see new technological advances particularly in the Indus Valley Civilization (modern day Pakistan), also known as the Harappan Civilization. **One notable achievement during this period was the technological development of complex drainage systems to prevent the spread of disease (+). These advancements reflect early cooperation and societal development, but also hint at the growing challenges of resource management, competition, and power struggles between emerging civilizations.**

The Harappan Civilization was superior in their urban planning, trade networks, and their architecture (like Mohenjo-Daro and Harappa).[33] As one of the earliest and most urbanized civilizations, the Harappans had a considerable influence on the trade and culture of South Asia.

Its decline around 1900 BCE is still a subject of debate, adding to its intrigue. Evidence pointing to a series of prolonged droughts around 1900 BCE would have severely impacted crop yields and reduced the region's capacity to sustain large urban centers like Harappa and Mohenjo-Daro. **Additionally, the lack of centralized**

---

[33] Kenoyer, J. M. (1998). *Ancient Cities of the Indus Valley Civilization*. Oxford University Press.

political power dynamics further weakened their ability to adapt to challenges (-), compounding the crisis rather than directly causing it. As droughts and declining resources weakened urban centers, trade networks suffered, further isolating communities, and accelerated the Harappan civilization's collapse.

While all three factors might have had some influence, the political power dynamics and environmental challenges were most influential and contributed the most to this society's decline.

3228 to 500 BCE – India's Religious Development: In 3228 BCE, the birth of Krishna in northern India marks a significant moment in the evolution of religious thought. Krishna is considered one of the earliest divine incarnations (avatars) of the god Vishnu on Earth. As depicted in the Bhagavad Gita, Krishna plays a significant role as a divine teacher, offering profound guidance on righteousness, duty, and spiritual liberation. **He symbolizes the restoration of cosmic order, the triumph of good over evil, divine protection on Earth, and the transformative power of love and devotion (+).**[34] Krishna's teachings and life serve as a foundational influence on Hindu philosophy and devotional practices, which will be explored in greater depth later.

By around 1500 BCE, the Vedic religion took shape in India, laying the groundwork for what would later become Hinduism. This early religion centered on elaborate ritual practices, hymns, and sacrifices, focusing primarily on appeasing deities like Indra, Agni, and Varuna. **It introduced foundational concepts such as karma (the law of action and consequence), dharma (duty or righteousness), and moksha (liberation from the cycle of rebirth) (+).**[35]

While the Vedic religion emphasized rituals over philosophical and devotional elements, around 500 BCE, Hinduism began to evolve beyond its Vedic roots. This period saw a significant expansion in beliefs, incorporating more diverse philosophical and devotional traditions, such as devotion to gods like Vishnu (in the form of Krishna) and Shiva. **These developments transformed Hinduism into a rich and multifaceted tradition, emphasizing not just ritual but also personal devotion, spirituality, and ethical living, which continue to define Hindu practice today (+).**

---

[34] Hawley, J. S., & Goswami, D. (1981). *Krishna: The Butter Thief*. Princeton University Press.
[35] Flood, G. (1996). *An introduction to Hinduism*. Cambridge University Press.

THE BRONZE AGE (3300 TO 1200 BCE)

3000 BCE – Mesopotamia: Sumer in Mesopotamia is often regarded as the first civilization due to the development of cuneiform writing (+), which is often seen foundational for Technological Advancements, Ideological Developments, and Political Power Dynamics. Written texts allowed for the recording of laws, trade, and religious texts. The rise of urban centers like Uruk and Ur and the invention of writing had a profound impact on human communication and record-keeping. This is critical because it marked the transition from prehistory to history. The development of writing not only influenced later Mesopotamian cultures (Akkadian and Babylonian) but also had an enduring impact on future civilizations globally.[36]

At the rise of writing, King Gilgamesh ruled Samaria. During this time, further advancements of the arts and philosophical achievements arose. The earliest known poem, Epic of Gilgamesh, reflects on the King's quest for immortality – as life beyond our basic needs expands, the quest for *more* is just beginning. In his poem, he writes, "Life which you look for, you will never find." In other words, death is inevitable and our thirst for more will never be quenched on earth. Texts such as these give us insight into the life and psychology of the earliest human societies in recorded history.

2700 BCE – Egypt: The idea of an afterlife continued to appear more in documented texts and artifacts. The Ancient Egyptians, during the time of the Old Kingdom in Egypt, were building the pyramids in order to preserve the Pharaohs in the afterlife. **The pharaohs, considered both political leaders and gods on Earth, were seen as intermediaries between the gods and the people, suggesting complex political power dynamics that may have contributed to the ideological degradation of human dignity (-) for the average person in Egypt.** When pharaohs died, they were mummified and laid to rest with their most important valuables to take into the afterlife. Pharaoh Djoser (2670 to 2640 BCE) was the first to be laid to rest in a pyramid, at Saqqara.[37] The pyramids were built as giant structures to enclose the tomb of the pharaoh, and to help guide them into the afterlife. Pharaoh Khufu, the fourth Dynasty of the Old Kingdom, built the famous Great Pyramid of Giza (2589 to 2566 BCE) for his afterlife. Today, Egypt is marked with many pyramids enclosing the

---

[36] Cooper, J. S. (1994). *Sumerian and Akkadian Cuneiform Texts*. Oxford University Press.
[37] Lehner, M. (1997). *The complete pyramids: Solving the ancient mysteries*. Thames & Hudson.

mummified tombs of the pharaohs.

The construction of the Egyptian pyramids and the Great Sphinx highlights the remarkable technological advancements and astronomical knowledge of ancient Egypt (+). The Egyptians used quarried limestone, granite, and sandstone, transporting massive blocks – some weighing up to 80 tons – through a combination of sledges, wooden rollers, and water lubrication to reduce friction on sandy surfaces. Their understanding of leverage, counterweights, and weight distribution allowed them to precisely position stones, demonstrating advanced mechanical principles.

Astronomically, the pyramids are aligned with the cardinal directions with incredible precision, achieved through observations of circumpolar stars.[38] Additionally, the pyramids' layout is thought to reflect the alignment with the Orion constellation, symbolizing the connection between the pharaoh's soul and the god Osiris.[39] The Great Sphinx faces directly east, likely linked to the rising sun and the equinoxes, emphasizing the Egyptians' deep understanding of solar cycles and their integration of architecture with celestial symbolism. **Advancements in their ideological symbolism reflect a comprehensive approach, where architecture, astronomy, and spirituality (+) were intertwined, underscoring the Egyptians' innovative capabilities.**

During the summer solstice (around June 21), the sun sets in perfect alignment between the Great Pyramid of Khufu and the Pyramid of Khafre as viewed from the Great Sphinx. This alignment suggests that the Sphinx was not only a symbolic guardian of the pyramids but also part of a larger astronomical design that emphasized the sun's movements. The direct gaze of the Sphinx toward the east at sunrise reflects the significance of the sun god Ra, reinforcing the Sphinx's symbolic role as a representation of both earthly and celestial order.

Technological advancements in their physical structures and ideological developments which promoted civilized society (+), often came at the cost of dehumanizing slave labor and sacrifice to their gods (-). The Old Kingdom solidified Egypt's place as a cultural and architectural leader of the ancient world, whose influence would stretch for millennia.[40] Although Egypt's political power

---

[38] Hawass, Z. (2006). *The Pyramids: The Mystery, Culture, and Science of Egypt's Great Monuments.* Smithsonian Books.

[39] Bauval, R., & Gilbert, A. (1994). *The Orion Mystery: Unlocking the Secrets of the Pyramids.* Crown Publishing Group.

[40] Shaw, I. (2003). *The Oxford History of Ancient Egypt.* Oxford University Press.

dynamics would shift, the Old Kingdom of Egypt still influences the world today. The origin of Ancient Egypt's technological and celestial knowledge is still unknown as archaeologists continue to uncover the history of ancient Egypt.

2334 BCE – Akkadian Empire in Persia: Back in the Persian Gulf and Mediterranean region in, the Akkadians overthrew the Sumerians. **The Akkadians, unlike previously controlled city-states, opted to form the Akkadian Empire under rule of Sargon of Akkad. This is the first known empire in history, marking a shift from the fragmented and often warring city-states of Sumer to a more unified political structure that controlled a vast region (+).**

After the conquering of the Sumerians, the Sumerian religion and language still existed, so to respect this, Sargon incorporated the religion into the Akkadian pantheon and allowed for the use of Sumerian language in the empire (although it eventually faded). **The respect for other religions (+) was a new ideological development within a society, as most groups to date had a singular belief system within their group.** Their centralized authority led to the establishment of *Ensi*, or governors, to lead various regions and city-states within Akkadia. This led to the rise of a military, administrative functions, and the establishment economic policies for the empire. Nothing had been seen on such a scale to date in human history. It demonstrated how a region could be held together through a combination of military power, strategic administration, and the integration of diverse cultures and languages.

The idea of an Empire through the Akkadian's political power dynamics showed increased complexity in human interaction with regard to decentralization of power and respect for smaller groups within a larger group dynamic (+). Future empires like the Babylonian and Assyrian empires would adopt and refine this model.[41]

2100 BCE – Xia Dynasty: Farther east, in China, we see the beginning of the Xia Dynasty.[42] The Xia Dynasty is credited with laying the groundwork for the dynastic system in China, which would continue through various dynasties for more than 3,000 years. **The dynastic system was a new political power dynamic that**

---

[41] Liverani, M. (2013). *The Ancient Near East: History, Society and Economy*. Routledge.
[42] Li, X. (2010). *Ancient China's early states: A comprehensive study of the Xia Dynasty*. Shanghai: Fudan University Press.

represented various forms of control over China, to include multiple ideological developments that influenced political leadership to benefit the rights of the people being governed (+).

According to legend, Yu the Great, the founder of the Xia Dynasty, was renowned for his role in controlling floods through large-scale water management, which symbolized the ruler's responsibility to maintain order in both nature and society. **The Xia rulers are said to have established hereditary rule (-), a political power dynamic which had little to do with ability to lead, but still became a defining feature of later dynasties.** The Xia controlled a significant part of the Yellow River valley, an area critical to Chinese agriculture and the development of Chinese civilization. This period may have also seen the emergence of early forms of Chinese writing, though the first unmistakable evidence of Chinese script comes from the later Shang Dynasty.

The Xia Dynasty's legendary history deeply influenced Chinese political philosophy. The concept of the Mandate of Heaven is a significant ideological development and change in political power dynamic which justified the rule of emperors through a divine power. It is said to have been introduced by the Xia and implemented most notably by the Zhou dynasty. **The mandate stated that rulers must govern virtuously to maintain their legitimacy (+).**[43] This became a central tenet of Chinese political thought.

It is interesting to note the similarities in divine influence being introduced into political power in both Egypt and China during this time, though no known relation exists to their origin post-cognitive revolution.

2000 BCE – The Prophet of the Jews, Christians, and Muslims: Around 2,000 BCE, a prophet named Abraham (Ibrahim in Islamic tradition) lived in the ancient Near East cities of Ur in Mesopotamia and Canaan (around modern-day Iraq, Türkiye, Syria, Israel, and Palestine) according to biblical and historical timelines. Although there is no remaining archaeological evidence of his life, the stories of Abraham's life in the Bible[44] and the Qur'an[45] align with the historical evidence, which promotes the credibility of his life during this time period. **Unique to prior spiritual beliefs and religions, he**

---

[43] Xu, H. (2015). The Mandate of Heaven in Chinese political history. *Shanghai Academy of Social Sciences Press.*
[44] Kitchen, K. A. (2003). *On the Reliability of the Old Testament.* William B. Eerdmans Publishing Company.
[45] Al-Khalidi, T. (2001). *Ibrahim: A Biography of the Prophet of Islam.* Islamic Publications International.

took responsibility for guiding his descendants in ethical living (+), setting an example of faith and commitment to god's laws.

Abraham and his wife, Sarah, were unable to conceive a child. In the Bible, Sarah suggested that Abraham have a child with Hagar (Sarah's Egyptian servant), which led to Ishmael's birth. So, Ishmael, the firstborn son of Abraham, was born to Hagar.[46] However, after Isaac was born, tension between Sarah and Hagar escalated, and Hagar and Ishmael were sent away at Sarah's request, though God promised Abraham that Ishmael, too, would be the father of a great nation.

Ishmael is seen as the ancestor of many Arab peoples, particularly in Islamic tradition. In Islam, Ishmael (called Isma'il in Arabic) holds a special place as a prophet and as the ancestor of the Prophet Muhammad, through whom Islam traces its lineage back to Abraham.

Eventually, Abraham and Sarah had a child together, named Isaac, when both were advanced in age. Isaac's birth is considered a fulfillment of God's promise to Abraham that he would father a great nation, specifically through Sarah. Isaac is significant in Jewish and Christian traditions as the child of God's covenant with Abraham.

In the biblical account, God tested Abraham's faith by commanding him to sacrifice Isaac, though at the last moment, God provided a ram to be sacrificed instead.[47] This story is central to Jewish and Christian theology, representing themes of faith, obedience, and divine intervention. Islamic tradition also has a version of the sacrifice story: Muslims believe that it was Ishmael, not Isaac, whom Abraham was commanded to sacrifice.[48] This story is commemorated annually during Eid al-Adha, a major Islamic festival. Isaac went on to Father Jacob (later named Israel) and Esau, with Jacob being the patriarch of the Israelites, making Isaac an ancestor of the Jewish people.

The lives of Isaac and Ishmael, while distinct, are deeply intertwined in the religious traditions of Judaism, Christianity, and Islam, symbolizing the shared heritage and ancestry of these Abrahamic faiths, despite the divergence in their theological narratives. **The intertwined story has created human-degrading conflict between the religions for millennia, which continue today (-); however, Abraham's respect for the dignity of humanity has been echoed in later teachings of Judaism, Christianity, and Islam (+).**[49]

---

[46] Genesis 17:15-21 (New International Version).
[47] Genesis 22:1-18 (New International Version).
[48] Qur'an 37:102-109 (Saheeh International).
[49] Levenson, J. D. (2012). *Inheriting Abraham: The Legacy of the Patriarch in Judaism, Christianity, and Islam.* Princeton University Press.

1894 to 1595 BCE – Old Babylonian Period: Going back to Mesopotamia, we see Babylonian Mesopotamia's leader create the legal system. **King Hammurabi's "Code of Hammurabi" promoted a significant ideological development which encouraged cooperation throughout the empire (+).** The legal system had 282 laws for King Hammurabi's people to follow.[50] Law 196, *An Eye for an eye, a tooth for a tooth*, is still echoed today. **The code encouraged political power dynamics founded in written code and diplomacy (+).** He created a society based on defined laws and created a caste system. Now, no matter where one fell in the hierarchy of society, it was defined rather than presumed, meaning that a person now had the ability to understand what was needed to move from one level of the hierarchy to another. The concept of written laws improved human rights because it allowed one to understand how society was viewed by those in power.

Hammurabi's code also developed the idea of *innocent until proven guilty*, which is a key theme to many justice systems in the world today. His code also furthered rights for families, inheritance, and property. The code was inscribed on a large stone stele and displayed publicly for all to see. This public display of laws was significant, as it established the king's role as a just ruler, while also making the laws accessible, ensuring that the people were aware of them. **The follow-on ideological developments that were inspired by Hammurabi's code often included defined principles (+), which allowed anyone to abide by cultural or group practices even if they were unfamiliar.**

1680 to 1650 BCE – Hittite Civilization: Less than A century later in modern day Türkiye, the Hittite civilization was being led by their first King, King Labarnas I. Labarnas and his successors played crucial roles in shaping the Hittite state, turning it from a small kingdom into a formidable empire by the mid-second millennium BCE.[51] **The Hittites were particularly noted for their technological advancements in military technology and their political power dynamics of statecraft and diplomacy (+).** They are credited with refining the use of chariots, which became a key element in their military dominance. They also used iron in their weaponry, which marked a critical transition from the Bronze Age to the Iron Age. The

---

[50] Richardson, S. (2010). Hammurabi's law code and the politics of justice in ancient Mesopotamia. *Journal of Ancient Near Eastern Law*, 10(2), 227-244.
[51] Bryce, T. (2005). *The Kingdom of the Hittites.* Oxford University Press.

development and use of iron tools and weapons transformed military and agricultural productivity, influencing later civilizations like the Assyrians.

Through their technological advancements (+), their territory expanded nearly all the way to Egypt in 1295 BCE. Similar to Hammurabi, the Hittites also developed a legal system which further defined political power dynamics to favor civilized society (+). The laws covered issues related to property, marriage, and crime, and they highlight the hierarchical nature of Hittite society. Their legal traditions would influence other Near Eastern cultures. **Additionally, their capital, Hattusa, would be a cultural and political hub in the region, influencing ideological developments through the publication and storage of legal, religious, and diplomatic texts in their archive system (+).**

1600 BCE – Mycenaean Greece: Mycenaean Greece was a powerful and militaristic society centered around fortified palace complexes, such as those at Mycenae and Pylos. Governed by a warrior elite, the Mycenaeans expanded their influence across the Aegean and Mediterranean through military conquest and trade. Their use of chariots and advanced bronze weaponry gave them a tactical advantage, and their raids, including the possible conquest of Minoan Crete, showcased their aggressive expansion.[52] **The Mycenaeans developed the Linear B script for administrative purposes, revealing a highly organized society (+) controlled by the palace-centered rulers.**[53] Although the civilization collapsed around 1100 BCE, likely due to internal strife and invasions, its **warrior ethos and heroic ideals influenced later Greek culture, especially as reflected in the Homeric epics. These warrior-ethos political power dynamics were often times oriented towards power and conquest with little regard for human dignity outside of their group (-), while their technological advances in writing and weaponry improved long term human flourishing (+).**

1600 BCE – Shang Dynasty: Back in China, The Shang Dynasty went on to replace the Xia dynasty. It was the second recorded Dynasty in Chinese history and is the earliest Chinese dynasty for which there

---

[52] Drews, R. (1993). *The End of the Bronze Age: Changes in Warfare and the Catastrophe ca. 1200 B.C.* Princeton University Press.
[53] Chadwick, J. (1976). *The Mycenaean World.* Cambridge University Press.

is direct historical evidence.[54] Ruling along the Yellow River, the Shang developed an early form of Chinese script on oracle bones, used for divination and communication with the gods. **Chinese script contributed to their ideological developments by allowing for communication of ethical behaviors and practices throughout the dynasty (+).** They practiced ancestor worship, with the king serving as both a political and religious leader. The dynasty's bronze weapons and military strength allowed them to maintain control over a vast region, while their highly stratified society placed the king and nobles at the top, with peasants and slaves at the bottom. **The Shang Dynasty's political power dynamics, once established, continued to place power at the top with little regard for human dignity (-), despite established laws and practices that would have allowed for growth and equality.** Thus, politically, the Shang did not show meaningful change from their predecessor's political leadership.

1295 to 1272 BCE – Hittite Civilization & Egypt: The Hittites fought the Egyptians most notably in the Battle of Kadesh in 1274 BCE. King Mutwalli II ordered troops to attack the Egyptian Neighbors who were led by Ramesses II. The battle was a territorial dispute particularly over Syria and Canaan. It was renowned for the massive use of chariots, which were the dominant military technology of the time. The Hittites, known for their expertise in chariot warfare, deployed over 3,000 chariots, outnumbering the Egyptian forces. However, Ramesses II was able to rally his troops and escape an ambush, turning the tide of the battle at a critical moment. Both armies withdrew, with neither side achieving a decisive victory. Though 40,000 Egyptians fought 20,000 Hittites, the battle ended in a draw.

Negotiations between King Mutwalli II and King Ramesses II met for peace talks after the battle and agreed to live separately in peace. The Hittites became known for their diplomacy, especially during the period after Labarnas' reign. They engaged in extensive diplomatic relations with other great powers of the time, including Egypt, Mitanni, and Assyria. **The Treaty of Kadesh (1274 BCE) with Egypt, signed much later in 1259 BCE, is one of the earliest recorded international peace treaties, showing the Hittites' prowess in political power dynamics through diplomacy (+).**[55] Through conflict resolution, the Hittites went on to teach the Egyptians

---

[54] Chang, K. C. (1980). *Shang Civilization*. Yale University Press.
[55] Beckman, G. (1996). Hittite diplomacy: Lessons from the past. *Journal of Ancient Near Eastern Studies*, 55(3), 99-112.

Metalwork, while the Egyptians taught the Hittites Agriculture, allowing both civilizations to prosper. **Technological advancement through cooperation and equity between civilizations was now seen as not only possible, but advantageous (+).**

After their conflicts with the Hittites and the subsequent peace treaty, Egypt continued to maintain and develop its established social hierarchy, which had existed long before these events. This hierarchy, often depicted as a pyramid, was essential to the structure of Egyptian society, with each class having a distinct role.

At the bottom were the peasants and slaves, who worked as farmers and laborers, providing the backbone of Egypt's agricultural economy and building of monumental structures. Above them were the artisans, including skilled workers like stonecutters and painters, responsible for creating Egypt's iconic monuments and artworks. The merchants facilitated trade along the Nile River and beyond, bringing goods to different regions of Egypt. The next tier consisted of the scribes, who mastered the art of hieroglyphics and recorded the daily life and decrees of the pharaohs. They were critical to maintaining Egypt's administrative system. Soldiers followed in rank, tasked with defending and expanding Egypt's borders, particularly during the New Kingdom. Above them were the bureaucrats, including viziers, who managed the resources of the empire, and priests, who ensured that the gods were honored through rituals and temple upkeep. Nobles governed the various regions of Egypt on behalf of the Pharaoh, owning vast estates and holding political and military power. At the top of this hierarchy was the Pharaoh, considered both a divine ruler and the mediator between the gods and the people.

Egyptian society was structured to serve the Pharaoh, who in turn served the gods, maintaining cosmic order (*ma'at*). This ensured that each class had a defined role, contributing to the stability of the Egyptian state.[56]

This complex hierarchy provided both a political power dynamic to promote stability (+) and ideological developments which encouraged cooperation as a whole of society (+). However, it explicitly led to inequality through slavery (-).

1250 BCE – The Jewish People & the Exodus from Egypt: The Exodus of Jews from Egypt is believed to have happened between 1300 to 1200 BCE. Jews were, at the time, a nomadic group who had

---

[56] Brewer, D. J., & Teeter, E. (1999). *Egypt and the Egyptians.* Cambridge University Press.

lived throughout Syria, Canaan, and Egypt. **They initially had a tribal political power dynamic in which they were led by local elders or judges rather than a centralized monarchy (+).** Jewish prophets, such as Isaiah, Jeremiah, and Amos, emerged as voices that challenged the monarchy and political leaders.

Jews emphasized adherence to ethical standards and denounced corruption, injustice, and idolatry among the elite through their thorough use of the Torah (+). The tradition of prophetic critique reinforced the idea that political leaders were accountable to divine law and the welfare of the people, rather than unchecked authority. **Welcomed for centuries in Egypt, Jews were enslaved as part of the Egyptian's political power dynamics which favored authoritarian rule over human dignity following the Treaty of Kadesh (-).**

According to Christian and Jewish history, in 1250 BCE, Moses freed the Israelites from Pharaoh Ramesses II in Egypt. Moses, born an Egyptian, was chosen by the Jewish people's God to lead the Exodus from Egypt, a defining moment in Jewish history. The Exodus story is crucial as it defines the Israelites' identity and their covenant with God, which includes receiving the Ten Commandments at Mount Sinai. While there is no direct connection between the Exodus and Hittite-Egyptian diplomacy, both events are part of the broader narrative of shifting powers and geopolitical migrations that shaped the Near East in this period. It is possible that the weakening of Egypt's hold on Canaan and other regions during this time created an environment that allowed smaller groups, such as the Israelites, to establish themselves in the region following their exodus. Moses became a key figure in the Religions of Judaism, Christianity, Islam, and other religions that stem from Abraham, to include the Baháʼí faith.

1200 BCE – Phoenician Civilization: One of the first signs of the end of the Bronze Age was the collapse of the Hittite Empire, which was due to internal strife, resource shortages, and military pressures. The final blow came from the Sea Peoples, whose invasions destabilized the region further.[57] The once-Hittite capital, Hattusa, was abandoned and eventually destroyed, marking the end of the Hittite civilization as a major political entity. The Sea Peoples did not limit

---

[57] Drews, R. (1993). *The End of the Bronze Age: Changes in Warfare and the Catastrophe ca. 1200 BC.* Princeton University Press.

their attacks to the Hittites; they also threatened the Egyptians and Mycenaean Greeks. The origins of the Sea Peoples remain a mystery, but theories suggest that they were composed of displaced populations from places such as Sardinia, Sicily, or the Balkans.

With the end of the bronze age, came the beginning of a significant moment in the Phoenician Civilization: The spread of the alphabet. **The Phoenicians were a seafaring people located in modern-day Lebanon who are credited with the development of one of the first alphabets, enabling more thorough communication of ideas (+).** They established colonies across the Mediterranean, including Carthage. As they interacted with major civilizations to include the Egyptians, Greeks, and Sicilians, their written language began to spread and be adopted. Their alphabetic system simplified writing, which had a major influence on literacy and communication in the ancient world.[58] **Their alphabet would later become the basis for many modern scripts, to include its influence on Greek and Latin, providing a platform for the multitude of ideological developments promoting ethical behavior (+) in the years to come via written text utilizing the phonetic alphabet.**

1200 to 400 BCE - The Americas: Around the same time, in the Americas, the Olmec civilization was establishing itself in what is now modern-day Mexico. This civilization, which lasted from approximately 1200 to 400 BCE, is often considered the "mother culture" of Mesoamerica, as it significantly influenced later civilizations such as the Maya and Aztec.[59] Much remains to be discovered about the Olmecs, especially due to the undeciphered hieroglyphs found in their artifacts, which are still being studied. One prominent theory suggests that the Olmec civilization may have served as a foundational culture for subsequent Mesoamerican civilizations, though their influence on Native American civilizations in the United States is uncertain. The Olmecs are famous for creating colossal stone heads, believed to represent their leaders. These monumental sculptures still exist today, though the identities of the figures remain unknown. **Additionally, their iconography, ball games, and religious practices shaped the later ideological developments through cooperation within the Maya and Aztec cultures (+).**

---

[58] Markoe, G. E. (2000). *Phoenicians.* University of California Press.
[59] Diehl, R. A. (2004). *The Olmecs: America's first civilization.* Thames & Hudson.

III.ii CLASSICAL ANTIQUITY AND THE IRON AGE
(1200 BCE TO 500 CE)

The Iron Age and Classical Antiquity saw a profound transformation in warfare, empire-building, and philosophical thought. **The technological advancements provided a shift to iron tools and weapons, which led to expansive empires, from Persia to Rome (+), and fostered larger and more organized military conflicts which exploited humanity on a scale yet to be seen (-).**

At the same time, **ideological developments – ranging from Greek democracy to Confucianism and the early monotheistic religions – introduced ideals that questioned power structures and human purpose, setting the groundwork for concepts of personal and societal dignity (+). However, these ideals often remained accessible only to certain groups, while political power continued to enforce a rigid hierarchy that could exclude and oppress the common people (-).** Conflicts during this period, therefore, reflected an evolving struggle between ideological beliefs and the political power dynamics that controlled them.

1046 to 256 BCE – Zhou Dynasty: The Zhou Dynasty eventually overthrew the Shang, marking the end of their reign, but their cultural and technological advancements had a lasting influence on Chinese civilization. **The shift from a centralized state to a more distributed form of rule influenced governance structures not just in China but echoed in feudal systems seen later in medieval Europe, which often led to inequal distribution of power (-).** This shift demonstrated how societies adapt governance models to deal with expanding territories, evolving **political power dynamics**, and local autonomy. **If managed fairly, distributed governance could work, but with the Zhou dynasty, leaders were often overpowered by corruption (-).** It also left philosophical implications, as the decentralized system created a complex web of obligations, leading to the ideological developments of social and ethical norms that governed the relationships between lords and vassals. **Confucianism later built on this, stressing the importance of familial and societal hierarchy and the moral duties between rulers and the ruled (+).**

The Zhou Dynasty became the longest lasting Chinese dynasty to

THE IRON AGE (1200 BCE TO 500 CE)

date.[60] It was divided into two major periods: the Western Zhou (1046 to 771 BCE) and the Eastern Zhou (770 to 256 BCE). Zhou continued the concept of a mandate from Heaven, which justified their rule by claiming divine approval. **These adopted ideological developments paired with political power dynamics often gave the emperor supreme rule (-).** The mandate had four principles: (1) Heaven grants the emperor the right to rule. (2) Since there is only one heaven, there can only be one emperor at any given time. (3) Emperor's virtue determines their right to rule. (4) No one Dynasty has a permanent right to rule.[61] Under the mandate, Emperors would lose favor from heaven (often through famine, floods, earthquakes), signaling the need for a new ruler.

Under the Zhou dynasty, feudalism became the dominant political structure, where regional lords governed territories on behalf of the king. Under feudalism, peasants farmed the lands, soldiers protected the lands, Lords owned the lands and gave some of the profits to the kings, and then the King governed it all. The peasants did not question this lifestyle because they were protected and allowed to live their day-to-day life without the immediate threat of losing basic needs; additionally, it aligned with eastern philosophy, started by Confucious.

The Eastern Zhou period is further divided into the Spring and Autumn Period and the Warring States Period, times of intense regional conflict but also of intellectual flourishing, as philosophies like Confucianism, Daoism, and Legalism emerged. **The Zhou are credited with technological advances in agriculture, bronze, and ironworking, which allowed for the support of larger bureaucracies and more citizen involvement to meet the required sophisticated administrative practices (+).** Despite internal strife and decentralization, the Zhou Dynasty and their feudal system left a profound legacy on Chinese governance, philosophy, and culture, which would shape Chinese civilization for centuries.

1020 to 586 BCE – Jews in the Near East: Back in the Near East, Saul became the first King of Israel around 1020 BCE, marking the transition from a tribal confederation (which had lasted since the Exodus several centuries earlier) to a centralized monarchy. His reign was largely defined by conflict with the Philistines. After Saul's death,

---

[60] Sima, Q. (1993). *Records of the Grand Historian.* (B. Watson, Trans.). Columbia University Press. (Original work published c. 91 BCE)

[61] Zhang, G. (2015). The political philosophy of the Mandate of Heaven in early Zhou China. *Journal of Chinese Historical Studies*, 21(3), 47-62.

David became king, uniting the tribes of Israel.

David was a significant figure for his military conquests and the establishment of Jerusalem as the capital. He established the Davidic Dynasty, from which the Messiah was prophesied to emerge.

Solomon, David's son, expanded Israel's wealth and influence. **His most famous achievement was the construction of the First Temple in Jerusalem in 957 BCE, which became the principal place of worship for the Hebrews, providing for a centralized location for ideological development (+).** The First Temple housed the Ark of the Covenant and was the central place of worship for the Jewish people. His reign was seen as a golden age of prosperity and wisdom. After Solomon's death, internal strife led to the division of the kingdom into two: the Northern Kingdom of Israel (comprising ten tribes) and the Southern Kingdom of Judah (with Jerusalem as its capital). This marked a period of decline, conflict, and foreign threats. In 722 BCE, The Assyrian Empire conquered the Northern Kingdom of Israel, leading to the dispersion of the Ten Lost Tribes. These tribes scattered across the Assyrian Empire and lost their distinct identity.

912 to 516 BCE – Neo-Assyrian & Neo-Babylonian Empires: In the Neo-Assyrian and Neo-Babylonian eras, Babylon and Assyria had a complex relationship marked by rivalry, intermittent cooperation, and cycles of conquest and rebellion.

The Neo-Assyrian Empire played a leading role in Mesopotamian history and the larger Near East, establishing one of the first truly imperial states through its aggressive military campaigns and innovations in governance and bureaucracy. Despite Babylon's distinct cultural identity and history, Assyrian kings saw the region as strategically and economically important, particularly for controlling the Mesopotamian trade routes and fertile lands. However, Babylonians resisted being suppressed, leading to frequent uprisings against Assyrian rule. The Assyrians developed advanced siege tactics and imposed vassalage across much of the Near East. Today, the Assyrian Empire is often seen as one of the first great militaristic empires, whose fall set the stage for the rise of Babylon empire and eventually the Persian Empire.[62]

To stabilize Babylon, some Assyrian rulers attempted diplomatic measures (+). For example, Esarhaddon (681 to 669 BCE) tried to govern Babylon with respect for its religious customs

---

[62] Liverani, M. (2013). *The Ancient Near East: History, Society, and Economy.* Routledge.

and even appointed his son as its king, recognizing Assyria as its own kingdom. **His successor, Ashurbanipal (669 to 631 BCE), also held Babylon in high regard and maintained Assyrian control while respecting Babylonian culture and religion (+).** This approach was aimed at easing Babylon's resistance, as Babylonians revered their city and religious heritage.

In 626 BCE, Babylon seized the opportunity to break free from Assyrian control, establishing the Neo-Babylonian Empire, which allied with the Medes to launch attacks on Assyrian territories. This coalition defeated Assyria, culminating in the fall of Nineveh in 612 BCE and the final collapse of the Assyrian Empire by 609 BCE.

Around 600 BCE, Under Nebuchadnezzar II, the Neo-Babylonian Empire reached its peak, with extensive technological advancements through building projects like the Ishtar Gate and the fabled Hanging Gardens (+). Ideological developments followed in Babylon, with an emphasis in cultural pride, leading to the Babylonian Exile of the Jewish people after the conquest of the Kingdom of Judah in 586 BCE, which **displayed degradation of human dignity and decaying ideological developments (-).**

During the conquest, Jerusalem and the First Temple were destroyed, and many Israelites were taken into Babylonian exile. This is a pivotal moment in Jewish history, as it leads to the development of key religious texts and the solidification of Jewish identity in exile.

Less than a century later, **the Neo-Babylonian fall to the Persians, led by Cyrus the Great in 539 BCE, opened a new era of cultural exchange (+) in Persia under the Achaemenid Empire.**[63] In 516 BCE, after the Jewish people returned to Jerusalem after the Babylonian Exile, the Jews used the original Temple Mount location of the First Temple to Construct the Second Temple. **This temple became the focal point of Jewish religious life, with rituals, sacrifices, and pilgrimages to the site (+).** The Second Temple was expanded and renovated by Herod the Great in the first century BCE, making it one of the grandest structures in the ancient world.

800 to 200 BCE – Axial Age: The Axial Age marked a profound transformation in human thought, laying the foundation for many of the world's religious and philosophical traditions (+).

---

[63] Kuhrt, A. (1995). *The Ancient Near East, c. 3000–330 BC*. Routledge.

We will cover these figures in the next sections, but names such as Zoroaster (Zarathustra) (circa 1000 to 500 BCE), Jeremiah (circa 650 to 570 BCE), Confucius (551 to 479 BCE), Laozi (500 BCE), Siddhartha Gautama "The Buddha" (563 to 483 BCE), Pythagoras (circa 570 to 495 BCE), Mahavira (circa 599 to 527 BCE), Heraclitus (circa 535 to 475 BCE), Parmenides (circa 515 to 450 BCE), Empedocles (circa 495 to 435 BCE), Mo Tzu (circa 470 to 391 BCE), Socrates (469 to 399 BCE), Democritus (circa 460 to 370 BCE), Plato (circa 428 to 348 BCE), and Aristotle (384 to 322 BCE) all emerged across different civilizations independently, yet contemporaneously.

These influential thinkers gave rise to religions such as Zoroastrianism, Judaism, Buddhism, Confucianism, and Taoism.[64] Further, a whole book could be written to elaborate how they were foundational to our understanding of science and the universe. **A central theme woven through each of these philosophers' teachings was that there exists a common truth to all of us through nature, regardless of social or political status (+)**. Many of these philosophers rejected the status quo of ritualism and hierarchical power and went on to find a personal way to ethically practice one's religion or beliefs through thoughts, works, and deeds. To this day, figures from this era continue to influence our understanding of ethics, society, and spirituality; moreover, they all advocate for the human rights of each individual.

800 to 500 BCE – Ancient Greece: Ancient Greece began to grow both in terms of population and economic complexity. Due to its naturally infertile land, especially in regions like Attica and Peloponnese, Greece could not fully support its growing population through agriculture. This prompted the Greeks to begin importing goods such as grain, timber, and metals from surrounding regions, particularly from places like Egypt, Anatolia, and the Black Sea region.[65] To sustain this expansion and secure access to resources, the Greeks embarked on a period of widespread colonization, establishing roughly 90 colonies along the Mediterranean and Black Sea coasts. These colonies stretched from Marseilles (ancient Massalia) in modern-day France to Rostov-on-Don (ancient Tanais) in modern-day Russia. The colonies were not just extensions of Greek territory but were independent city-states that maintained strong trade and cultural links

---

[64] Jaspers, K. (1953). *The origin and goal of history*. Routledge & Kegan Paul.
[65] Boardman, J. (1999). *The Greeks Overseas: Their Early Colonies and Trade*. Thames & Hudson.

with their mother cities. **Greek colonization led to the decline of small city-states housing Indigenous peoples (-); however, it significantly influenced the spread of Hellenic culture, language, and political structures across the Mediterranean, contributing to the eventual rise of classical Greek civilization (+).**

Greece's spread of Hellenic identity spurred exposure to new regions and challenges encouraged Greek colonies to experiment with various forms of political power dynamics, from oligarchies to early forms of democracy. Colonies facilitated trade and resource exchange, which boosted prosperity and stability for many Greek city-states, enabling them to fund infrastructure, arts, and military advancements that strengthened their political influence. These experiments and exchanges led to the rise of a fierce rivalry between Athens and Sparta, which had a deep impact on daily life and the region's political landscape.

Sparta was unique in its organization, revolving around a militaristic system established by the Lycurgan reforms, which took place around 650 BCE. **These reforms emphasized a rigid social hierarchy, military discipline, and a dual kingship system.** Sparta's primary concern was military strength, and its society was divided into three main groups: the Helots (state-owned serfs, often prisoners of war), free non-citizens (known as Perioikoi, who were soldiers and craftsmen without political rights), and the Spartiates (the ruling warrior class). **Spartan life centered on discipline, warfare, and the subjugation of the Helot population, which had an overall negative impact to human dignity outside of Sparta (-).**

Athens began to rise in prominence during the seventh century BCE, particularly after the establishment of democracy under Cleisthenes around 508 to 507 BCE (+). Although the official rise of democracy is notable, earlier political and legal reforms by Draco and Solon in the seventh and sixth centuries BCE laid the groundwork for Athenian democracy.

Athens became a cultural, economic, and intellectual hub, excelling in philosophy, the arts, and architecture, with a strong emphasis on civic participation through its democratic institutions (+), sparking both positive ideological developments and political power dynamics. Under Cleisthenes, the Council of 500 was created, with 50 citizens chosen by lottery from each of the ten tribes to serve for one year. Every citizen (defined as free males born to Athenian parents) had a vote in the Assembly. In the assembly, laws were passed, military generals were elected, and other governmental decisions were made. Those who were not citizens (women, slaves, and foreigners) were excluded from the assembly.

Athens' influence peaked during the fifth century BCE, particularly under the leadership of Pericles. This period, known as the Golden Age of Athens, saw the construction of the Parthenon and the flourishing of democracy, drama, and philosophy.

753 BCE – The Beginning of Rome: According to Roman legend, the city of Rome was founded in 753 BCE. While Rome was not a direct result of Greek colonization, it was heavily influenced by neighboring Etruscan and Greek cultures in the broader Mediterranean region. The foundation myth of Rome centers around the twin brothers, Romulus and Remus, who were said to be the sons of Rhea Silvia and the god Mars. According to the legend, the twins were abandoned as infants and later rescued and nurtured by a she-wolf (Lupa), a symbol that became deeply ingrained in Roman identity.

As the story goes, the brothers grew up and eventually decided to establish a new city. However, a conflict arose between them over where to build the city and who would rule it. In the ensuing battle, Romulus killed Remus and became the sole founder and first king of Rome.[66] Romulus named the city after himself, and his reign began the legendary era of the Roman Kingdom.

The foundation myth of Rome reflects early Political Power Dynamics involving the struggle for authority between Romulus and Remus, leading to Romulus's rise to power through violence (-). This myth symbolizes the early establishment of power struggles within Roman identity, shaping Rome's long-standing association with power and conquest.

550 to 530 BCE – Persia & India: In 550 BCE, Cyrus the Great of Persia overthrew the Median Empire and established the Achaemenid Empire, which would become one of the largest empires in the ancient world. King Astyages of Medes, who was Cyrus's maternal grandfather, is said to have had a prophecy that Cyrus would one day rise to power. In response, Astyages allegedly attempted to eliminate him as a child. However, Cyrus survived and, as an adult, raised an army to challenge his grandfather. The conflict culminated in 550 BCE, when Cyrus defeated and captured Astyages. Rather than killing him, Cyrus allowed Astyages to live in peace after taking control

---

[66] Wiseman, T. P. (1995). *Remus: A Roman Myth*. Cambridge University Press.

THE IRON AGE (1200 BCE TO 500 CE)

of the Median Empire. **Cyrus's administrative innovations and technological advancements helped him efficiently govern a diverse empire, promoting tolerance and adaptability (+).**

As mentioned previously, **Cyrus famously conquered Babylon in 539 BCE, where he was welcomed as a liberator due to his benevolent rule, respecting local customs and religions (+).** With the conquest of Babylon, Cyrus became the ruler of Mesopotamia and extended his empire to the Indus Valley.[67] His policies of tolerance and administrative innovations helped solidify his rule over such a vast and culturally diverse empire. **By adopting benevolent policies, Cyrus set a precedent for governance that balanced power with respect for local traditions (+).** Cyrus also turned his attention westward, conquering Ionia, a region of Greek colonies in Asia Minor.

After creating an expansive Persian Empire, Cyrus died in 530 BCE during a military campaign against the Massagetae in Central Asia. The empire was inherited by Cyrus' son, Cambyses II, and later, by Darius the Great, who continued to expand and consolidate the empire further.

Around the same time in India, Prince Siddhartha Gautama lived in a palace in the Kingdom of Magadha. Prince Gautama was surrounded by beauty within his palace, but he was well aware of the broken nature of humanity. He spent most of his time reflecting on how the human experience was not perfect and sublime – it was death. When he grew up, he left the palace and went on to study and meditate with teachers, eventually forming Buddhism.

As the teacher of Buddhism, he had transcended the limitations of the ego and came to be in touch with universal consciousness through, what he called, *Enlightenment*. Siddartha became known as "Buddha," or the "Awakened one." The rise of Buddhism under Siddhartha Gautama represents a transformative Ideological Development. **His teachings on enlightenment and compassion (+) offered a contrast to the often rigid and divisive beliefs within societies of that time.** His teachings introduce the cessation of suffering through the Eightfold Path. **The Eightfold path consisted of eight practices: right view, right resolve, right speech, right conduct, right livelihood, right effort, right mindfulness, and right meditative awareness (+).**[68] Through these practices, one could achieve enlightenment.

---

[67] Wiesehöfer, J. (2001). *Ancient Persia: From 550 BC to 650 AD*. I.B. Tauris.
[68] Gethin, R. (1998). *The foundations of Buddhism*. Oxford University Press.

CONFLICT

490 to 356 BCE – Persia & Greece: The Persians attacked the Athenians in Marathon in 490 BCE. In this battle, the Persians lost over 6,000 soldiers before retreating, while the Athenians lost less than 200. It was after this battle that an Athenian soldier named Pheidippides ran 26.2 miles from Marathon to Athens to proudly state that the Athenians defeated the Persians. Persia's Mardonius restructured his military to reattempt multiple attacks on Greece both by land and sea. The Greek city-states, though undermanned, used fiords and terrain to tactically defeat the Mardonius and the Persians, marking an end to Persia's attacks on Greece. The Persian Wars highlight Greece's resilience and strategic use of terrain to fend off a larger Persian force.

The end of the Persian wars for Greece led to a period of thriving and unity through technological innovation, architecture, and cultural growth through arts and philosophy. The unity did not last long though, as power and prosperity rebirthed a competition between the Athenians and Spartans, leading to the Peloponnesian War from 431 to 404 BCE, where Sparta eventually defeated Athens.[69] **The Peloponnesian War reflected a recurring theme of political power-seeking at the expense of human dignity (-).** Athens' attempts to conquer Syracuse in Sicily in 413 BCE led to their ultimate downfall after they nearly destroyed their Naval fleet.[70] Eventually, Sparta defeated Athens and took over the Athenian city-state, leading to the end of Ancient Greece's prosperity.

At the height of the Peloponnesian war, a philosopher named Plato was prominently researching democracy in Athens. Plato was a student of Socrates and the teacher of Aristotle, and he founded the Academy in Athens, one of the earliest institutions of higher learning in the Western world. He was critical of the democratic system. In Book VI of The Republic, Plato argued that selecting rulers randomly from the population, as was the case with many positions in Athenian democracy, was akin to letting unskilled sailors steer a ship. He contended that only those who had studied philosophy and learned wisdom, logic, and justice – what he called the "philosopher-kings" – were truly fit to rule. Plato famously wrote, "There will be no end to the troubles of states, or indeed of humanity, until philosophers become kings, or until those we now call kings and rulers really and

---

[69] Raaflaub, K. A. (1998). Democracy, Oligarchy, and the Power Struggle in Athens and Sparta. *The Cambridge Ancient History: Vol. 5* (pp. 254-280). Cambridge University Press.
[70] Lazenby, J. F. (2004). *The Peloponnesian War: A Military Study.* Routledge.

truly become philosophers."[71]
Plato's criticism of democracy through his concept of "philosopher-kings" (+) introduced a new ideological perspective on leadership and the value of wisdom in governance, emphasizing the role of virtue over sheer power.

475 to 221 BCE – China's Warring States Period: In China, the Warring States Period was marked by continuous conflict between competing states due to the fragmentation of the Zhou Dynasty and uncertain economic and cultural factors. **The constant warfare of this time led to the rise of Legalism, a philosophy of governance based on the idea that people act primarily out of self-interest and require strict laws and punishments to maintain order (-).** The Legalist system was advocated by thinkers like Shang Yang and Han Feizi, who formalized its principles during the late Zhou Dynasty. Han Feizi, in particular, emphasized a rigid system of rewards and punishments to ensure compliance and reinforced state power.[72] Under Legalism, the ruler held absolute control over the state, including the economy, military, and society, to maintain stability and unity. **The rise was in direct response to the chaotic Political Power Dynamics of constant warfare. This harsh approach, while intended for stability, often disregarded individual dignity, and contributed to a culture of authoritarian rule (-).**

Legalism was not the only proposed form of governance; Confucian ideas about governance through benevolence were proposed, while Daoist ideals of non-interference were also proposed. These competing schools of thought introduced enduring questions about the nature of power, the role of the state, and the moral responsibilities of leaders.[73] Due to the internal strife caused by the warring states, the intellectual and military innovations of the time profoundly influenced Chinese history and governance, shaping the ideological and political structures of future dynasties. **As such, Confucianism continued to grow as an ideological development, shaping future Chinese generations by emphasizing a ruler's moral rectitude and integrity (+) as the basis for a stable and just government.**

---

[71] Plato. (2003). *The Republic* (C. D. C. Reeve, Trans.). Hackett Publishing Company.
[72] Pines, Y. (2013). *The Everlasting Empire: The Political Culture of Ancient China and Its Imperial Legacy.* Princeton University Press.
[73] Schwartz, B. I. (1985). *The World of Thought in Ancient China.* Harvard University Press.

CONFLICT

500 to 200 BCE – Zapotec Civilization: Meanwhile, in Mesoamerica, the Zapotec civilization thrived in its capital, Monte Albán, a city overlooking the Oaxaca Valley. The Zapotecs developed a clear social hierarchy, with the elite residing in Monte Albán, while artisans and farmers lived in the surrounding valleys.[74] Zapotecs were highly skilled in agriculture, particularly in the cultivation of maize. They also developed an early hieroglyphic writing system, using symbols and numbers, which remains one of the oldest known writing systems in Mesoamerica. In addition, they had an advanced calendar system, based on solar observations, which was used to track seasonal changes and ritual events.

356 to 160 BCE – Greece's Alexander the Great: Back in Greece, Alexander the Great was born, and grew up with teachers such as Aristotle, one of history's most renowned philosophers. Aristotle personally taught Alexander about key ideas, including the scientific method, philosophical reasoning, ethical considerations, and the value of the arts. At the age of 20, Alexander's father, Philip II of Macedonia, was assassinated. Alexander, having been shaped by Aristotle's teachings, took his father's place as King of Macedonia.

Alexander quickly raised a large army, consolidating his rule over Greece by defeating rebellious city-states. In 336 BCE, he began his campaign against the Persian Empire, defeating Darius III's forces in modern-day Türkiye. Alexander the Great went on to conquer the Persian Empire, including Judea, in 333 BCE. This led to the spread of Hellenistic (Greek) culture in Jewish lands, which influenced religious, cultural, and political life. By 331 BCE, Alexander had defeated Darius again in battles near Mosul and Babylon, pushing the Persian army further east. By 330 BCE, Alexander had captured the Persian capital, Persepolis, and extended his conquests into Iran and Afghanistan.[75] He continued his military campaign into the Hindu Kush mountains and India, where he fought the local rulers, including forces of the Mauryan Empire. **Alexander's use of technological advancements and military strategies (+) allowed him to extend Greek culture across vast regions, integrating diverse societies.**

However, Alexander's troops, having already achieved significant victories over Persia, grew weary and questioned the necessity of further conquests. As a result, Alexander's push for power was halted,

---

[74] Marcus, J., & Flannery, K. V. (1994). *The Zapotecs: Lords of the Clouds.* Thames & Hudson.
[75] Bosworth, A. B. (1988). *Conquest and empire: The reign of Alexander the Great.* Cambridge University Press.

THE IRON AGE *(1200 BCE TO 500 CE)*

forcing him to return to Greece without fully defeating the Mauryans. **Alexander's political power dynamics through expansionist ambitions caused large-scale displacement and upheaval (-), highlighting the human costs of empire-building.**

Meanwhile, in India, Ashoka the Great of the Mauryan Empire built up a powerful army in response to the threat posed by Alexander's incursions. After conquering the Kingdom of Kalinga, Ashoka witnessed the immense destruction caused by war, with over 100,000 people perishing.[76] Unable to justify the mass death, Ashoka embraced the teachings of Buddhism, promoting non-violence, respect for all religions, and the abolition of slavery within his realm. Ashoka's conversion to Buddhism after witnessing war's devastation was a pivotal Ideological Development. **His subsequent policies promoted non-violence and religious tolerance (+), contrasting sharply with the previous emphasis on conquest (-).** His conversion still impacts the region's ideology towards war today.

Alexander the Great died in Babylon in 323 BCE, at the age of 32. Following his death, his empire was divided among his generals into three major realms: the Ptolemies in Egypt, the Seleucids in the East, and the Antigonids in Greece.

323 to 146 BCE – Alexander's Legacy: Alexander the great left a legacy that would echo through history for centuries. After his death, regions of his Empire were divided.[77] Ptolemy I Soter, a general of Alexander the Great, took control of Egypt after Alexander's death. He established the Ptolemaic Dynasty, which ruled Egypt for 300 years. He built the library of Alexandria, which was one of the first major western educational institutions. This library attracted scholars, scientists, and philosophers from across the Mediterranean, housing many works of Plato, Aristotle, and other prominent thinkers. Alexandria became a hub of knowledge, especially in the areas of philosophy, science, mathematics, and astronomy, playing a critical role in the dissemination of Hellenistic culture.[78]

Meanwhile, Seleucus I Nicator founded the Seleucid Empire, another of Alexander's generals. Seleucus claimed vast territories that stretched from modern-day Türkiye to parts of Central Asia, including Babylon, Syria, and Persia. The empire was characterized by its

---

[76] Thapar, R. (2002). *Ashoka and the decline of the Mauryas* (3rd ed.). Oxford University Press.
[77] Green, P. (1990). *Alexander to Actium: The Historical Evolution of the Hellenistic Age.* University of California Press.
[78] Fraser, P. M. (1972). *Ptolemaic Alexandria.* Oxford University Press.

multiculturalism, incorporating Greek, Persian, and Asian traditions. The Seleucids continued to expand, but their control was often challenged by local rulers and internal revolts. By 223 BCE, Antiochus III the Great had ascended the throne and sought to reconsolidate the empire. Antiochus undertook campaigns to restore Seleucid power, fighting against Ptolemaic Egypt in the Fifth Syrian War and expanding into India and Anatolia. His reign represented the height of Seleucid influence, though it also set the stage for eventual conflict with Rome.[79]

Hannibal Barca, a Carthaginian military commander, launched one of the most famous attacks against Rome during the Second Punic War (218 to 201 BCE). In 218 BCE, Hannibal famously crossed the Alps with a massive army that included war elephants, catching the Roman forces by surprise. His campaign in Italy was marked by a series of significant victories, including the crushing Roman defeat at the Battle of Cannae in 216 BCE. Hannibal's strategic genius posed the greatest threat to Rome's dominance, but despite his initial successes, he was unable to capture the city of Rome itself. Over time, the Romans regrouped and under Scipio Africanus, they defeated Hannibal at the Battle of Zama in 202 BCE, leading to the decline of Carthage and its eventual destruction in 146 BCE.[80]

In Macedonia, The Antigonid Dynasty controlled Macedonia and parts of Greece. After the death of Alexander, the region fell under the rule of Antigonus I Monophthalmus and later his descendants. The Antigonids maintained a strong military presence in Greece and frequently clashed with other Hellenistic powers. They played a significant role in maintaining Greek independence from the growing influence of Rome and engaged in several wars with the Achaean League and Sparta. However, by 168 BCE, the Antigonid Dynasty fell to the Romans, marking the beginning of Roman dominance in the region.[81]

Around 167 BCE in Jerusalem, in response to the forced Hellenization and the desecration of the Temple by Antiochus IV, the Maccabees, a Jewish rebel group, rose up to reclaim Jerusalem. Today, this event is commemorated by the festival of Hanukkah.

221 to 96 BCE – China's Qin & Han Dynasties: Meanwhile, back in China, a new dynasty – the Qin Dynasty – rose to power in 221

---

[79] Bevan, E. R. (1902). *The House of Seleucus.* Edward Arnold.
[80] Lazenby, J. F. (1996). *Hannibal's War: A Military History of the Second Punic War.* University of Oklahoma Press.
[81] Walbank, F. W. (1984). *The Hellenistic World.* Harvard University Press.

THE IRON AGE (1200 BCE TO 500 CE)

BCE, driven by the new principles of Legalism. The Qin Dynasty, though short-lived, made significant strides toward unifying China.[82] Under the leadership of Qin Shi Huang, the first Emperor of China, the empire was divided into 36 commanderies, each governed by a civil governor, military commander, and imperial inspector. Qin Shi Huang, in response to the warring states period, believed in ruling through strict laws, based on the Legalist understanding that humans are inherently selfish and require strict discipline to maintain order. **His regime enforced harsh laws and centralized power to ensure unity, leading to widespread resentment (-).**

Qin Shi Huang's unexpected death in 210 BCE from illness, after his quest for immortality, contributed to the dynasty's fall. Some viewed his death as a sign of the Mandate of Heaven, carrying through with the overthrow of ineffective or immoral rulers. Due to internal rebellions and leadership struggles, the Qin Dynasty lasted only 14 years.

The Han Dynasty followed, beginning in 206 BCE. The Han rulers took a different approach to governance, incorporating the teachings of Confucius, which emphasized virtue, moderation, and piety. Under the Han, technology and economics flourished, particularly with the development of the silk industry. Silk production became the backbone of Chinese trade and led to the establishment of the Silk Road, the world's largest trade network at the time.[83] **The Silk Road connected civilizations, allowing for the exchange of goods and ideas, promoting intercultural engagement (+).**

In 96 BCE, China attempted to extend its influence to Rome by establishing diplomatic and trade ties, but this effort was thwarted by the Parthians in Mesopotamia. The Parthians, positioned between the major powers of Rome and China, functioned as intermediaries, often using deceptive tactics to control trade and maintain their influence.

86 to 26 BCE – The Spread of Roman Authority: Back in Greece, the Romans sought to take over the Greek city of Athens. They succeeded in 86 BCE during the First Mithridatic War, under the command of the Roman general Lucius Cornelius Sulla. This conquest marked the beginning of broader Roman influence in Greece. **It was also a precursor to Rome's larger expansion through military means (-).** Over the next century, Rome would go on to conquer

---

[82] Loewe, M. (2006). *The Government of the Qin and Han Empires: 221 BCE to 220 CE*. Hackett Publishing.
[83] Hansen, V. (2012). *The Silk Road: A New History*. Oxford University Press.

territories such as Jerusalem, Carthage, Eastern Spain, and the Celtic lands in modern-day France, Switzerland, Austria, and Germany.

In 52 BCE, Rome sent the military general Julius Caesar to lead fierce campaigns in Gaul (modern-day France), culminating in the siege of Alesia, where the Gallic leader Vercingetorix surrendered to Caesar. After this victory, Caesar continued to conquer much of Gaul, effectively turning it into a Roman province. Many of the Gauls were offered Roman citizenship, while others were enslaved.

Seeing Caesar's rapid success, the Roman Senate grew concerned over his growing power and demanded that he halt his conquests or be declared an "enemy of the state." This ultimatum marked the beginning of the Roman Civil War (49 to 45 BCE), which pitted Julius Caesar against his former ally and son-in-law, Pompey the Great. Caesar emerged victoriously, leading to sizable political restructuring in Rome.

During the civil war, Egypt was brought into Rome's in-fighting. This led to Caesar defeating Ptolemy XIII, after which he established Cleopatra and her brother Ptolemy XIV as co-rulers of Egypt. Following his conquests and victory in the civil war, Caesar sought to make Rome a more sophisticated civilization by leveraging the knowledge and technologies of the lands Rome had conquered. **Under Caesar, Rome developed infrastructure such as roads, bridges, aqueducts, as well as advances in arts, sciences, and political reforms (+); however, he did this at the expense of the people and resources that were conquered through war (-).**

Caesar also introduced significant legal reforms and expanded Roman citizenship to people in the newly conquered provinces. He implemented the Julian calendar, which, with modifications, is still in use today. However, in 44 BCE, Julius Caesar's reign ended abruptly when Cassius and Brutus assassinated him on the floor of the Senate.

After his death, Caesar's adopted son Octavian (later known as Augustus) and Mark Antony, one of Caesar's top lieutenants, worked together to defeat the assassins at the Battle of Philippi in 42 BCE.[84] However, in 31 BCE, tensions between Octavian and Antony resulted in a final conflict, with Octavian defeating Antony at the Battle of Actium. Following this defeat, Antony fled to Egypt with his lover Cleopatra, where they both died by suicide. In 27 BCE, the Roman Senate granted Octavian the title of Augustus, officially marking the beginning of the Roman Empire.[85]

---

[84] Southern, P. (2014). *Augustus*. Routledge.
[85] Boatwright, M. T., Gargola, D. J., & Talbert, R. J. A. (2004). *The Romans: From Village to Empire*. Oxford University Press.

3 BCE to 70 CE - Christianity: In the Roman province of Judea, a man named Jesus was born. This event is traditionally placed during a time when Rome was conducting a census, as mentioned in the Gospel of Luke in the Bible, which was intended to count the population of the Roman Empire for taxation purposes. Jesus' mother, Mary, and her husband Joseph traveled from Nazareth to Bethlehem, a journey of 150 kilometers, to participate in the census. When they arrived in Bethlehem, the inns were full due to the influx of people for the census, so Jesus was born in a manger, as described in Christian tradition.

Bethlehem holds special significance in Jewish prophecy as the birthplace of the future Messiah,[86] and many who witnessed Jesus' birth and early life believed him to be the prophesied savior. His teachings and miracles reaffirmed this belief for many Jews. However, the Roman Empire, which controlled Judea at the time, grew wary of Jesus' influence. In 33 CE, during the reign of Tiberius Julius Caesar Augustus, the Roman governor Pontius Pilate ordered Jesus' crucifixion, viewing him as a threat to Roman authority and stability in Judea. This execution, however, did not quell the movement. Instead, it sparked the rise of Christianity, with his followers proclaiming Jesus as the Son of God. **The rise of Christianity through Jesus' teachings introduced a new worldview that emphasized compassion, forgiveness, and salvation through faith (+). However, its monotheistic challenge to Rome's polytheistic and imperial structure (-) led to significant tensions, resulting in persecution and suppression of Christians.**

Saul of Tarsus, later known as the apostle Paul, posed a significant challenge to the Roman Empire's established order, contributing to Christianity's spread. After Jesus' death, Paul wrote thirteen of the twenty-seven books of the New Testament, known as the Pauline Epistles, which include letters to various early Christian communities, such as the Romans, Corinthians, and Galatians. In these letters, he continually stressed the monotheistic teachings of Jesus over the polytheistic ideologies of Rome.[87] The rise of monotheism through Christianity directly undermined the authority of the emperor and the traditional Roman religious practices.[88]

In 64 CE, a great fire destroyed two-thirds of the city of Rome. The Emperor Nero blamed Paul and the Christians for starting the fire,

---

[86] Micah 5:2 (New International Version).
[87] Acts 9:1-19, 13:1-3; Galatians 1:11-24 (New International Version).
[88] Kelly, C. (2006). *The Roman Empire: A Very Short Introduction.* Oxford University Press.

leading to widespread persecution of Christians throughout the empire, to include Paul's beheading in Rome after the fire. In the aftermath of the fire, Nero printed copious amounts of currency to fund reconstruction, leading to hyperinflation. Discontent spread, particularly in the provinces, as inflation exacerbated economic disparities.

In 66 CE, Jerusalem revolted against Roman rule, initially defeating Roman forces. However, in 70 CE, the Roman army, led by Titus, besieged Jerusalem, cutting off food and water supplies. The siege of Jerusalem ended in a devastating defeat for the Jewish population, with the Second Temple being destroyed and many people killed, effectively ending major resistance to Roman rule in the region.[89] **The opposition of the Roman state to Christianity showcases the rigid Political Power Dynamics that resisted any threat to the established order (-).**

The Roman empire expanded to the largest it would ever be, under Emperor Trajan (98 to 117 CE).[90] Roman control of Britain had been established under Emperor Claudius in 43 CE, but Trajan further consolidated and defended the region. Trajan's conquest of Dacia (modern-day Romania) in 106 CE was one of his most famous victories, enriching the empire with Dacia's vast gold mines. In his later campaigns, Trajan successfully captured parts of Mesopotamia (modern Iraq), extending Roman territory to the Persian Gulf. At its peak, the Roman Empire stretched from Britain in the west to the Persian Gulf in the east, and from the North African coast to the Rhine and Danube rivers in northern Europe. This vast empire encompassed a wide range of cultures, languages, and peoples, unified under Roman law and governance. **Roman expansion during Trajan's rule prioritized powerful control and resource extraction, often at the expense of local populations' autonomy and dignity (-).**

100 to 650 CE – The Americas: Back in central Mexico, Teotihuacan was one of the largest cities in the ancient world at its peak, with a population of over 100,000. The city was known for its massive pyramids, particularly the Pyramid of the Sun and the Pyramid of the Moon.[91]

The Teotihuacan civilization in the Americas reflected the advanced architectural capabilities and technological

---

[89] Goodman, M. (2008). *Rome and Jerusalem: The Clash of Ancient Civilizations*. Penguin Books.
[90] Bennett, J. (1997). *Trajan: Optimus Princeps*. Routledge.
[91] Cowgill, G. L. (2015). *Ancient Teotihuacan: Early Urbanism in Central Mexico*. Cambridge University Press.

THE IRON AGE (1200 BCE TO 500 CE)

advancements that enhanced social organization and cultural expression (+). However, by around 650 CE, Teotihuacan had declined and was eventually abandoned, though its cultural and architectural influences persisted in later Mesoamerican civilizations, such as the Toltecs and Aztecs.

Meanwhile in Mesoamerica in the Andean region, civilizations in modern day Peru and Chile were beginning to take shape, such as the Moche civilization and the Nazca civilization. Both civilizations are known to have complex social structures and beliefs. Located primarily along the northern coast of Peru, the Moche civilization is known for its highly sophisticated irrigation systems and agricultural techniques, which allowed them to thrive in an arid environment.

Moche society had a clear hierarchy with rulers, priests, warriors, and artisans, depicting a clear political power dynamic intended for the good of the community (+), but limited people within their layer of the hierarchy (-).[92] **When it came to ideology and technology, they were particularly famous for their intricate ceramic pottery and metalwork, which often depicted gods, warriors, and daily life (+). The Moche also practiced human sacrifice as part of their religious rituals (-),** as indicated by archaeological evidence found at sites like Huaca de la Luna.

South of the Moche, the Nazca civilization was located in the southern coastal region of Peru. The Nazca were recognized for their pottery and vibrant textile production. Today, the Nazca civilization's geoglyph "Nazca lines" depict unique shapes and animals.[93] These designs, such as the hummingbird, spider, and monkey, can only be fully appreciated from the air due to their enormous scale, spanning hundreds of meters. The exact purpose of the Nazca Lines remains debated, with theories suggesting they were linked to astronomy, religious ceremonies, or water rituals. It is unclear even today how they developed such exact designs on such a large scale.

The Nazca and Moche civilizations were part of a broader Andean cultural tradition that influenced the development of later empires, particularly the Inca Empire. Their innovations in water management, social organization, and artistic expression left a lasting legacy in the region. Furthermore, both civilizations illustrate the broader human capacity to adapt to harsh environments, demonstrating how technology, art, and religious practices can be deeply intertwined with

---

[92] Quilter, J. (2010). *The Moche of Ancient Peru: Media and Messages.* Peabody Museum Press.
[93] Reinhard, J. (1998). *The Nazca Lines: A New Perspective on their Origin and Meaning.* National Geographic Research.

ecological and geographical challenges.

Both the Nazca's and Moche's impacts are still visible today, from the preservation of the Nazca Lines to the ongoing archaeological discoveries that continue to reveal the complexity of Moche society. These civilizations not only contributed to the development of pre-Columbian cultures in South America but also offered insights into the ways ancient societies managed natural resources, governed their people, and expressed their beliefs through art and architecture. Following the decline of the Moche, the Wari and Tiwanaku cultures rose to prominence in the Andean region starting around 500 CE.

25 to 220 CE – The Fall of China's Han Dynasty: Back in China, during the early Eastern Han period, the Han dynasty was thriving economically thanks to the Silk Road and intellectually through the philosophies of Buddhism, Daoism, and Confucianism, which reinforced values within the different aspects of the dynasty.[94] Confucianism continued to serve as the intellectual backbone of governance, but Daoism and emerging Buddhist influences created a more diverse spiritual and philosophical landscape. During this period, these schools of thought often coexisted, with individuals sometimes blending elements of Confucian ethics, Daoist mysticism, and Buddhist spiritual practices.

By the middle of the second century CE, the Han Empire began to decline due to the weakening of imperial authority, the rise of the use of eunuchs (men who were castrated for specific reasons, often acting as key players in the social, political, or administrative purposes within an empire), economic strain, use of warlords to maintain regional order, political infighting, corruption, and popular revolts (-).[95] The increasing power of eunuchs and warlords, thanks to relatively inexperienced emperors – to include Emperor Huan (146 to 168 CE) and Emperor Ling (168 to 189 CE) – were keys to the fall of the Han empire.

Under their rule, officials often secured their positions through bribery, and many were more interested in personal gain than serving the empire. **As the dynasty weakened, rulers and officials increasingly deviated from Confucian ideals, leading to corruption and moral decay (-).** This shift undermined public trust in the government and contributed to social unrest. This resulted in

---

[94] Yü, Y. L. (1986). *Trade and Expansion in Han China: A Study in the Structure of Sino-Barbarian Economic Relations.* University of California Press.
[95] Bielenstein, H. (1980). *The Bureaucracy of Han Times.* Cambridge University Press.

mismanagement of the empire's resources and further weakened the government's ability to address crises.

In its earlier years, the Han Dynasty benefited from technological advancements in agriculture (like the use of iron tools and better irrigation techniques). However, by the end of the dynasty, technological stagnation and neglect of infrastructure contributed to food shortages and discontent among the population. This decline (-) reduced people's quality of life and strained social stability.

Toward the late second century, powerful aristocratic families, and warlords, such as the Cao family (with Cao Cao[96] rising to prominence), began to wield greater power, often superseding the emperor's authority. **The inability to innovate and sustain an effective defense system (-) both within and outside its borders left the empire vulnerable to invasions, further eroding stability.** The imperial family struggled to maintain control, and powerful families and generals began to challenge the emperor's authority.

One of the most significant crises was the Yellow Turban Rebellion in 184 CE, a massive peasant revolt driven by economic distress and the influence of millenarian religious movements. The assassination of Emperor Ling in 189 CE triggered a power struggle between warlords like Dong Zhuo, Yuan Shao, and Cao Cao, which led to the eventual fragmentation of the empire. **Millenarian movements reflected a rejection of the existing order and were often met with brutal suppression, exacerbating human suffering (-).** In 220 CE, Emperor Xian, the last Han emperor, was forced to abdicate, and Cao Pi, son of Cao Cao, established the Cao Wei dynasty, marking the official end of the Han Dynasty and the beginning of the Three Kingdoms period.

The Three Kingdoms Period was a brief but highly impactful era in Chinese history, characterized by war, political fragmentation, and the rise of powerful warlords. Although the period ended in 280 CE with the reunification of China under the Jin Dynasty, it left a lasting legacy on Chinese culture and history. Not only was it considered a time of intense warfare, political intrigue, and heroic figures, but it was also an era of cultural development and technological innovation.

---

[96] De Crespigny, R. (2010). *Imperial Warlord: A Biography of Cao Cao 155–220 AD*. Brill.

117 to 280 CE – Emperor Hadrian: Back in Rome, Hadrian ruled the Roman Empire from 117 to 138 CE. He is remembered for both his military and diplomatic achievements, including his construction of Hadrian's Wall in Britain to suppress tribes in Scotland who were not willing to live under Roman conquest. The wall stretched 80 Roman miles (73 miles/117 kilometers) from the River Tyne in the east to the Solway Firth in the west. **Hadrian's wall was a massive fortification (+), providing security for the Roman Empire's northern frontier and allowing for a more stable and controlled border with the tribes of Scotland. While it improved the safety and organization of Roman territories, the wall also symbolized the separation between Romans and local tribes, sometimes contributing to resentment and conflicts (-).** It served not only as a military fortification but also as a symbol of Roman power, marking the northernmost boundary of the Roman Empire at the time.[97]

In addition to his defensive strategies, Hadrian also faced the brutal task of suppressing internal revolts, most notably Bar Kokhba Revolt in Judea (132 to 136 CE). The revolt erupted after Hadrian implemented policies that deeply antagonized the Jewish population, such as his decision to build a Roman city, Aelia Capitolina, on the ruins of Jerusalem and his ban on circumcision, a critical Jewish religious practice. The revolt, led by Simon Bar Kokhba, initially saw Jewish forces recapture Jerusalem and declare independence. **However, Hadrian's response was brutal: he dispatched his general Julius Severus and reinforcements from across the empire to mercilessly crush the rebellion (-).**[98] After years of fighting, the Romans regained control, and the Jewish people suffered devastating consequences. Hundreds of thousands of Jews were killed, and many survivors were sold into slavery or exiled (-). Hadrian renamed Judea as "Syria Palaestina" in an attempt to erase Jewish ties to the land and forbade Jews from entering Jerusalem.[99] This marked a turning point in Jewish history, leading to the Jewish Diaspora and a shift in Jewish identity from a political to a more spiritual framework.

These events highlight the dual nature of Hadrian's reign, as both an authoritarian consolidator of Roman power and a harsh enforcer of imperial rule (-). His strict measures to suppress dissent, particularly the heavy military and economic costs, are precursors to

---

[97] Breeze, D. J. (2006). *Hadrian's Wall: A History of Archaeological Thought*. Kendall Hunt Publishing.
[98] Schäfer, P. (2003). *The Bar Kokhba War Reconsidered: New Perspectives on the Second Jewish Revolt Against Rome*. Mohr Siebeck.
[99] Eusebius, *Ecclesiastical History* (4.6.2).

THE IRON AGE *(1200 BCE TO 500 CE)*

the challenges that would contribute to the fall of the Roman Empire.

224 to 651 CE – Sassanian Dynasty: In the middle east, Ardashir I was the founder of the Sassanian Empire and reigned as Shahanshah (King of Kings) of Persia from 224 CE to 242 CE. He established the Sassanian Dynasty after defeating the last ruler of the Parthian Empire, Artabanus V, in the Battle of Hormozdgan in 224 CE, marking the end of the Parthian Empire and the beginning of Sassanian rule in Persia.

By improving infrastructure, reviving the economy, and unifying the empire under a single legal and religious framework, he contributed to social stability, economic prosperity, and the consolidation of cultural identity (+).

By promoting Zoroastrianism, he supported a structured ethical framework that emphasized truth, justice, and righteousness (+). However, Ardashir's efforts to centralize **Zoroastrianism as the dominant faith came at the expense of other religions and belief systems (-).** The suppression of religious minorities, including Christians, Jews, and followers of other local cults, diminished the religious freedom and dignity of those who did not adhere to Zoroastrian beliefs. This contributed to social tensions and conflicts. His legacy set the foundation for four centuries of Sassanian rule in modern day Iran, which would become one of the dominant empires in the region.[100]

250 to 900 CE – Classical Period in Mayan Culture: The Maya civilization reached its peak during the Classic Period. The Maya inhabited what is now southern Mexico, Guatemala, Belize, and parts of Honduras and El Salvador.

The Maya had a highly stratified society with a rigid class system. The ruling elite, including kings and priests, held significant power, while the common people had limited social mobility. **This hierarchy often resulted in social inequality, with the lower classes shouldering the burden of labor and tribute to support the ruling elite (-). While the Mayan society was patriarchal, there is evidence that women of noble birth could hold positions of power (+), particularly in times of political transition or as regents for young rulers.**

Their large footprint is attributed to Mayan knowledge in agriculture and engineering. **They developed sophisticated**

---

[100] Frye, R. N. (1983). *The History of Ancient Iran.* C.H. Beck.

agricultural techniques, such as terracing, raised fields, and irrigation systems, which enhanced their ability to feed a growing population. These innovations improved food security and economic stability (+).

Mayans were also known for their sophisticated knowledge of astronomy, mathematics, and the development of a complex calendar system. Their technological advancements also created the only fully developed writing system in pre-Columbian America (+).[101] During the Classical period, major Maya cities like Tikal, Palenque, Copán, and Calakmul flourished, with monumental architecture such as pyramids, temples, and palaces.

The concept of the *popol vuh* (creation myth) and the intricate beliefs about life, death, and the afterlife shaped their worldview. **The Mayan religious structure provided meaning, purpose, and social cohesion, enhancing the sense of dignity for those who adhered to it (+). However, the religious ideology also included practices such as human sacrifice, bloodletting rituals, and other offerings to appease gods. Captives from warfare were sometimes used for sacrifices, highlighting how political and religious systems could intersect to justify violence (-).**

The Mayan civilization was composed of independent city-states rather than a centralized empire. **While this allowed for cultural diversity and local autonomy (+), it also led to frequent warfare among city-states as they competed for resources, land, and captives (-). This warfare was often ritualistic, creating a need for unnecessary human-degrading conflict due to the capture and sacrifice of prisoners.**

Around 900 CE, many of the major Maya cities in the southern lowlands experienced a mysterious decline, due to environmental degradation, drought, warfare, and internal political collapse. However, the northern Maya cities, like Chichén Itzá, continued to thrive into the Postclassic Period (900 to 1200 CE).[102] **While the Mayan civilization made remarkable contributions to human knowledge, culture, and technology, the benefits of these advancements were limited to the elite (-) and came at the expense of those who were marginalized or sacrificed (-) for religious or political purposes.**

---

[101] Martin, S., & Grube, N. (2008). *Chronicle of the Maya Kings and Queens.* Thames & Hudson.
[102] Demarest, A. A. (2004). *Ancient Maya: The Rise and Fall of a Rainforest Civilization.* Cambridge University Press.

THE IRON AGE *(1200 BCE TO 500 CE)*

265 to 420 CE – China's Jin Dynasty: The Jin Dynasty was founded by Sima Yan, who established the Western Jin after overthrowing the Wei state in 265 CE, effectively ending the Three Kingdoms Period. By 280 CE, the Jin had successfully reunified China after conquering the state of Wu. However, the Western Jin was plagued by internal strife, particularly during the War of the Eight Princes (291 to 306 CE), a conflict that severely weakened the state. The Western Jin ended in 316 CE when nomadic invaders, the Xiongnu, captured the capital Luoyang, leading to the dynasty's collapse in northern China.[103]

The Eastern Jin was established in 317 CE by remnants of the Jin royal family, who retreated south of the Chang Jiang and set up their capital in Jiankang (modern-day Nanjing). The Eastern Jin maintained control over southern China, while the north was fragmented into various states ruled by nomadic groups during the Sixteen Kingdoms period.

The Jin Dynasty, especially during the Eastern Jin period, became a center for cultural and intellectual growth, particularly in literature, philosophy, and art (+). Philosophically, Neo-Daoism (Xuanxue), a revival of Daoist thought and metaphysical speculation, flourished during the Jin Dynasty, influencing intellectual circles. Figures like Wang Bi contributed to the philosophical interpretation of Daoist and Confucian classics, blending Daoism with Confucian ethics (+).[104]

The Eastern Jin period played a key role in the spread of Buddhism in China. Although Buddhism had already been introduced to China during the Han Dynasty, it gained greater prominence and acceptance during the Jin Dynasty. Several Buddhist texts were translated into Chinese during this time, and Buddhist communities began to establish monasteries and temples, influencing Chinese culture and spirituality.

The Jin aristocracy also played a key role in shaping the administrative structures that influenced later Chinese dynasties. The aristocratic families of the Jin were highly influential in local and central governance, setting the stage for later power dynamics in Chinese political culture.[105] **The dynasty was marked by a division between the ruling Jurchen elite and the Han Chinese majority, with the**

---

[103] Graff, D. A. (2002). *Medieval Chinese Warfare, 300–900*. Routledge.
[104] Chan, A. (2011). *Two Visions of the Way: A Study of the Wang Bi and the Guo Xiang Commentaries on the Laozi*. SUNY Press.
[105] Twitchett, D. C., & Loewe, M. (Eds.). (1986). *The Cambridge History of China: Volume 1, The Ch'in and Han Empires, 221 BC–AD 220*. Cambridge University Press.

CONFLICT

Jurchens maintaining a privileged status. The Han Chinese were often subjected to higher taxes and discriminatory policies, which led to social tensions and periodic rebellions (-).

Despite internal challenges and military pressures, the Eastern Jin survived until 420 CE, when General Liu Yu seized power and founded the Liu Song Dynasty, marking the end of the Jin Dynasty.[106]

284 to 325 CE – Rome's Acceptance of Christianity: Back in Rome, a significant turning point in European history occurred: the era of the tetrarchy and eventual acceptance of Christianity. Leading up to this, Diocletian recognized that Rome was becoming too large, so he created the tetrarchy of Rome. Diocletian divided the empire into four regions, each ruled by an emperor or a deputy, in order to bring stability and reduce the chances of civil war.[107] Diocletian formally established the Tetrarchy in 293 CE, appointing Maximian as his co-emperor (or Augustus) in the West, while Diocletian himself remained as *Augustus* in the East. To further strengthen the system, two junior emperors, known as *Caesars*, were appointed: Constantius Chlorus in the West and Galerius in the East. The idea of a Junior Emperor was to ensure smoother transition processes between emperors moving forward.

Diocletian pushed for military and administrative reforms, in addition to economic stability, which focused on defense from external threats, rather than continued expansion (+). These changes improved the defense capabilities of the empire, but they also placed significant strain on the population through heavy taxation to fund the enlarged military forces (-). By dividing the empire into more manageable regions, he was able to station armies closer to areas of conflict and ensure quicker responses to invasions.[108] Administratively, the Tetrarchy also allowed each emperor to oversee specific areas, reducing the overwhelming burden on any single ruler. Economically, he introduced the Edict on Maximum Prices in 301 CE, which sought to control prices and wages throughout the empire. While the edict had limited success, it reflected Diocletian's broader concern for stabilizing the economy and reducing inequality.

Despite its initial success in stabilizing the empire, the Tetrarchy system began to unravel after Diocletian's retirement in 305 CE. The system relied on the cooperation of the emperors, and once Diocletian was no longer in power, in-fighting and struggles for dominance among

---

[106] Mote, F. W. (1999). *Imperial China 900–1800*. Harvard University Press.
[107] Potter, D. (2004). *The Roman Empire at Bay, AD 180-395*. Routledge.
[108] Kelly, C. (2006). *Ruling the Later Roman Empire*. Harvard University Press.

the emperors' heirs resurfaced. By 312 CE, the Tetrarchy effectively ended when Constantine (heir to Constantius Chlorus) defeated Maxentius (heir to Maximian) at the Battle of the Milvian Bridge, where Constantine famously led his troops into battle with Christian crosses painted on their shields after having a vision. His victory not only consolidated power but also marked a turning point for Christianity in the Roman Empire.

In 313 CE, Constantine, alongside Licinius (heir to Galerius), issued the Edict of Milan, which granted religious tolerance to Christians and allowed them to practice their faith openly.[109] While Constantine ruled the Western Roman Empire, Licinius governed the East. **A series of conflicts between the two emperors – to include Licinius' pagan background and continued unjust rule of Christians in the east – eventually led to war (-).** After several battles, Constantine defeated Licinius decisively at the Battle of Chrysopolis in 324 CE, bringing an end to Licinius' reign and making Constantine the sole ruler of the Roman Empire.[110] The Eastern Roman Empire's capital was renamed from Byzantium to Constantinople (modern-day Istanbul, Türkiye). Licinius was initially spared but was later executed, along with his son, in 325 CE.

The Council of Nicaea, convened by Constantine in 325 CE, not only aimed to resolve the immediate theological dispute caused by Arianism, which questioned the nature of Christ's divinity, but also set a precedent for the role of the Roman Empire in religious affairs. The council's outcome – the Nicene Creed – affirmed the co-eternality of Christ with the Father, rejecting Arius's teachings and establishing the foundation of Christian orthodoxy. By issuing this creed, the council provided a unified Christian doctrine, which would shape the theological landscape of Christianity for centuries.[111]

Constantine's involvement marked a significant shift: the Roman emperor now had a personal stake in maintaining religious unity to stabilize his empire, intertwining the Church and state in a way that had lasting political ramifications (-). The Nicene Creed not only solidified Christian orthodoxy but also led to the eventual recognition of Christianity as the official religion of the Roman Empire under Theodosius I in 380 CE. This event formalized the integration of Christian doctrine into imperial policy and laid the groundwork for the imperial Church model that would dominate the

---

[109] Lenski, N. (2006). *The Cambridge Companion to the Age of Constantine*. Cambridge University Press.
[110] Odahl, C. M. (2004). *Constantine and the Christian Empire*. Routledge.
[111] Kelly, J. N. D. (1978). *Early Christian Doctrines* (5th ed.). HarperCollins.

Byzantine Empire and later European kingdoms. The council's long-term effects shaped the religious and political structure of both the Eastern and Western Christian worlds, leading to continued doctrinal debates and the centralization of ecclesiastical authority under imperial oversight.

370 to 476 CE – The Huns in Central Asia: The Huns, a nomadic group from Central Asia, began their westward movement in the late fourth century CE. By 375 CE, they had displaced the Ostrogoths (German goth tribes), forcing both the Ostrogoths and Visigoths toward Roman territory, contributing to increasing pressure on the Roman Empire. **The Huns excelled in mounted warfare, using the composite bow and highly mobile cavalry tactics to kill their enemies with their technological advancements (-).** This type of pressure was felt particularly after the death of Roman Emperor Theodosius I in 395 CE. Theodosius, the last emperor to rule both the Eastern and Western Roman Empires as a unified entity, had kept the empire stable, but after his death, he had a plan in place to divide the empire between his two sons, Honorius in the West, and Arcadius in the East.

The Huns, under leaders such as Uldin and later Attila, saw the division of the empire as a strategic weakness and began their invasions in the early fifth century CE. **The Huns did not establish a unifying ideological or religious framework, instead relying on charismatic leadership and tribal loyalty (-) to consolidate power, reflecting a barbaric mindset.** Although the Huns did not immediately invade the city of Rome, their movements in Eastern Europe displaced other groups, such as the Visigoths, who eventually sacked Rome in 410 CE. The Visigoths later established their own kingdom in 418 CE in modern-day Spain. Despite the sack of Rome, the city remained under Roman control.[112]

In 434 CE, Attila the Hun, and his brother Bleda inherited joint control of the Hunnic Empire, following the death of their uncle Rugila. Initially, they maintained an uneasy peace with the Roman Empire, particularly the Eastern Roman Empire (Byzantine Empire), through treaties. In 441 CE, Attila the Hun endured ruthless conquests throughout the Balkans and up to the Danube River frontier. His armies devastated cities like Naissus (modern Niš, Serbia) and Sirmium, and pushed toward Constantinople, but did not directly threaten the

---

[112] Collins, R. (2004). *Visigothic Spain, 409–711*. Blackwell Publishing.

capital until later campaigns.

Under leaders like Attila, the Huns created a loosely organized confederation that exerted political pressure on the Roman Empire, exploiting its divisions and demanding tribute (-). In 443 CE, His armies reached within striking distance of Constantinople, forcing Roman Emperor Theodosius II to pay a hefty annual tribute to secure peace.

After Attila assassinated his brother Bleda in 445 CE, he became the sole ruler of the Huns and turned his attention to further expansion and conquest. In 447 CE, Attila resumed his assault on the Eastern Empire, defeating Roman forces at the Battle of the Utus River. The Eastern Romans, financially strained, were forced to increase their tribute payments significantly. Attila's most significant campaign in the West was his invasion of Gaul (modern-day France) in 451 CE. His Hunnic forces allied with various barbarian groups, including the Franks and Burgundians, and sought to conquer the rich Roman provinces. The Battle of the Catalaunian Plains (also known as the Battle of Châlons) in 451 CE was a significant moment where a coalition of Roman and Visigothic forces halted Attila's advance into the Western Roman Empire.[113] In 452 CE, Attila invaded Italy, where he sacked several cities, including Aquileia, Milan, and Pavia. However, Attila withdrew after a mysterious meeting with Pope Leo I near the city of Mantua. The reasons for his withdrawal remain unclear, but factors may have included famine, disease, or the logistical difficulties of continuing the campaign.[114]

In 453 CE, Attila died unexpectedly on the night of his wedding to a young bride named Ildico. He died in the Pannonian Basin, a region located in modern-day Hungary. The cause of death is debated – some sources suggest he choked to death from a nosebleed, while others hint at assassination. Following his death, the Hunnic Empire quickly disintegrated as internal struggles and revolts from subject peoples, such as the Gepids and Ostrogoths, fragmented the once-Hunnic confederation. The Huns faded from the historical stage after the Battle of Nedao in 454 CE, where a coalition of Germanic tribes decisively defeated Attila's sons. **Without a strong and charismatic leader like Attila, the Hunnic Empire collapsed because it had failed to distribute wealth, power, and responsibility to anyone other than Attila (-).**

---

[113] Kelly, C. (2009). *The End of Empire: Attila the Hun and the Fall of Rome.* W.W. Norton & Company.
[114] Heather, P. (2005). The Fall of the Roman Empire: A New History of Rome and the Barbarians. Oxford University Press.

CONFLICT

The eventual collapse of the Western Roman Empire in 476 CE was influenced by a combination of factors to include economic decline, internal instability, general bureaucracy, and political divide; however, the primary acceleration of the instability and collapse of the Roman Empire is attributed to the Huns ransacking the empire with the help of various Germanic Barbarian tribes (Visigoths, Ostrogoths, Vandals, and Franks).[115] The Ostrogoths eventually took reign of modern day Italy following the fall of the Roman Empire. Odoacer, who had been serving as a general in the Roman army as an Ostrogothic warlord, declared himself king of Italy and sent the imperial insignia to the Eastern Roman Emperor Zeno, marking the symbolic end of the Western Roman Empire. Although the empire's power had been in decline for decades, this event is traditionally seen as the fall of the Western Roman Empire.[116]

The Visigoths in Spain, the Ostrogoths in Italy, the Franks in Gaul, and the Vandals in North Africa established new political orders that maintained many Roman traditions but also marked a significant transformation of Europe. The Franks, under Clovis I, eventually united much of Gaul and established the Merovingian dynasty. **These new kingdoms laid the foundation for the medieval order in Western Europe, blending Roman, Christian, and Germanic elements into a new cultural and political synthesis (+).**[117]

400 to 628 CE – Gupta Empire in India: The Gupta Empire led the Golden Age of India, marked by significant advancements in science, technology, mathematics, literature, and astronomy. **The Gupta rulers, particularly Chandragupta I, Samudragupta, and Chandragupta II, fostered an environment that encouraged intellectual growth and scholasticism. Centers of learning, such as Nalanda University, flourished, creating a lasting influence on intellectual development both in India and abroad (+).**

Aryabhata (lived 476 to 550 CE), one of the earliest and most influential astronomers and mathematicians of ancient India, is best known for his work, the Aryabhatiya, written when he was only 23 years old. In this treatise, Aryabhata calculated the circumference of the Earth with remarkable accuracy, estimating it to be about 24,835 miles (39,968 km), which is impressively close to the actual value of 24,901 miles (40,075 km). His work laid the foundation for future

---

[115] Ibid.
[116] Halsall, G. (2007). *Barbarian Migrations and the Roman West, 376–568*. Cambridge University Press.
[117] Collins, R. (1991). *Early Medieval Europe, 300–1000*. St. Martin's Press.

THE IRON AGE *(1200 BCE TO 500 CE)*

advancements in trigonometry and planetary motion.[118]

Brahmagupta (lived 598 to 668 CE) also made significant contributions in mathematics and astronomy. His most important work, the Brahmasphutasiddhanta, written in 628 CE, introduced the concept of zero as a number rather than merely a placeholder and provided rules for arithmetic operations involving zero. He also developed rules for solving quadratic equations and formulated methods for calculating the area and volume of geometric shapes, such as circles and spheres. In astronomy, Brahmagupta made significant advancements by calculating the motions of planets and accurately predicting eclipses.[119]

The Guptas established a decentralized administration politically, allowing regional leaders some autonomy while maintaining control over a vast and culturally diverse empire (+).

Hinduism and Buddhism flourished, with the Gupta era being known as the Golden Age of Indian culture, emphasizing art, literature, and religious tolerance. **Such Tolerance, paired with intellectual advancement, had a lasting influence, with the works of Aryabhata and Brahmagupta being translated and studied by later civilizations, including the Islamic world, where they contributed to the development of medieval science (+).**

420 to 581 CE – China's North and South Dynasties: After the fall of the Jin Dynasty, a period known as the Northern and Southern Dynasties took place in China, marking a time of political fragmentation in China.[120]

Nearly 200 years of human-degrading conflict ensued (-). In the south, power shifted between various dynasties: the Liu Song Dynasty (420 to 479 CE) was founded by Liu Yu but was marred by political instability and internal political conflicts (-); the Southern Qi Dynasty (479 to 502 CE), established by Xiao Daocheng, was short-lived and plagued by corruption (-); the Liang Dynasty (502 to 557 CE), under Xiao Yan, experienced a flourishing of culture and intellectual pursuits (+), though it later weakened due to internal rebellions (-); and finally, the Chen Dynasty (557 to 589 CE), led by Chen Baxian, was the last of the Southern Dynasties before its conquest by the Sui Dynasty (-).

Meanwhile, the northern region saw its own succession of rulers.

---

[118] Shukla, K. S. (1976). *Aryabhata and His Contributions.* Indian Journal of History of Science.
[119] Sarma, K. V. (2001). *Brahmagupta and His Contribution to Mathematics.* Journal of Indian History.
[120] Ebrey, P. B. (1999). *The Cambridge Illustrated History of China.* Cambridge University Press.

The Northern Wei Dynasty (386 to 534 CE), founded by the Tuoba clan of the Xianbei, succeeded in unifying northern China (+) and became known for its promotion of Buddhism, which provided spiritual guidance during tumultuous times (+). However, internal strife led to its split into Eastern Wei (534 to 550 CE) and Western Wei (535 to 557 CE) (-). The Northern Qi Dynasty (550 to 577 CE), which emerged from Eastern Wei, struggled with decadence and poor governance (-), falling to the Northern Zhou Dynasty (557 to 581 CE), which managed to reunify northern China and set the stage for the Sui unification (+).

Despite ongoing warfare, technological advancements in agriculture – such as improved irrigation techniques – helped sustain the population (+). The cultural landscape, particularly in the south, flourished with developments in art, literature, and Buddhist philosophy (+), offering spiritual peace amidst political upheaval. While elites enjoyed periods of relative stability, much of the population faced the challenges of war, heavy taxation, and social instability (-), reflecting both resilience and suffering during this fragmented era in Chinese history.[121]

481 to 786 CE – Frankish Kingdom: Meanwhile, in Europe, the Frankish Kingdom (modern-day France and Southwest Germany) began to form. The most significant early event in the formation of the kingdom was the rise of Clovis I, who became king of the Salian Franks in 481 CE. Clovis unified the various Frankish tribes and expanded their control over much of Gaul. **The Franks were known for developing the heavy plow, which significantly improved agricultural productivity in Northern Europe, leading to economic stability and population growth (+).**

In 496 CE, Clovis famously converted to Catholic Christianity after his victory at the Battle of Tolbiac, marking a turning point in European history. The Franks were the first Germanic tribe to adopt Catholic Christianity rather than Arianism, the form of Christianity practiced by many other Germanic groups at the time. This conversion helped Clovis secure the support of the Catholic Church and the Gallo-Roman population of Gaul. In 786 CE, Charlemagne, later known as Charles the Great, became the leader of the Franks. The Frankish Kingdom played a pivotal role in shaping medieval Europe, eventually

---

[121] Holcombe, C. (2011). *A History of East Asia: From the Origins of Civilization to the Twenty-First Century.* Cambridge University Press.

giving rise to the Carolingian Empire under Charlemagne, and laying the foundation for the future kingdoms of France and Germany.[122]

The kingdom not only unified the Franks but also strengthened ties with the Roman Catholic Church, which later became a cornerstone of Western European identity (+). Charlemagne's support of education and the establishment of schools led to a cultural revival known as the Carolingian Renaissance, fostering intellectual and religious growth (+).

---

[122] James, E. (1988). *The Franks.* Blackwell Publishing.

CONFLICT

III.iii THE MIDDLE AGES
(500 TO 1500 CE)

In the Medieval period, political power often consolidated within feudal systems, binding individuals to rigid class structures and frequently restricting personal freedoms. **Although some ideological developments (religious movements and philosophies) began to champion the sanctity of life and community (+), ideologies were entangled with political power dynamics seeking dominance and power, exemplified in the Crusades and religious schisms (-).** Technological advancements, though slow, facilitated territorial expansions and conflicts. **This era exemplifies how political power, while maintaining social order, often hindered the development of human rights by enforcing strict hierarchies and limiting social mobility, where the worth of an individual was defined by their status and adherence to dominant belief systems.**

500 to 1600 CE – The Americas: In the Americas, civilizations were continuing to rise throughout the Andean region, Mesoamerica, and North America.

In North America, **in the southwest of what is now the United States, the Ancestral Puebloans (formerly known as the Anasazi) built impressive cliff dwellings and pueblos, exemplifying advanced architectural and agricultural techniques (+). By around 1000 CE, they had developed large communities such as Chaco Canyon in modern-day New Mexico, which became centers of trade and religious ceremonies (+).** These societies practiced agriculture, focusing on maize, and were skilled in pottery and weaving. **The Ancestral Puebloans thrived until around 1200 CE, when environmental stress, including drought (-), led to the decline of many of their major settlements.**[123]

To their Northeast, in what is now the midwestern United States, the Mississippian culture emerged around 800 CE and is known for its large earthen mounds, complex chiefdoms, and monumental earthen mounds such as the most famous Mississippian site, Cahokia, located near modern-day St. Louis. **Cahokia was home to a large population – impressive earthworks, including the largest earthen structure in North America, provided geographic visualization of political power dynamics and ideology of the time (+).** Cahokia became a

---

[123] Lekson, S. H. (2009). *A History of the Ancient Southwest.* SAR Press.

major trade and religious center until its decline around 1600 CE.[124] **Its decline was attributed to resource depletion and political fragmentation (-)**.

Further north, the Cherokee, Navajo, and Inuit tribes developed distinct cultural identities, often adapting to harsh environments with innovative technologies, such as the Inuit's use of igloos and seal hunting (+). **The Navajo migrated to the Southwest around 1400 CE, while the Inuit spread across the Arctic, showcasing resilient social systems built on cooperation and shared resources (+)**.

In Mesoamerica, the Toltec civilization emerged after the decline of Teotihuacan in modern day Central Mexico. The Toltecs were known for their military prowess, trade networks, and religious influence over the region. **The Toltecs established themselves as a dominant power from around 900 CE until their decline in the mid-12th century, which was marked by internal strife (-) and invasions from northern groups like the Chichimeca.**[125]

In the Andean region, following the decline of the Moche, the Wari and Tiwanaku cultures rose to prominence in the Andean region. **Centered in the central highlands of Peru, the Wari built extensive road systems and urban centers (+), establishing a powerful empire that lasted from around 500 to 1000 CE.**[126] Located near Lake Titicaca in modern-day Bolivia, the **Tiwanaku civilization thrived during the same period and was known for its monumental architecture and sophisticated agricultural techniques, including raised-field farming (+)**.

Both cultures developed complex religious and political systems that fostered stability (+), but they eventually collapsed due to environmental challenges and internal political fragmentation (-). This led to a decentralization of power and the decline of their once-prosperous urban centers.

After the fall of the Wari and Tiwanaku, the Chimú civilization emerged along the northern coast of Peru, centered around their capital city, Chan Chan. **The Chimú built an impressive urban society and maintained a strong economic system based on agriculture and trade (+).**[127] Both the Wari and Tiwanaku civilizations collapsed

---

[124] Pauketat, T. R. (2004). *Ancient Cahokia and the Mississippians.* Cambridge University Press.
[125] Cowgill, G. L. (2015). *Ancient Teotihuacan: Early Urbanism in Central Mexico.* Cambridge University Press.
[126] Isbell, W. H. (2008). *Wari and Tiwanaku: International Identities in the Central Andean Middle Horizon.* University of Iowa Press.
[127] Moseley, M. E. (1992). *The Incas and Their Ancestors: The Archaeology of Peru.* Thames & Hudson.

due to a combination of environmental degradation and internal political fragmentation (-). As prolonged droughts strained their agricultural systems, both empires faced food shortages that weakened their economies, long-distance trade networks, and central authority. This allowed local elites to assert more control, leading to the decentralization of power and the eventual abandonment of major urban centers. By the 11th century, both the Wari and Tiwanaku civilizations had disintegrated, leaving a power vacuum in the Andean region that would later be filled by the Inca Empire.

527 to 610 CE – The Byzantine & Sassanid Empires: In the Eastern Roman Empire, Justinian I ruled the Byzantine Empire from 527 to 565 CE, based in Constantinople. **Justinian is most famous for his efforts to reconquer lost Western Roman territories, his comprehensive legal reforms known as the Corpus Juris Civilis which codified all Roman laws (+) and became the basis of European laws today, and his architectural achievements, including the construction of the Hagia Sophia (+).** His reign marked a high point in Byzantine imperial power, although his ambitious campaigns in Italy and North Africa, compounded with his reforms strained the empire's resources, and eventually led to overstretching Byzantine defenses.[128]

Meanwhile, the Sassanid Empire to the east (in modern day Iran) had just been revitalized by Khosrow I, who increased military, administrative, and economic reforms during his reign from 531 to 579 CE. Remembered as one of the empire's greatest rulers, his reign marked a high point in Sassanid strength and saw extensive military campaigns against the Byzantine Empire.

Khosrow I's wars with the Byzantine emperor Justinian I were part of a long-standing political rivalry between the two empires (-). These wars were primarily fought over control of the Caucasus region, Armenia, and strategic locations in Mesopotamia and Syria. Khosrow I's military campaigns against the Byzantines included several victories that expanded Sassanid influence, particularly in the eastern Mediterranean, and forced Justinian to pay large sums of tribute to maintain peace.[129]

Khosrow I supported the arts and sciences, establishing schools and libraries (+), which further solidified the Sassanid

---

[128] Cameron, A. (2011). *The Mediterranean World in Late Antiquity: AD 395–700*. Routledge.
[129] Greatrex, G., & Lieu, S. N. C. (2002). *The Roman Eastern Frontier and the Persian Wars: Part II, AD 363–630*. Routledge.

Empire as a cultural and intellectual hub in the region. The administrative and tax reforms he implemented helped strengthen the central government and increased the empire's capacity to wage war.

In the seventh century, the rivalry between the Sassanid Empire and Byzantium intensified under Khosrow II (590 to 628 CE). This period saw one of the most significant and destructive conflicts in the history of the Near East: the Byzantine-Sassanid War of 602 to 628 CE. Khosrow II launched a series of successful campaigns against the Byzantine Empire, exploiting internal weaknesses in Byzantium. **His forces captured key Byzantine cities, including Antioch, Damascus, and even Jerusalem in 614 CE, taking the True Cross, a revered Christian relic, back to Ctesiphon, the Sassanid capital.**[130] **This was a devastating blow to the Byzantine Empire, both militarily and religiously (-).** At its height, Khosrow II's empire stretched from the Caucasus to Egypt, and the Sassanids controlled more Byzantine territory than at any other point in history. However, these victories came at a high cost, and the prolonged conflict left both empires severely weakened.

570 to 610 CE – The Birth of Muhammad: To the southwest, in Mecca (modern day Saudi Arabia), the Quraysh and other Arab tribes in the region maintained their independence from both the Byzantine and Sassanid empires. Within the Quraysh tribe, the prophet Muhammad was born in 570 CE, to Abdullah. Although born into a noble family, Muhammad was orphaned at an early age – his father died before he was born, and his mother passed away when he was six. He was then raised by his grandfather, Abdul Muttalib, and later by his uncle Abu Talib, who protected him and played a significant role in his early life. Muhammad's lineage, in Islamic tradition, traces back to the prophet Abraham.

Muhammad worked as a merchant and was known for his honesty and integrity, earning the nickname Al-Amin (The Trustworthy). At the age of 25, he married Khadijah, a wealthy widow and businesswoman, with whom he had several children, including Fatimah, who became a prominent figure in early Islam. His marriage to Khadijah provided him with financial stability, allowing him time for spiritual contemplation.

Around 610 CE, at the age of 40, Muhammad began retreating to the Cave of Hira, located on the mountain of Jabal al-Nour near Mecca, to meditate. It was during one of these retreats that he received his first

---

[130] Kaegi, W. E. (2003). *Heraclius: Emperor of Byzantium*. Cambridge University Press.

revelation from the Archangel Gabriel (Jibril in Arabic). This moment is considered the beginning of his role as a prophet. Gabriel instructed Muhammad to "Recite!" (or "Read!"), and the first verses of what would become the Qur'an were revealed to him (Surah Al-'Alaq, 96:1-5).[131] Over the next 23 years, Muhammad continued to receive revelations that form the Qur'an, the holy book of Islam.

Muhammad began preaching a message of monotheism, calling for the worship of one God (Allah) and urging people to abandon the polytheistic pagan practices prevalent in Mecca. **His message emphasized social justice, equality, and the need for compassion toward the poor and marginalized (+).** Initially, his message was accepted by many, but faced resistance from the Quraysh elites, who were invested in the polytheistic traditions that drew pilgrims to the Kaaba and contributed to Mecca's wealth.

622 to 700 CE – The Fall of Empires & Rise of Islam: The Byzantine Emperor Heraclius (610 to 641 CE) managed to turn the tide against the Sassanids. From 622 to 628 CE, Heraclius launched a counteroffensive, eventually defeating the Sassanids in a series of decisive battles. In 627 CE, the Byzantines dealt a crushing blow to the Sassanid army at the Battle of Nineveh, which forced Khosrow II to flee and led to his assassination in 628 CE.[132]

Meanwhile to the south, as Muhammad's following grew, he and his followers faced increasing persecution from the Quraysh leaders. In 622 CE, after enduring years of hostility, Muhammad and his followers migrated to the nearby city of Yathrib (later renamed Medina), an event known as the Hijra. The Hijra marks the beginning of the Islamic calendar and is one of the most pivotal moments in Islamic history. In Medina, Muhammad was welcomed as a leader, and he established a growing community of Muslims, consolidating both religious and political authority.

In Medina, Muhammad successfully united various tribes, including Jewish and Christian communities, under the Constitution of Medina, which outlined the ideological principles of governance and coexistence (+). He became both a spiritual and political leader, implementing Islamic law (Sharia) and organizing the Muslim community, known as the Ummah. As his influence grew, so did the opposition from Meccan elites, leading to a

---

[131] Esposito, J. L. (2005). *Islam: The Straight Path.* Oxford University Press.
[132] Howard-Johnston, J. (2006). *The Last Great War of Antiquity: Heraclius and Khosrow II.* Oxford University Press.

series of military confrontations, including The Battle of Badr (624 CE): A key victory for the Muslims against the Quraysh; The Battle of Uhud (625 CE): A defeat for the Muslims, but a turning point in solidifying their resolve; and finally, The Battle of the Trench (627 CE): A successful defense of Medina against a larger Quraysh force.

At the same time, the wars between the Sassanids and Byzantines in the sixth and seventh centuries had far-reaching consequences for both empires. By the end of the Byzantine-Sassanid War in 628 CE, both empires were severely weakened. Their economies were drained, and their military forces were exhausted, leaving them vulnerable to new external threats. As a post-war effort, the Byzantine Empire regained control of Jerusalem from the Sassanids in 629 CE, following their earlier capture of the city during the Byzantine-Sassanid War in 614 CE.

The weakening of both empires created a political power vacuum (-) in the Near East that would soon be filled by the rapid expansion of Islam. In the years following the war, the newly unified Arab tribes under Muhammad and his successors, the Rashidun Caliphs, took advantage of the political instability in the region. Upon entering the city of Mecca in 630 CE, Muhammad ordered the destruction of the idols housed in the Kaaba, symbolizing the triumph of monotheism over polytheism. He rededicated the Kaaba to the worship of Allah, and most of the Meccan population converted to Islam. This event marked the final consolidation of Islam in Arabia, and Mecca became the spiritual center of the Muslim world.

In 632 CE, Muhammad died. Within a few decades of Muhammad's death, the Muslim armies swiftly conquered both Persia and large parts of the Byzantine Empire, including Syria, Palestine, and Egypt.[133] In 636 CE, the Muslims, under the command of Khalid ibn al-Walid, achieved a decisive victory over the Byzantines at the Battle of Yarmouk, which effectively opened the door to Muslim control over Greater Syria, including Jerusalem.

The Muslim Siege of Jerusalem lasted for several months until Patriarch Sophronius, the Byzantine leader of the city, agreed to surrender Jerusalem to Caliph Umar on the condition that he would personally receive the keys to the city. Umar traveled to Jerusalem, where he accepted the city's peaceful surrender. **After the conquest of Jerusalem, Umar ensured religious freedom for the city's**

---

[133] Kennedy, H. (2004). *The Prophet and the Age of the Caliphates: The Islamic Near East from the Sixth to the Eleventh Century.* Pearson Education.

Christian and Jewish inhabitants (+). He famously prayed outside the Church of the Holy Sepulchre to avoid setting a precedent that could later turn the church into a mosque. This event is remembered for its display of tolerance.

Only a few years later, in 641 CE, Muslim forces conquered Egypt, taking control of Alexandria. The collapse of the Sassanid Empire in 651 CE marked the end of a centuries-long rivalry with Rome/Byzantium and paved the way for the Islamic Caliphates to dominate the Near East. The geopolitical landscape of the region was permanently transformed by the rise of Islam, which replaced both the Sassanid and Byzantine influences in large parts of the Middle East, North Africa, and Central Asia.

While the Muslim empire expanded rapidly, internal divisions began to emerge over the rightful leadership of the community. Ali eventually became the fourth caliph after the assassination of the third caliph, Uthman ibn Affan, in 656 CE. However, his leadership was contested, and his reign was marked by internal conflict. Notably, a civil war between various factions within the Muslim community occurred, known as the First Fitna (656 to 661 CE). Ali faced political opposition from Muawiyah, the governor of Syria, who eventually established the Umayyad dynasty after Ali's assassination in 661 CE.

In stark conflict, Sunnis believed that the caliph should be chosen by consensus among the community's leaders and do not hold that the leader must be from the Prophet's family; meanwhile, Shia Muslims believed that leadership of the Muslim community should have stayed within the family of the Prophet, beginning with Ali and continuing through his descendants, known as imams. The defining event that solidified the Sunni-Shia split was the Battle of Karbala in 680 CE, in which Husayn ibn Ali, the son of Ali and grandson of Muhammad, was killed by the forces of the Umayyad caliph Yazid I. Husayn's martyrdom became a central event in Shia belief and is commemorated annually during Ashura. **His death is seen as a symbol of the struggle against tyranny and injustice, and it deepened the violent rift between Shia and Sunni Muslims (-).**

Despite this rift, as Islam became an established religion, Muhammad's life had a profound and lasting impact on world history. **Although the internal political conflicts after Muhammad's death led to enduring schisms (-), he is still regarded by Muslims as the final prophet in a line of prophets that includes Abraham, Moses, and Jesus, and his revelations form the core of Islamic theology.**

THE MIDDLE AGES (500 TO 1500 CE)

His leadership not only founded a new religious movement but also reshaped the political and cultural landscape of the Near East.

589 to 907 CE – China's Sui & Tang Dynasties: Back in China, The Sui Dynasty (581 to 618 CE) marked the reunification of North and South China. The Sui Dynasty was founded by Yang Jian, also known as Emperor Wen of Sui, who reunified China after centuries of fragmentation by conquering the Chen Dynasty in 589 CE. **The Sui implemented wide-ranging political reforms and technological advancements, including centralizing government, building the Grand Canal, and standardizing coinage and the legal code (+). However, the dynasty was short-lived due to military overreach, particularly in attempts to conquer Korea (-).** The Sui Dynasty was succeeded by the Tang Dynasty in 618 CE, marking the beginning of a new golden age in Chinese history.

The Tang Dynasty was led through means of Confucianism and Buddhism. **Their adoption of Confucianism and Buddhism promoted cultural cohesion and supported a flourishing era of literature and thought, aligning with human dignity (+).** The dynasty was founded by Emperor Gaozu (Li Yuan) and reached its height under Emperor Taizong and later Emperor Xuanzong.[134] The Tang Dynasty expanded China's borders into Central Asia, Korea, and Vietnam, strengthening its military and creating a vast empire, as well as for its flourishing of Buddhism, literature, and poetry.[135]

The Tang era is famous for the works of great poets such as Li Bai and Du Fu, whose contributions have shaped Chinese literary tradition. It was also during this period that China saw significant trade expansion, particularly along the Silk Road, which facilitated exchanges with Persia, the Byzantine Empire, and the Islamic Caliphates.[136]

However, the dynasty's decline began in the mid-eighth century, exacerbated by internal strife, including the Lushan Rebellion (755 to 763 CE), and economic challenges arising from the rebellion (-). The Tang Dynasty officially ended in 907 CE, leading to a period of fragmentation known as the Five Dynasties and Ten Kingdoms period.[137]

---

[134] Gernet, J. (1996). *A History of Chinese Civilization*. Cambridge University Press.
[135] Twitchett, D., & Fairbank, J. K. (Eds.). (1979). *The Cambridge History of China: Volume 3, Sui and Tang China, 589–906 AD*. Cambridge University Press.
[136] Hansen, V. (2012). *The Silk Road: A New History*. Oxford University Press.
[137] Adshead, S. A. M. (2004). *T'ang China: The Rise of the East in World History*. Palgrave Macmillan.

CONFLICT

711 to 1021 CE – Muslim Conquests & A Christian Empire: As Muslim expansion continued, Kingdoms that took place of the West Roman Empire began to fall. To mark a shift in ideology, the Umayyad Caliphate constructed the Al-Aqsa Mosque in 709 CE under Caliph Al-Walid I. **The mosque was built on the site of the Temple Mount (-), which was one of the holiest sites in Judaism, and remains a holy site for Jews, Christians, and Muslims today.**

The Umayyad Caliphate continued its conquests of the western world, when it conquered the Visigothic Kingdom in Spain in 711 CE, amid the Sunni-led Muslim conquest of the Iberian Peninsula. **Muslim forces under Tariq ibn Ziyad crossed the Strait of Gibraltar and began the conquest of the Iberian Peninsula (modern-day Spain and Portugal) (-).** Back in the Near East, in 717 CE, The Siege of Constantinople by Sunni-led Muslim forces failed, halting further expansion into Byzantine territory.[138]

Following this, one of the most significant developments in the Byzantine Empire was the Iconoclasm movement, which began in 726 CE under the reign of Emperor Leo III. Iconoclasm was a period of religious conflict marked by the rejection and destruction of religious images, known as icons, within the empire. Leo III and his successors, such as Constantine V, viewed the veneration of icons as idolatry, which they believed had caused divine displeasure, contributing to military defeats and natural disasters. This period led to a deep schism between the Eastern and Western Christian worlds, with the Pope in Rome condemning the movement. **This ideological shift was intended to strengthen religious devotion but, in practice, it led to social conflict and persecution of those who continued to venerate icons (-).** The Iconoclastic Controversy (726 to 787 CE) not only intensified religious divisions but also played a role in strengthening the unique identity of the Eastern Roman Empire by emphasizing imperial authority over church affairs, a hallmark of Caesaropapism - a political-religious system in which the secular ruler, often an emperor or monarch, has authority over the Church, including its doctrines, administration, and practices (-). This period solidified the cultural and religious differences between the Eastern Byzantine and Western Latin worlds, contributing to the eventual Great Schism in 1054 CE.[139] **The intent behind the iconoclastic reforms was to purify religious practices and protect what was seen as the**

---

[138] Nicolle, D. (2008). *The Great Islamic Conquests AD 632-750.* Osprey Publishing.
[139] Brubaker, L., & Haldon, J. (2011). *Byzantium in the Iconoclast Era, c. 680-850: A History.* Cambridge University Press.

integrity of the Christian faith (+); however, the differences in practice led to division (-).

Back in the Iberian Peninsula in 732 CE, Sunni-led Muslim forces were halted in their advance into Western Europe at the Battle of Tours (modern day France) by the Frankish leader Charles Martel.[140] This was as far west as Sunni Muslim expansion would go.

A few decades later, in 750 CE, the Abbasid Revolution led to the overthrow of the Umayyad dynasty and the establishment of the Abbasid Caliphate, based in Baghdad.[141] **Under the Abbasid Caliphate, Islam began to shift its focus from territorial expansion (-) to cultural and intellectual pursuits (+), ushering in the Golden age of Islam, which lasted roughly 150 years.** Sunni leaders such as Harun Al-Rashid contributed to the flourishing of knowledge by establishing institutions like the House of Wisdom in Baghdad. The House of Wisdom hosted scholars from around the world and even translated significant works from other academic institutes in Greece and Egypt.[142] **This era saw major advancements in science, medicine, philosophy, and art, with scholars from the House of Wisdom making significant contributions to fields such as algebra, sociology, and chemistry (+).**

Meanwhile in modern day western Europe, Frankish leader Charlemagne continued to skillfully expand his empire through military campaigns (-) in support of Christianity. He conquered large parts of what is now France, Italy, Germany, and parts of Spain, further consolidating his influence in Western Europe.[143]

Charlemagne's support of Christianity culminated when he was crowned as the Holy Roman Emperor on Christmas Day in 800 CE by Pope Leo III. This event symbolized the close alliance between the Papacy and the Frankish monarchy, marking the foundation of what would become the Holy Roman Empire. Leo III's papacy was not without challenges; facing internal struggles in Rome, he sought Charlemagne's protection and, in turn, used the crowning to assert the papal authority over secular matters as well as religious ones.[144]

While Pope Leo III had goodwill in crowning Charlemagne, his actions – especially in aligning the Papacy with a powerful

---

[140] Bachrach, B. S. (1977). *Charles Martel and the Battle of Tours-Poitiers: A reconsideration.* Speculum, 52(2), 334-346.
[141] El-Hibri, T. (2010). *The Abbasid Caliphate: A history.* Cambridge University Press.
[142] Gutas, D. (1998). *Greek Thought, Arabic Culture: The Graeco-Arabic Translation Movement in Baghdad and Early 'Abbasid Society (2nd–4th/8th–10th Centuries).* Routledge.
[143] McKitterick, R. (2008). *Charlemagne: The Formation of a European Identity.* Cambridge University Press.
[144] Collins, R. (2009). *Charlemagne.* University of Toronto Press.

CONFLICT

Christian ruler – contributed to the evolving political-religious landscape of Europe (-). This alliance of European states under one Christian ruler, amid the spread of Islam in neighboring states, laid important groundwork that indirectly contributed to the political and religious dynamics that would unfold in coming centuries.

After Charlemagne's death in 814 CE, his vast empire – which included much of modern-day France, Germany, and Italy – was passed to his son Louis the Pious. Louis had three sons – Lothair, Louis the German, and Charles the Bald – who each vied for control of the empire after their father's death in 840 CE. Internal divisions after Charlemagne's death, especially among his grandsons, led to the fragmentation of the empire through the Treaty of Verdun in 843 CE, setting the stage for the eventual formation of modern European states. The Treaty of Verdun is often seen as a key moment in the development of medieval Europe. It not only divided Charlemagne's once-unified empire but also set the stage for the emergence of European states as we know them today. It solidified divisions that would influence the political, cultural, and territorial makeup of Western Europe for centuries to come.[145]

Going back to the Abbasid Empire in the ninth century, between 826 and 828 CE, Arab forces from North Africa and Al-Andalus (Muslim Spain) launched significant military campaigns, extending their influence in the Mediterranean by conquering Crete, Sicily, and raiding Sardinia. These islands, under Byzantine control prior to being conquered and raided by the Muslims, were strategically important for controlling trade routes and projecting naval power in the Mediterranean.[146] The Arab conquests of Crete, Sicily, and raids on Sardinia between 826 and 828 CE represented a major expansion of Muslim influence in the Mediterranean and dealt a significant blow to the Byzantine Empire's naval and commercial dominance in the region. These islands would serve as bases for Arab maritime activities, including piracy, trade, and military campaigns, further cementing Arab control over key Mediterranean routes for centuries to come.

Shortly after the raids of mediterranean islands, the Abbasid Empire began to lose control over parts of the empire, including North Africa, Spain, and Persia, as local rulers worked to establish independent dynasties (e.g., the Shia Fatimids in North Africa, Sunni Aghlabids in the mediterranean islands, Sunni Umayyads in Spain, and

---

[145] McKitterick, R. (1983). *The Frankish Kingdoms under the Carolingians, 751-987*. Longman.
[146] Treadgold, W. (1997). *A History of the Byzantine State and Society*. Stanford University Press.

THE MIDDLE AGES *(500 TO 1500 CE)*

Sunni Samanids in Persia and Central Asia).[147] The Sunni-led Abbasids continued to exist as a religious authority, but their political and military power diminished significantly as their dynasties functioned autonomously.

The Fatimid Caliphate, an Ismaili Shia dynasty, established its rule in North Africa in 909 CE and eventually expanded into Egypt, founding the city of Cairo in 969 CE. **Although the Fatimids were ideologically and politically separate from the Sunni Abbasids, they promoted Islam as the unifying faith in their territories, even while asserting their own line of Shia imams as legitimate rulers (+).**

In Spain, Prince Abd al Rahman I established the Emirate of Córdoba in 929 CE, his descendant Abd al-Rahman III proclaimed the Caliphate of Córdoba, further asserting independence from the Abbasid caliphs in Baghdad. Despite political fragmentation, the Umayyads of Spain upheld Sunni Islam and played a key role in fostering a rich intellectual and cultural golden age, which contributed to the larger Islamic civilization.

The Samanid dynasty, based in Persia and Central Asia, also established an independent Sunni state while maintaining nominal allegiance to the Abbasid caliphs. The Samanids were instrumental in reviving Persian culture and fostering the development of Islamic scholarship, particularly through the Hanafi school of Sunni Islamic jurisprudence. Their efforts to Islamize Central Asia and spread Persian Islamic culture helped further integrate new regions into the broader Islamic civilization, even while the Abbasid caliphate weakened.

While the rise of the Shia Fatimids, Sunni Umayyads, and Sunni Samanids illustrated the political fragmentation of the Muslim world during the ninth and tenth centuries, the shared commitment to Islam as the guiding religious and legal framework maintained a sense of religious unity across these independent states. **As Islamic states pursued their own political ambitions, they contributed to the expansion, cultural flourishing, and intellectual development of the broader Islamic civilization, thus ensuring that Islam remained a unifying force towards dignity (+) despite the political divisions (-).**

In 1009 CE, Fatimid Caliph Al-Hakim bi-Amr Allah (996 to 1021 CE) began taking steps to consolidate his authority and exert pressure on Byzantine political power (-). Al-Hakim was

---

[147] Morgan, D. (1986). *The Mongols.* Blackwell Publishing.

known for his erratic and often extreme policies, which included periods of intense persecution of non-Muslims, particularly Christians and Jews, within his realm. His actions were influenced by a belief that such religious sites were symbols of idolatry, which ran contrary to his strict interpretation of Islam. His reign was marked by periods of religious fanaticism where he sought to enforce Islamic orthodoxy.

His extreme beliefs led to the destruction of Christian churches and Jewish synagogues, most notably the destruction of the Church of the Holy Sepulchre in Jerusalem in 1009 CE (-), a major holy site for Christians, traditionally believed to be the site of the crucifixion, burial, and resurrection of Jesus Christ. In addition to the destruction of the Church of the Holy Sepulchre, numerous other Christian and Jewish religious sites were targeted in Jerusalem and throughout the Fatimid Caliphate.

Such actions led to widespread outrage in Christian Europe and contributed to growing tensions between the Muslim and Christian worlds.[148] It marked a stark contrast to the earlier Caliph Umar's conquest of Jerusalem in 639 CE, when Umar displayed religious tolerance by allowing Christians to continue practicing their faith and refrained from praying in the Church of the Holy Sepulchre to preserve its sanctity as a Christian site.[149] **In response to the destruction of Holy land, Pope Sergius IV sent a letter to all churches, calling for a Holy Fight (-) in the Middle East and for the expulsion of Muslims from the Holy Land, sparking an era of retaliatory Crusades (-).** It would take nearly a century for the European Christians to adequately unite an army for such a fight.

793 to 1066 CE – The Vikings & Rise of a unified England: Meanwhile, an influential group was rising in the north – Vikings. They were uncivilized pagans from Scandinavia, who sought out equality by benefiting from elites' wealth. **In 793 CE, the Vikings launched one of their most infamous raids on the Lindisfarne Monastery in Northumbria (-), located on the east coast of England. This raid marked the beginning of the Viking Age (793 to 1066 CE) and sent shockwaves across Europe.** The attack on Lindisfarne was particularly shocking because monasteries were seen as places of peace, learning, and religion, yet they were undefended, making them ideal

---

[148] Canard, M. (1965). *Al-Hakim bi-Amr Allah*. In P. Bearman et al. (Eds.), *Encyclopaedia of Islam* (2nd ed.). Brill.
[149] Gil, M. (1997). *A History of Palestine, 634-1099*. Cambridge University Press.

targets for Viking raids.¹⁵⁰

The raid on Lindisfarne in 793 CE marked the beginning of a series of Viking raids on monasteries, towns, and coastal villages across Britain, Ireland, and Frankish territories. **These early raids were characterized by hit-and-run tactics (-), where small Viking fleets would land, plunder for resources, and escape before local defenses could be mobilized.**¹⁵¹

As the Vikings became more organized, they began to settle in the lands they raided. They went on to conquer and establish settlements in Danelaw, England in the early 800s, Dublin, Ireland in the mid-ninth century,¹⁵² Iceland in 874 CE, the establishment of Normandy, France in 911 CE,¹⁵³ Greenland in 985 CE, and were the first Europeans to reach as far as the Americas to Vinland (modern day Newfoundland) in 1000 CE. In 1066 CE, the Norman Conquest of England occurred, which was led by William the Conqueror (a descendant of Vikings from Normandy). This was the final Viking expansion.

After the Viking conquests and raids during the ninth century, Alfred the Great became King of Wessex in 871 CE. He worked diligently to defend his kingdom against continued Viking incursions. One of his major contributions was the creation of a network of fortified towns known as burhs. These fortifications were strategically placed across Wessex and beyond to protect against Viking attacks and provide refuge for local populations. In addition to building burhs, Alfred also reorganized his military, creating a system in which part of his army could defend the realm while the other part maintained essential agricultural work. **Alfred's efforts, along with his alliances with other Anglo-Saxon kingdoms, such as Mercia, helped secure the defense of Wessex and eventually contributed to the unification of England under his descendants, fostering identity and stability in the region (+).**¹⁵⁴

Athelstan ruled England from 924 to 939 CE and is widely regarded as the first king to unify the Anglo-Saxon kingdoms into a single entity. His reign saw the consolidation of power over the British Isles, particularly after his victory at the Battle of Brunanburh in 937 CE, which secured his dominance over rival kingdoms, including the Vikings, Scots, and Welsh.¹⁵⁵ As the grandson of Alfred the Great and

---

[150] Forte, A., Oram, R., & Pedersen, F. (2005). *Viking Empires*. Cambridge University Press.
[151] Sawyer, P. H. (1971). *The Age of the Vikings* (2nd ed.). Palgrave Macmillan.
[152] Ó Corráin, D. (1972). *Ireland before the Normans*. Gill & Macmillan.
[153] Bates, D. (2001). *William the Conqueror*. Yale University Press.
[154] Abels, R. P. (1998). *Alfred the Great: War, Kingship, and Culture in Anglo-Saxon England*. Longman.
[155] Foot, S. (2011). *Æthelstan: The First King of England*. Yale University Press.

the son of Edward the Elder, he played a significant role in uniting the English territories and defeating external threats. Athelstan's rule marked a significant step in the consolidation of England as a single kingdom, and he is often considered the first King of a unified England.

Aside from England, The Viking raids continued to have a profound impact on the political structure of medieval Europe, contributing to the rise of feudalism (-). Much like the Zhou Dynasty in 1000 BCE China, where people sought protection and security through a system that decentralized power, Europeans turned to feudalism as a way to safeguard their lands. In this system, lords controlled vast estates that were farmed by freemen, vassals provided military service in exchange for land, and peasants/serfs worked the land in return for protection. Kings retained ownership of the land and received tribute from the people, benefiting from the economic output of their subjects. **Unlike China's Feudal political power, the King was often in lockstep with the Christian Bishop, who was controlled by the Pope. Therefore, the Pope often controlled the Feudal states in Europe in an effort to reinforce beliefs (-) which encouraged peace (+).**

Feudalism became a popular and practical solution during the time of the Vikings, as it offered increased defenses against raids (+). Local lords could raise armies to defend their territories, and the decentralized nature of feudalism allowed for quicker and more localized responses to external threats.

By the end of the 11th century, Viking raids had decreased significantly, thanks to a few factors. First, the strengthening of European kingdoms and their defenses made it harder for Vikings to conduct successful raids. Second, **The Christianization of Scandinavia led to the Vikings' integration into broader European society both culturally and politically (+).** Finally, as the power of the Vikings increased, internal conflicts shifted their focus away from external raids.

800 to 1000 CE – The Eurasian Steppe & The Magyars: The nomadic Magyar lived in the Pontic-Caspian steppe (modern-day Ukraine and southern Russia) in the early 800s, where they formed a confederation of tribes called Etelköz.[156] **The Magyar people were engaged in raiding and warfare, often as mercenaries (-) for the**

---

[156] Kristó, G., & Makk, F. (1996). *The Early History of Hungary*. Akadémiai Kiadó.

THE MIDDLE AGES (500 TO 1500 CE)

Byzantine Empire and other regional powers.
These nomads originated from the Eurasian Steppe, which is a vast region of grasslands and savannas that stretches across the continent of Eurasia from Eastern Europe to Central Asia. It is one of the largest continuous expanses of grassland in the world, covering parts of modern-day Ukraine, Russia, Kazakhstan, Mongolia, and China.

The nomadic cultures from this region were Finno-Ugric – a group of people who shared major branch of the Uralic language family and have cultural similarities despite modern geographical separation. They all spoke a language whose foundations are distinct from Indo-European languages, such as English, French, German, or Russian; instead, the languages of Finnish, Estonian, Hungarian, Sámi, Komi, Mordvin, Mari, Udmurt, and Khanty all share distinct characteristics within the Finno-Ugric grouping.

Culturally, there are ties that are emblematic to the Finno-Ugric practices in the Eurasian steppe, to include the csikós mounted horsemen in Hungary[157] and reindeer herders in Finland,[158] both of whom have deep connections to the similar traditional ways of life that are closely tied to the land and animals that their ancestors cared for in the Eurasian step.

As the Magyars migrated westward in the eighth and ninth centuries, they reached the Carpathian Basin in the winter of 895–896 CE, led by Grand Prince Árpád.[159] **The Magyar migration was partly driven by pressure from the Pechenegs, another nomadic group, and partly by opportunities for plunder (-) and settlement in the more fertile lands to the west. Once they settled in the Carpathian Basin, the Magyars continued their raiding lifestyle (-), conducting military campaigns across Western Europe until their defeat at the Battle of Lechfeld in 955 CE by Otto I of Germany, which marked the end of their large-scale raids into Western Europe.**[160] In 962 CE, Otto I was coronated as the new Holy Roman Emperor by Pope John XII as a reward for stopping the Magyars.

After settling in the Carpathian Basin, the Magyars gradually adopted Christianity and became sedentary, particularly under Stephen I, who was crowned the first Christian king of Hungary in 1000 CE.

---

[157] Kontler, L. (2009). *A History of Hungary: Millennium in Central Europe.* Palgrave Macmillan.
[158] Beach, H., & Stammler, F. (2006). *Human-Animal Relations in Pastoralism* (Sámi reindeer herding). In Ingold, T. (Ed.), *Animals and Human Society: Changing Perspectives* (pp. 201-220). Routledge.
[159] Molnár, M. (2001). *A Concise History of Hungary.* Cambridge University Press.
[160] Pálóczi-Horváth, A. (1989). *Pechenegs, Cumans, Iasians: Steppe Peoples in Medieval Hungary.* Corvina Press.

CONFLICT

802 to 1431 CE - The Khmer Empire: One of the most powerful empires in Southeast Asia, the Khmer Empire, existed from the ninth century CE to the 15th century CE. It was centered in modern-day Cambodia and, at its peak, controlled territories across present-day Thailand, Laos, Vietnam, and Myanmar. **Jayavarman II founded the empire around 802 CE, who declared himself a god-king (Devaraja) and united the Khmer people, despite his oppressive declaration as a god-king (-).** The capital, eventually moved to Angkor, became a thriving center of culture and politics.[161]

By the 12th and 13th centuries, especially under **Jayavarman VII, the empire shifted towards Mahayana Buddhism, which emphasized compassion, the welfare of the people, and the king as a benevolent ruler serving his subjects (+).** This transition helped soften the previous authoritarian structures and promoted more inclusive governance. **Eventually, the Khmer Empire fully adopted Theravada Buddhism, which rejected the Devaraja cult entirely, focusing instead on the individual's path to enlightenment and reducing the emphasis on the divine authority of kings (+).**

The Khmer were renowned for their sophisticated irrigation systems and construction techniques, enabling large-scale agriculture and the building of monumental structures (+). The empire reached its height under rulers like Suryavarman II and Jayavarman VII. Suryavarman II built Angkor Wat, the largest religious monument in the world, originally dedicated to the Hindu god Vishnu. Under Jayavarman VII, the empire expanded significantly, and Buddhism became more prominent.[162]

At its peak, the empire's centralized monarchy, exemplified by rulers like Jayavarman VII, consolidated power through military campaigns and infrastructure projects (+). However, overexpansion, internal strife, and pressure from neighboring states eventually led to its decline (-). Ironically, the ideological shift from god-like kings towards equality, led to a decrease in centralized authority, which would eventually contribute to the empire's fragmentation during its decline. By 1431 CE, the empire effectively ended when the Siamese sacked Angkor. The legacy of the Khmer Empire, particularly through its monumental architecture like Angkor Wat, remains a defining symbol of Cambodia's cultural heritage.[163]

---

[161] Coedès, G. (1968). *The Indianized States of Southeast Asia*. University of Hawaii Press.
[162] Chandler, D. P. (2008). *A History of Cambodia*. Westview Press.
[163] Higham, C. F. W. (2001). *The Civilization of Angkor*. University of California Press.

882 to 1240 CE – The rise of the Kievan Rus': The origins of the Russian state can be traced back to the Kievan Rus', a federation of Pagan Slavic and Finno-Ugric tribes, established in the ninth century CE by Varangians (Vikings) who came from the north. In 882 CE, the Varangian prince Oleg of Novgorod captured the city of Kyiv (modern-day Kyiv), making it the capital of Kievan Rus'. Later, in the late tenth century, Prince Vladimir I sought to consolidate his power and unify his people under a single religion, seeing Christianity as a way to enhance political and cultural ties with the Byzantine Empire, which was one of the most powerful and influential states at the time. **The consolidation of power by these early rulers created a strong centralized state that controlled important trade routes along the Dnieper River. The strategic alliances and military campaigns led to the expansion of Kievan Rus territory, which bolstered its political influence (+).**

The Kievan Rus' grew into a powerful state, with Prince Vladimir the Great converting to Eastern Orthodox Christianity in 988 CE, a decision that marked the official adoption of Eastern Orthodox Christianity as the state religion of Kievan Rus' and linked the region culturally and religiously to the Byzantine Empire.[164] This ideological move, which can also be seen as political, not only solidified the religious unity of the state but also provided a moral and cultural framework that legitimized the authority of the rulers. Kievan Rus' laid the foundation for the future Russian, Ukrainian, and Belarusian identities. **The influence of Orthodox Christianity promoted literacy, arts, and a cohesive cultural identity among the diverse Slavic tribes (+); however, it also reduced local autonomy (-).**

The trade of furs, honey, and slaves with the Byzantine Empire and the Islamic Caliphates brought wealth and resources that fueled the development of their cities (+). The decline of Kievan Rus' began in the 12th century due to internal divisions and external pressures. **The Mongol invasion from 1237 to 1240 CE further fragmented the region (-), leading to the dominance of the Mongol Golden Horde over many of the former Kievan Rus' territories. During this time, the city of Moscow (Muscovy) began to rise as a center of power.**

987 to 1200 CE – The West Franks: King Louis V's death without an heir allowed for the rise of Hugh Capet, a nobleman who

---

[164] Franklin, S., & Shepard, J. (1996). *The Emergence of Rus 750–1200*. Longman.

was elected king of the Franks in 987 CE. **Capet used his ties with the Church to solidify their authority and control (-), often creating conflicts between secular and religious authorities. The alliance between the monarchy and the Church helped maintain social cohesion, while fostering the idea of divine kingship (+).** This marked a turning point in French history, as the Capetian dynasty established itself and gradually centralized power in France over the following centuries.

1037 to 1194 CE – The Seljuk Empire: The Seljuk Empire was a major medieval Turkic empire that spanned large parts of Central Asia, the Middle East, and Anatolia (modern-day Türkiye) from approximately 1037 to 1194 CE.[165] The empire was founded by the Seljuk dynasty, a branch of the Oghuz Turks, with Tughril Beg capturing Merv and Nishapur in 1037 CE and later taking Baghdad in 1055 CE, assuming power over the Abbasid Caliphate.[166]

Under Alp Arslan (reigned 1063 to 1072 CE) and Malik Shah I (reigned 1072 to 1092 CE), the Seljuks reached their peak, achieving a decisive victory over the Byzantines at the Battle of Manzikert in 1071 CE, which opened Anatolia to Turkic settlement.[167] **Malik Shah's reign marked the high point of Seljuk power, with the empire flourishing culturally and intellectually (+).** In 1076, they captured Medinah, and in 1077, they went on to capture Mecca, the holiest city of Islam.

After Malik Shah's death in 1092 CE, the empire fragmented into smaller, semi-independent states, such as the Sultanate of Rum in Anatolia, weakening centralized stability and control (-). The arrival of the Crusades by Pope Urban II and internal ideological disputes further weakened the empire (-).[168] By 1194 CE, the Seljuk Empire effectively ended after the defeat of Toghrul III by the Khwarazmian Empire.

1095 to 1291 CE - The Crusades & The Holy Land: Following Pope Sergius IV's call to a Holy fight following the destruction of the Church of the Holy Sepulchre in Jerusalem, Pope Urban II called for

---

[165] Peacock, A. C. S. (2015). *The Great Seljuk Empire*. Edinburgh University Press.
[166] Frye, R. N. (1996). *The Heritage of Central Asia: From Antiquity to the Turkish Expansion*. Princeton University Press.
[167] Cahen, C. (1968). *Pre-Ottoman Turkey: A General Survey of the Material and Spiritual Culture and History*. Taplinger Publishing Co.
[168] Bosworth, C. E. (1968). *The Political and Dynastic History of the Iranian World (A.D. 1000-1217)*. Cambridge University Press.

the Council of Clermont in 1095 CE, which called for all Christians to free the Holy lands.[169]

By 1098, Christians from all over Europe made their way to the middle east and took the county of Edessa (modern day Türkiye), and eventually recaptured the Holy City of Jerusalem in 1099. **The ambitious gains led to conflicts, both among European powers and with the Muslim world, especially when political power often overshadowed religious motives (-).**

In 1144 CE, the Muslim leader Imad ad-Din Zengi, saw an opportunity to attack Edessa while the city's defenses were weakened. The city fell, and a large number of its Christian inhabitants were massacred as they were defenseless (-). Zengi allowed the Armenian Christians to remain, but Latin Christians faced execution or enslavement (-). The fall of Edessa was the first major defeat for the Crusader states in the Levant. It shocked the Christian world and led directly to the calling of the Second Crusade by Pope Eugene III in 1145 CE. It demonstrated that the Crusader states were vulnerable to organized and united Muslim forces.

The Second Crusade (1147 to 1150 CE) was launched by King Louis VII of France and Holy Roman Emperor Conrad III in an attempt to reclaim the lost territory of Edessa. However, the Second Crusade ended in failure, and the Crusaders were unable to recapture Edessa or make significant gains.

The Third Crusade (1189 to 1192 CE) was initiated in response to Saladin's capture of Jerusalem in 1187 CE, led by notable European monarchs, including Richard the Lionheart of England, Philip II of France, and Holy Roman Emperor Frederick I (Barbarossa).[170] While the Crusaders failed to recapture Jerusalem, they did secure some coastal cities, such as Acre, and negotiated a treaty with Saladin that allowed Christian pilgrims access to Jerusalem.

The Fourth Crusade (1202 to 1204 CE), originally intended to recapture Jerusalem, was diverted by political and financial issues, leading to the sack of Constantinople in 1204 CE. **The Fourth Crusade's diversion to Constantinople was not originally planned; it was the result of a combination of financial difficulties, opportunistic leaders, and broken political promises (-).** While it began as a campaign to reclaim the Holy Land from the Muslims, it ended in the devastating sack of the greatest Christian city

---

[169] Riley-Smith, J. (2005). *The Crusades: A History* (2nd ed.). Yale University Press.
[170] Tyerman, C. (2006). *God's War: A New History of the Crusades.* Belknap Press of Harvard University Press.

in the East, deepening the divide between the Eastern Orthodox and Roman Catholic Churches. **This unplanned event weakened the Byzantine Empire and created a deep divide between the Eastern Orthodox and Roman Catholic churches (-).**

The Later Crusades (1208 to 1291 CE) followed, including the Albigensian Crusade (against the Cathars in France), the Fifth Crusade (attempting to conquer Egypt) led by King Andrew II of Hungary and Duke Leopold VI of Austria, and the Sixth Crusade, led by Frederick II of the Holy Roman Empire, which resulted in a peaceful handover of Jerusalem in 1229 CE (though it was recaptured by Muslims a decade later). The Seventh and Eighth Crusades were led by Louis IX of France but failed to achieve lasting results in the Holy Land. The fall of Acre in 1291 CE, the last major stronghold of the Crusaders in the Holy Land, is considered the end of the Crusades.

The Crusades were driven by a complex interplay of political, ideological, and technological factors. While they initially achieved some of their objectives, they led to centuries of conflict, deepening religious divisions (-) and shifting the balance of power in the Mediterranean region (-). The long-term consequences leave negative legacies of distrust between the Western Roman Catholics, Eastern Orthodox, and Muslim worlds (-).

1206 to 1271 CE – The Mongols: The rise of the Mongols in the early 13th century was one of the most remarkable expansions of power in world history, transforming a group of nomadic tribes into the largest contiguous empire the world has ever seen. The Mongols, a group of steppe nomads from the Mongolian Plateau, were initially divided and engaged in frequent internal conflicts. However, by the late 12th century, a charismatic leader named Temujin began uniting the Mongol clans. In 1206 CE, after successfully bringing together a number of the Mongol tribes under his rule, he was proclaimed Genghis Khan, meaning "universal ruler."[171] This event marked the formal beginning of the Mongol Empire.

The Mongols' superior military tactics and innovations, such as their expertise in horseback archery, efficient communication systems, and siege technology (often acquired from conquered cultures), allowed them to conquer diverse territories swiftly and maintain control over vast regions. **These technological strengths enabled**

---

[171] Weatherford, J. (2004). *Genghis Khan and the Making of the Modern World*. Crown.

THE MIDDLE AGES (500 TO 1500 CE)

the Mongols to form the largest contiguous land empire in history, facilitating the rapid spread of goods, ideas, and culture across Eurasia (+).

Under Genghis Khan's leadership, the Mongols rapidly expanded their territory. Known for their superior military tactics – including exceptional use of horseback archery, mobility, and psychological warfare – the Mongols were able to defeat much larger and more established empires. **One of Genghis Khan's first major targets was the Khwarezmian Empire in Persia (modern-day Iran), which he decisively conquered by 1221 CE, using brutal tactics that terrified other enemies into submission (-).**[172] The Mongols' remarkable adaptability and incorporation of local technologies, as well as their highly organized military hierarchy, contributed significantly to their success. **The Mongols were also flexible in adopting and respecting various religious practices and cultural beliefs of the people they conquered (+), facilitating trade and diplomatic relations.** This tolerance supported stability and growth within their territories, as they encouraged scholars, artisans, and traders from many backgrounds.

Following Genghis Khan's death in 1227 CE, the Mongol Empire was divided among his sons, yet the empire continued to expand under the leadership of his descendants. His grandson, Kublai Khan, conquered China and established the Yuan Dynasty in 1271 CE, marking the first time a non-Han dynasty ruled all of China.[173] The Mongol Empire reached its greatest extent in the late 13th century, stretching from Eastern Europe to the Pacific Ocean and from Siberia to the Indian subcontinent. **The Mongols facilitated trade across the Silk Road, linking Europe and Asia and fostering an exchange of goods, culture, and ideas (+), despite their reputation for violence and conquest (-).**[174]

1215 to 1295 CE – England's Magna Carta & Parliament: The Magna Carta, also known as the Great Charter, was written, and sealed on June 15, 1215, at Runnymede near the River Thames in England. **It was a result of the conflict between King John of England and a group of rebellious barons, who were unhappy with the king's heavy taxation and arbitrary justice (-).** The Magna Carta is widely regarded as one of the most important legal documents in

---

[172] Man, J. (2011). *Genghis Khan: Life, Death, and Resurrection.* St. Martin's Press.
[173] Rossabi, M. (1988). *Khubilai Khan: His Life and Times.* University of California Press.
[174] Morgan, D. (1986). *The Mongols.* Blackwell.

the history of democracy, influencing constitutional law and individual rights for centuries (+).

The Magna Carta was originally intended as a practical solution to the political crisis in 13th-century England. It established that the king was subject to the law, not above it, and introduced the idea that the monarch must govern according to agreed-upon rules (+). One of its most significant clauses (Clause 39) states that no free man shall be imprisoned or stripped of his rights without the lawful judgment of his peers, laying the groundwork for the principle of habeas corpus and the right to a fair trial (+).[175]

While many of the specific grievances in the Magna Carta were about feudal rights and privileges, its broader implications were revolutionary. The document limited royal authority, establishing that the monarchy could not impose taxes without the "common counsel of the kingdom," which eventually led to the development of Parliament.[176] Although King John sought to annul the Magna Carta shortly after its issuance, the document was reissued several times by subsequent monarchs and became a foundation for English law. Its legacy reached far beyond England, influencing legal systems worldwide, including the United States Constitution and the Bill of Rights.[177]

The Magna Carta remains a powerful symbol of freedom and justice. While it was originally focused on protecting the rights of the nobility (-), over time, it came to be seen as a broader statement of the principle that all individuals have rights that even the sovereign must respect (+). Its impact on the development of constitutional law continues to be felt in legal traditions around the world today.

In 1295 CE, King Edward I of England convened what is known as the Model Parliament, an event considered a foundational moment in the development of the English parliamentary system. This parliament was notable because it included representatives from not only the nobility and clergy but also from the common people – namely, knights from the shires and burgesses (town representatives). Edward I's decision to summon a broad-based parliament was partly driven by the need to raise funds for military campaigns against Scotland and France. The inclusion of commoners in Parliament

---

[175] Holt, J. C. (1992). *Magna Carta* (2nd ed.). Cambridge University Press.

[176] Carpenter, D. (2015). *Magna Carta: A Very Short Introduction*. Oxford University Press.

[177] Linebaugh, P. (2008). *The Magna Carta Manifesto: Liberties and Commons for All*. University of California Press.

marked a significant shift toward a more representative form of governance in England and established a model that would influence the future structure of the English Parliament.[178]

1299 to 1453 BCE – The Fall of the Byzantine Empire: The Ottoman Empire began its rise in the late 13th century, founded by Osman I in 1299 CE in northwestern Anatolia. The Ottomans quickly expanded their territory through a combination of military conquests, alliances, and the use of skilled diplomacy. By the 14th century, they had absorbed many neighboring Turkic states and began to encroach upon Byzantine territories in the Balkans and Anatolia. Key victories, such as the Battle of Kosovo (1389) and the Battle of Nicopolis (1396), solidified Ottoman dominance in the Balkans. Under Sultan Murad I and Sultan Bayezid I, the empire continued to expand, but it was under Sultan Mehmed II (reigned 1444 to 1446, and 1451 to 1481) that the Ottomans launched their most ambitious campaign to capture Constantinople and end the Byzantine Empire.[179]

The fall of Constantinople on May 29, 1453, marked the culmination of Ottoman expansion and the end of the Byzantine Empire. Sultan Mehmed II, known as Mehmed the Conqueror, led the siege with a well-equipped army and advanced artillery, including massive cannons designed to breach the city's walls. Despite a valiant defense by Emperor Constantine XI and the outnumbered Byzantine forces, the Ottomans overwhelmed the city after two months of siege and bombardment by artillery. **The capture of Constantinople allowed the Ottomans to establish the city as their new capital, renaming it Istanbul and transforming it into a major center of Islamic culture and trade.** The fall of Constantinople is often seen as a pivotal moment, symbolizing the end of the Middle Ages and the rise of the Ottoman Empire as a dominant power in southeastern Europe and the eastern Mediterranean.[180]

1312 to 1337 CE – Mansa Musa & The Mali Empire: Mansa Musa I (reigned 1312 to 1337 CE) was the tenth emperor of the Mali Empire in West Africa and is often regarded as one of the wealthiest individuals in history. He came to power following the reign of his predecessor, Abu Bakr II, and under his rule, the Mali Empire expanded to include vast territories, covering parts of modern-day

---

[178] Maddicott, J. R. (2010). *The Origins of the English Parliament, 924-1327.* Oxford University Press.
[179] Finkel, C. (2005). *Osman's Dream: The History of the Ottoman Empire.* Basic Books.
[180] Runciman, S. (1965). *The Fall of Constantinople 1453.* Cambridge University Press.

Mali, Mauritania, Senegal, and Guinea. Mansa Musa's reign is particularly noted for the empire's wealth, which was derived from the control of gold and salt mines, and for his promotion of Islam and learning within the empire.[181]

One of the most significant events in Mansa Musa's life was his pilgrimage to Mecca (Hajj) in 1324 to 1325 CE. His journey is legendary for the extraordinary display of wealth that accompanied him. He traveled with a caravan of 60,000 men, including slaves and soldiers, and carried vast amounts of gold. **Along the way, Mansa Musa generously distributed gold to the poor and to cities such as Cairo and Mecca, which temporarily destabilized local economies due to the influx of wealth (-).** His pilgrimage not only displayed the immense wealth of the Mali Empire but also established diplomatic and trade relations with the Islamic world.[182]

Upon his return to Mali, Mansa Musa focused on enhancing the cultural and intellectual life of his empire. He commissioned the construction of several mosques, most notably the famous Djingareyber Mosque in Timbuktu, which became a center of Islamic learning. **Under his reign, Timbuktu flourished as a hub of trade, religion, and education, attracting scholars, poets, and theologians from across the Islamic world (+).** Mansa Musa's legacy as a patron of learning and a devout Muslim helped cement Mali's reputation as a powerful and wealthy empire.[183]

1325 to 1521 CE – The Aztec City of Tenochtitlan: Tenochtitlan was the capital city of the Aztec Empire and one of the most impressive cities in the pre-Columbian Americas. It was founded in 1325 CE by the Mexica people (who would later be known as the Aztecs) on an island in Lake Texcoco, in what is now Mexico City. Tenochtitlan became the heart of the Aztec civilization, both politically and religiously, and at its height, it is believed to have had a population of over 200,000 people, making it one of the largest cities in the world at the time.[184]

Tenochtitlan was the center of Aztec power and a symbol of their empire. Its strategic location on a lake island gave the Aztecs a natural defense against invaders, and the city was connected to the mainland

---

[181] Levtzion, N. (1973). *Ancient Ghana and Mali*. Methuen.

[182] Robinson, D. (2004). *Muslim Societies in African History*. Cambridge University Press.

[183] Hunwick, J. O., & Boye, A. M. (2003). *The Hidden Treasures of Timbuktu: Rediscovering Africa's Literary Culture*. Thames & Hudson.

[184] Smith, M. E. (2008). *Aztec City-State Capitals*. University Press of Florida.

THE MIDDLE AGES *(500 TO 1500 CE)*

by a series of causeways. **These causeways were designed with removable sections to protect the city in case of attack. The city had a complex system of canals that allowed transportation throughout the city by canoe, and it was known for its remarkable organization and advanced infrastructure, including aqueducts that brought fresh water to the city from nearby springs (+).**[185]

At the heart of Tenochtitlan was the Templo Mayor, a large pyramid that was the focal point of Aztec religious life. The Templo Mayor was dedicated to two gods: Huitzilopochtli, the god of war and the sun, and Tlaloc, the god of rain and agriculture. **Human sacrifices were a regular feature of Aztec religious ceremonies (-),** and the Templo Mayor served as the stage for these rituals, believed to ensure the survival of the world and the fertility of the land.[186]

1337 to 1453 CE – France & England's 100 Years' War: The Hundred Years' War was a series of conflicts fought between the kingdoms of England and France over claims to the French throne and territorial disputes. The war began when Edward III of England claimed the right to the French crown through his mother, a French princess, after the death of the French king Charles IV. This claim was contested by the Valois dynasty, which took control of France. The conflict was fueled by long-standing tensions between the two kingdoms, as well as competition for control over territories in France, particularly the Duchy of Aquitaine.[187] The war spanned several phases, including significant battles such as Crécy (1346), Poitiers (1356), and Agincourt (1415), where the English, particularly under Henry V, achieved major victories due to their use of longbowmen and tactical innovations.[188]

However, the tide turned in favor of the French in the latter part of the war. Amid the rise of Joan of Arc – a 17-year-old woman who rallied French forces and lifted the siege of Orléans in 1429 – France was able to implement key political and military strategies to win the war. France's efforts, along with internal strife in England and French territorial advantages, led to the eventual defeat of the English.

Joan of Arc was captured on May 23, 1430, by Burgundian forces – French allies of the English – during the siege of Compiègne. She

---

[185] Townsend, R. F. (2009). *The Aztecs*. Thames & Hudson.
[186] López Luján, L. (2005). *The Temple of Quetzalcoatl at Tenochtitlan*. Thames & Hudson.
[187] Allmand, C. (1988). *The Hundred Years War: England and France at War c.1300–c.1450*. Cambridge University Press.
[188] Sumption, J. (1990). *The Hundred Years War: Trial by Battle*. University of Pennsylvania Press.

was later sold to the English, who saw her as a dangerous threat. Joan was put on trial in Rouen, which was under English control at the time. The trial was overseen by Pierre Cauchon, the Bishop of Beauvais, a pro-English cleric. The primary charges against Joan were heresy and witchcraft, with an emphasis on her claims of divine visions and her wearing of male clothing, which was considered a violation of church law. **On May 30, 1431, Joan was taken to the marketplace in Rouen, where she was publicly executed by burning at the stake (-).**

By 1453, England had lost nearly all its territories in France except for the port of Calais. The war significantly shaped the development of both nations, leading to the centralization of the French monarchy and the decline of feudalism, while in England, it fueled the later Wars of the Roses.[189]

In 1456, a posthumous retrial of Joan of Arc was held at the request of Charles VII, the French king whom Joan had helped crown. **The retrial concluded that her original trial had been biased and unjust, and Joan was exonerated of all charges (+).** She was declared a martyr for the French cause and canonized a saint by the Catholic Church in 1920.

1347 CE – The Bubonic Plague: The Bubonic Plague, or Black Death, was a devastating pandemic that struck Europe, Asia, and North Africa in the mid-14th century. It is believed to have originated in Central Asia and spread to Europe via trade routes, particularly through the Silk Road and merchant ships. The disease, caused by the bacterium Yersinia pestis, was transmitted by fleas that infested black rats, common aboard ships. The plague first arrived in Sicily in 1347 CE and quickly spread across the continent, decimating populations. By 1351 CE, the plague killed an estimated 25 to 30 million people in Europe, or about one-third of its population.[190] The symptoms included fever, painful swellings (buboes), and black spots on the skin, leading to death within days in most cases. **The rapid spread and high mortality rate caused panic and social upheaval (-).**

The impact of the Black Death extended beyond the immediate loss of life. It had profound economic, social, and religious consequences across Europe. **Labor shortages due to the death toll led to higher wages for peasants and workers, weakening the feudal system**

---

[189] Seward, D. (1978). *The Hundred Years War: The English in France 1337-1453*. Penguin Books.
[190] Ziegler, P. (1998). The Black Death. Harper Collins.

and shifting the balance of power between landowners and laborers (+). **The Church's inability to explain or stop the plague also led to declining faith in religious institutions, while some people turned to extreme religious practices or blamed minority groups like Jews, leading to persecution (-).**[191] In the long term, the devastation caused by the plague reshaped European society, contributing to the eventual decline of feudalism and the rise of the Renaissance. It it killed an estimated 75 to 200 million people throughout Europe, Asia, North Africa, and the Middle East.

1350 to 1600 CE – The Renaissance in Europe: The Renaissance, which began in Florence, Italy in the late 14th century and flourished through the 15th and 16th centuries, marked a cultural, intellectual, and artistic revival rooted in the rediscovery of classical antiquity. **Central to this movement was humanism, a philosophy emphasizing the value of human potential and achievement (+).**

Key figures like Leonardo da Vinci (1452 to 1519), who painted the iconic Mona Lisa (1503 to 1506), and Michelangelo Buonarroti (1475 to 1564), known for his masterpieces such as the *Sistine Chapel ceiling* (1508 to 1512) and the sculpture of *David* (1501 to 1504), revolutionized Western art with their mastery of form, anatomy, and expression. Writers such as Dante Alighieri (1265 to 1321), Petrarch (1304 to 1374), and Giovanni Boccaccio (1313 to 1375) were instrumental in developing vernacular literature, while Niccolò Machiavelli's *The Prince* (1513) explored the dynamics of political power.[192] **While *The Prince* is often viewed as pragmatic and even ruthless in its advice to rulers, it touches on the responsibilities of leadership, how freedom can be manipulated, and the complex relationship between power and moral accountability (+).**[193]

The Renaissance had far-reaching consequences, not only transforming European culture but also shaping the modern world. **Johannes Gutenberg's invention of the printing press around 1440 revolutionized communication (+), allowing for the mass production of books and the spread of ideas.** This facilitated the Protestant Reformation and the Scientific Revolution in the following centuries. The era also saw the rise of notable scientists such as Galileo Galilei (1564 to 1642) and Nicolaus Copernicus (1473 to 1543), whose heliocentric theory challenged the Church's geocentric model of the

---

[191] Benedictow, O. J. (2004). The Black Death 1346–1353: The Complete History. Boydell & Brewer.
[192] Burke, P. (1987). *The Italian Renaissance: Culture and Society in Italy*. Princeton University Press.
[193] Machiavelli, N. (1513/2008). *The Prince*. (W. K. Marriott, Trans.). Oxford University Press.

universe. **However, the Renaissance coincided with the Age of Exploration, beginning with Christopher Columbus's voyage in 1492, which led to European colonization and exploitation of the Americas (-).**[194] The Renaissance's emphasis on reason, empirical evidence, and humanism influenced the Enlightenment and laid the foundation for modern Western thought and institutions.

1368 to 1644 – China's Ming Dynasty: The Ming Dynasty marked a return to native Chinese rule following the overthrow of the Mongol-led Yuan Dynasty. It was founded by Zhu Yuanzhang, a former peasant and rebel leader who became Emperor Hongwu after successfully leading an uprising against the Yuan.

Under Hongwu's rule, the Ming Dynasty re-established Confucian principles and restored the civil service examination system, which had been neglected under the Mongols.[195] **This period was characterized by the strengthening of centralized control and numerous reforms aimed at improving the livelihoods of peasants, including reducing taxes and promoting agricultural expansion (+).**[196]

One of the most significant periods of the Ming Dynasty occurred during the reign of Emperor Yongle (reigned 1402 to 1424 CE). Under his leadership, China experienced a series of major maritime expeditions led by the famed admiral Zheng He. From 1405 to 1433, Zheng He's fleets sailed to Southeast Asia, India, the Persian Gulf, and the East African coast, displaying Chinese power and facilitating trade and diplomacy. These voyages were unprecedented in scale and ambition but were eventually discontinued by the dynasty as they turned their focus inward. **The Ming period also saw significant cultural achievements, particularly in the production of fine porcelain and literature (+).**

As they turned inward, the later Ming emperors focused on ways to defend from the Mongols and northern tribes. In doing so, they ordered the reconstruction of the Great Wall of China as we know it today. Although the wall had existed as early as the warring states period in the 7th century BCE, the Ming fortified the wall using bricks, stones, and other durable materials, creating a structure designed to resist artillery, which included watchtowers, garrisons, and signal stations.

---

[194] Brotton, J. (2006). *The Renaissance Bazaar: From the Silk Road to Michelangelo.* Oxford University Press.
[195] Mote, F. W. (1999). *Imperial China 900-1800.* Harvard University Press.
[196] Tsai, S. H. (2001). *Perpetual Happiness: The Ming Emperor Yongle.* University of Washington Press.

THE MIDDLE AGES *(500 TO 1500 CE)*

Despite its early successes, the Ming Dynasty eventually declined due to a combination of corruption, natural disasters, and strategic military weaknesses (-). By the late 16th century, internal strife, and external threats – most notably from the Manchus – destabilized the empire. In 1644, after a series of rebellions and invasions, the Ming Dynasty fell to the Manchus, who established the Qing Dynasty, marking the end of Ming rule.[197]

1462 to 1721 CE – Russian Independence: By the late 15th century, Ivan III (Ivan the Great) of Moscow (1462 to 1505 CE) consolidated power and ended Mongol rule over Russia in 1480 CE, marking the beginning of the unification of the Russian lands. Ivan was born in 1440 CE to Vasily II, the Grand Prince of Moscow, and was part of the Rurik dynasty, which claimed descent from the legendary Varangian prince Rurik, the founder of the first ruling dynasty of Kievan Rus'. The Rurik dynasty had ruled various parts of what is now Russia since the ninth century. Ivan III adopted the title of "Grand Prince of All Rus'", establishing Moscow as the new center of Russian political life.[198]

Ivan's marriage to Sophia Palaiologina, the niece of the last Byzantine Emperor, in 1472 also played a significant role in shaping his legacy. This marriage allowed him to claim continuity from the Byzantine Empire, adopting the title of Tsar (derived from Caesar) and positioning Moscow as the "Third Rome," a spiritual and political successor to the Byzantine Empire after the fall of Constantinople in 1453.

In 1547 CE, Ivan III's grandson, Ivan IV (Ivan the Terrible), declared himself Tsar of All Rus', formally establishing the Tsardom of Russia. **Ivan IV expanded Russian territory significantly, pushing into Siberia and establishing the foundations for future Russian imperial expansion (-).** With expansion, he constructed significant Russian infrastructure and architecture, to include St. Basil's cathedral in Moscow. **His reign, though marked by significant military successes, was also characterized by internal strife and autocratic rule (-).**[199] As his reign continued, he became known for striking down anyone who disagreed with his decisions, which gave him the nickname "Ivan the Terrible." This period set the stage for the later

---

[197] Brook, T. (1999). *The Confusions of Pleasure: Commerce and Culture in Ming China.* University of California Press.
[198] Vernadsky, G. (1953). *Kievan Rus.* Yale University Press.
[199] Hosking, G. (2001). *Russia and the Russians: A History.* Harvard University Press.

transformation of the Tsardom of Russia into the Russian Empire under Peter the Great in 1721 CE, a period marked by modernization and territorial expansion.[200]

1492 to 1600 CE – The European Arrival in the Americas: In 1492, Christopher Columbus, an Italian explorer sailing under the Spanish flag, made his first voyage across the Atlantic Ocean in search of a westward route to the Indies. Instead, he famously "discovered" the Americas when he landed in the Bahamas on October 12, 1492, believing he had reached Asia. Sponsored by the Catholic Monarchs of Spain, King Ferdinand II and Queen Isabella I, Columbus's expedition was motivated by the pursuit of new trade routes and wealth. Though not the first European to reach the Americas, his voyages initiated widespread exploration and colonization by European powers, which would drastically reshape the history of the Western Hemisphere.[201] Columbus's four voyages between 1492 and 1504 opened the way for the Spanish conquest of the Caribbean and the eventual colonization of vast parts of North and South America.[202]

When explorers and conquistadors like Christopher Columbus, Hernán Cortés, and Francisco Pizarro arrived in the Americas, they unknowingly brought with them diseases such as smallpox, measles, and influenza (-). Indigenous populations had no prior exposure or immunity to these diseases, which spread rapidly and caused catastrophic epidemics. It is estimated that up to 90% of the Indigenous population in some regions died from these diseases, severely weakening societies like the Aztecs and Incas before significant battles even occurred.[203]

One of the first regions to experience this decline was the Caribbean, where Indigenous groups like the Taíno and Arawak were among the first to come into contact with Spanish explorers, beginning with Christopher Columbus in 1492. **Within a few decades, these populations were nearly extinct due to smallpox, enslavement, and brutal exploitation under the encomienda system, a labor system imposed by the Spanish to "civilize" and Christianize the local populations (-).**[204] Similarly, the Mississippian cultures in North

---

[200] Riasanovsky, N. V. (2000). *A History of Russia* (6th ed.). Oxford University Press.
[201] Fernández-Armesto, F. (1991). *Columbus*. Oxford University Press.
[202] Morison, S. E. (1942). *Admiral of the Ocean Sea: A Life of Christopher Columbus*. Little, Brown and Company.
[203] Diamond, J. (1997). *Guns, Germs, and Steel: The Fates of Human Societies*. W. W. Norton & Company.
[204] Cook, N. D. (1998). Born to Die: Disease and New World Conquest, 1492–1650. Cambridge University Press.

America, including the powerful city of Cahokia, faced disruptions due to the spread of European diseases and loss of trade networks. By the time European settlers began moving inland in the 16th and 17th centuries, many of these complex societies had already collapsed or diminished significantly.[205]

The Aztec city of Tenochtitlan end came with the arrival of the Spanish in 1519 CE, led by Hernán Cortés. **Despite friendly relations amid language and cultural barriers, tensions between the Spanish and the Aztecs escalated, and in 1521 CE, after months of siege, the Spanish and their indigenous allies destroyed Tenochtitlan (-).** The defeat of the Aztecs marked the end of their empire, and Tenochtitlan was replaced by Mexico City, which became the capital of New Spain. **The Incan Empire would go on to last until 1533, until Francisco Pizarro of Spain would conquer it, only two years after the arrival of his voyagers (-).**[206]

In Mesoamerica, beyond the Aztecs, smaller civilizations like the Mixtec and Zapotec also faced devastation, both from European diseases and the collapse of regional economies under Spanish rule. In South America, the Mapuche people in the southern regions of Chile and Argentina resisted European conquest for centuries but experienced profound disruptions from European-introduced diseases and the pressures of colonial encroachment. **In North America, many Indigenous nations such as the Powhatan Confederacy in the present-day United States initially engaged in trade with European settlers but were later displaced or annihilated by warfare and disease (-). The decimation of native populations led to significant cultural loss, as religious practices, languages, and traditional ways of life were undermined by European colonization, missionary efforts, and assimilation policies (-).**[207]

---

[205] Mann, C. C. (2005). *1491: New Revelations of the Americas Before Columbus.* Knopf.
[206] Hemming, J. (1970). *The Conquest of the Incas.* Harcourt Brace Jovanovich.
[207] Crosby, A. W. (2003). *The Columbian Exchange: Biological and Cultural Consequences of 1492.* Praeger.

III.iv AGE OF EXPLORATION AND EARLY MODERNITY
(1500 TO 1800 CE)

The Age of Exploration and Early Modernity introduced a rapidly expanding world, where technological advances and navigational prowess opened paths to interconnect new continents and cultures (+), but also gave rise to exploitation, disease, and colonization (-). Political power dynamics became more internationally oriented (+), but European nations established colonies and enforced their own laws and structures on Indigenous populations (-). Ideological developments during the period gave rise to the Enlightenment, bringing forth new ideas on human rights and governance, challenging existing hierarchies, and suggesting that all individuals might possess an inherent dignity (+). However, these emerging ideals often clashed with the colonial practices of the time, where economic and political agendas overrode philosophical principles (-), leading to intercultural conflicts that undermined the dignity of countless societies.

1500 to 1800 – The Atlantic Slave Trade: The Atlantic slave trade began in the early 16th century and lasted until the 19th century, involving the forced transportation of millions of Africans to the Americas (-). European powers, including Portugal, Spain, Britain, and France, played a major role in this brutally inhumane form of trade (-). The system operated on a triangular route: European goods were traded in West Africa for enslaved people, who were then transported across the Atlantic Ocean in horrific conditions known as the Middle Passage. The enslaved Africans were sold in the Americas to work on plantations, producing cash crops such as sugar, tobacco, and cotton, which could in turn be shipped back to Europe. The demand for labor in the growing colonies fueled the expansion of this inhumane enterprise, with profound consequences for both Africa and the Americas.[208]

The impact of the slave trade on African societies was devastating – it contributed to the collapse of kingdoms (-), caused widespread depopulation (-), and intensified internal conflicts as African leaders and traders, under pressure, participated in the capture and sale of their own people.

---

[208] Klein, H. S. (2010). *The Atlantic Slave Trade*. Cambridge University Press.

Communities were torn apart, and traditional social structures were disrupted as millions of Africans were forcibly removed from their homelands. In the Americas, the reliance on enslaved labor not only enriched European colonial powers but also shaped the economic and social structures of the Americas, leading to deep racial divisions that persist to this day.[209]

The slave trade not only contributed to the exploitation of personal value, but it led to accepted forms of discrimination, exclusion, and dehumanization. **The infamous triangular trade passage in the Atlantic allowed Europeans to successfully exploit foreign lands (-) on the American continents and exploit foreign peoples (-) on the African continent.**

1500 to 1529 – The Reach of the Ottoman Empire: Suleiman the Magnificent (reigned 1520 to 1566), the tenth and longest-reigning sultan of the Ottoman Empire, significantly expanded the empire's territory through a series of successful military campaigns across Europe, Asia, and Africa. Suleiman's conquests began early in his reign, with the capture of Belgrade in 1521, which opened the way for Ottoman control in the Balkans. In 1526, he defeated the Kingdom of Hungary at the Battle of Mohács, leading to the fall of Budapest and the eventual incorporation of much of Hungary into the Ottoman realm. Suleiman also laid siege to Vienna in 1529, marking the height of Ottoman expansion into central Europe, though the siege ultimately failed. To the east, he waged campaigns against the Safavid Empire, capturing Baghdad in 1534 and solidifying Ottoman control over Mesopotamia (modern-day Iraq). Suleiman's empire also expanded in the Mediterranean and North Africa, with the conquest of Rhodes in 1522 and the vassalization of Algiers in 1529, extending Ottoman influence across the Mediterranean Sea and the Barbary Coast.[210] **He also conquered Jerusalem and Mecca in the Middle East, two internationally-known lands that represented ideologies of world religions (-).**

These conquests transformed the Ottoman Empire into a vast, multi-ethnic, and multi-religious empire, stretching from the gates of Vienna in the west to the Persian Gulf in the east, and from the Crimean Peninsula in the north, to North Africa in the south.

---

[209] Thornton, J. (1998). *Africa and Africans in the Making of the Atlantic World, 1400–1800.* Cambridge University Press.
[210] Imber, C. (2002). *The Ottoman Empire, 1300-1650: The Structure of Power.* Palgrave Macmillan.

CONFLICT

1517 – The Protestant Reformation: Martin Luther (lived 1483 to 1546) was a German monk and theologian whose criticism of the Catholic Church sparked the Protestant Reformation. In 1517, Luther famously posted his 95 Theses on the door of the Wittenberg Castle Church, challenging the Church's practice of selling indulgences – a way to reduce the punishment for sins in exchange for money. Luther argued that salvation could not be bought and must come from faith alone ("sola fide") and grace alone ("sola gratia"), rather than through the Church's sacraments and financial transactions.[211] His theses quickly spread across Europe, aided by the printing press, and attracted widespread support as well as condemnation from the Catholic Church. In 1521, Pope Leo X excommunicated Luther from the Catholic Church, but his ideas continued to gain traction among those seeking reform.

The Protestant Reformation that followed Luther's actions radically transformed the religious, political, and social landscape of Europe. Luther's doctrine emphasized the freedom of the individual to interpret the Bible without relying on Church authority, thereby promoting a sense of personal responsibility in one's faith. This shift from institutional control to personal conscience represented a fundamental change in how Christians understood their relationship with God and the Church. By advocating for the priesthood of all believers, Luther underscored the inherent dignity and autonomy of every person in their spiritual life, challenging the hierarchical structure of the Catholic Church, which at the time centralized power in the clergy.[212]

Luther's emphasis on the equality of believers before God provided a theological foundation for the idea of human dignity, suggesting that all people, regardless of status, have equal value and intrinsic worth (+). However, this newfound religious freedom also led to political and social tensions, as different Protestant movements emerged, sometimes leading to violent conflicts in Europe (-).[213]

1527 to 1616 – The Church of England & The Renaissance: The Church of England was established in the 16th century as a direct result of King Henry VIII's (1491 to 1547) break from the Roman Catholic Church. The initial cause of this separation was Henry's desire

---

[211] Luther, M. (1957). *Martin Luther's Ninety-five Theses*. Fortress Press.
[212] Bainton, R. H. (1950). *Here I Stand: A Life of Martin Luther*. Abingdon Press.
[213] McGrath, A. E. (1993). *Reformation Thought: An Introduction*. Blackwell Publishers.

to annul his marriage to Catherine of Aragon, with whom he had failed to produce a male heir. In 1527, Henry sought an annulment from Pope Clement VII, but the Pope refused, due to political pressures from Charles V, Holy Roman Emperor, and nephew of Catherine. Frustrated by the papal authority, Henry decided to take matters into his own hands, leading to a historic break with the Roman Catholic Church.[214]

In 1534, the English Parliament passed the Act of Supremacy, which declared the king as the Supreme Head of the Church of England, thus formalizing the creation of a separate English church. This was a political and religious turning point, as it transferred authority over spiritual matters from the pope to the English monarch. **Henry dissolved monasteries, seized church lands, and appropriated significant wealth from the Catholic Church (-).** Although theologically Henry remained conservative and opposed many of the Protestant reforms taking place elsewhere in Europe, his establishment of the Church of England laid the groundwork for future Protestant reforms under his successors.

After Henry VIII's death, the religious character of the Church of England began to shift more clearly towards Protestantism under his son, Edward VI (reigned 1547 to 1553), who introduced reforms such as the Book of Common Prayer in 1549, designed to standardize worship in English. The subsequent reign of Mary I (reigned 1553 to 1558), who sought to return England to Catholicism, temporarily reversed these changes. However, under Queen Elizabeth I (reigned 1558 to 1603), the Elizabethan Religious Settlement of 1559 solidified the Church of England as a distinct Protestant church, while maintaining some Catholic traditions. This settlement allowed for a degree of religious compromise, ensuring that the Church of England would become a permanent institution in England.[215]

Queen Elizabeth I is often associated with the flourishing of the English Renaissance. Her reign, known as the Elizabethan Era, marked a period of great cultural, artistic, and intellectual revival in England. Under her rule, England saw the rise of major achievements in literature, theater, music, and the visual arts, with figures like William Shakespeare, Christopher Marlowe, and Edmund Spenser becoming central to this cultural movement. Elizabeth's patronage of the arts and

---

[214] Guy, J. (1988). *Tudor England*. Oxford University Press.
[215] Haigh, C. (1993). *English Reformations: Religion, Politics, and Society Under the Tudors*. Oxford University Press.

her political stability enabled England to become a cultural hub.[216]

One of the most significant figures of the Elizabethan Renaissance was William Shakespeare lived (1564 to 1616). **Shakespeare's works – which include iconic plays such as Hamlet (1600), Romeo and Juliet (1597), Macbeth (1606), and A Midsummer Night's Dream (1595) – captured the complexity of the human experience and continue to influence literature and theater globally (+).** He was a key figure in the rise of the English theater, and his plays were performed at the Globe Theatre in London. **The themes of power, love, ambition, and tragedy in his works were reflective of the Renaissance's humanistic emphasis on individual experience and moral complexity (+).** Shakespeare's mastery of language, as well as his innovative use of iambic pentameter and dramatic structure, solidified him as one of the greatest playwrights in history.[217]

Elizabeth I's reign also fostered significant developments in education, science, and exploration, contributing to the Renaissance spirit of curiosity and discovery. The Elizabethan Age is often regarded as the "Golden Age" of English history, partly due to the extended period of peace and prosperity that allowed the arts to thrive. The queen herself was an educated and cultured monarch, fluent in several languages, and her court was a center for the arts. Although Elizabeth ruled during a time of religious conflict, her policies promoted relative religious tolerance, which helped maintain the social stability necessary for the blossoming of English culture.

1527 to 1714 – Spanish Succession: King Philip II of Spain (1527 to 1598) was one of the most powerful monarchs in European history, reigning from 1556 to 1598 during the height of the Spanish Empire's global influence. He inherited vast territories, including Spain, the Netherlands, parts of Italy, and Spanish colonies in the Americas and the Philippines. Philip was a staunch defender of Catholicism, leading him to engage in conflicts with Protestant powers, most notably during the Anglo-Spanish War against Elizabeth I of England. **In 1588, Philip launched the Spanish Armada in an unsuccessful attempt to invade England (-), a significant military defeat that marked the beginning of Spain's gradual decline as Europe's dominant power.** Philip II is also known for consolidating the Spanish Inquisition and enforcing religious conformity, and overseeing the

---

[216] Doran, S. (2003). *Elizabeth I and Her Circle*. Oxford University Press.
[217] Greenblatt, S. (2004). *Will in the World: How Shakespeare Became Shakespeare*. W. W. Norton & Company.

annexation of Portugal in 1580, further expanding Spain's empire.[218]

Archduke Charles VI of Austria (1685 to 1740), also known as Holy Roman Emperor Charles VI, played a key role in the War of the Spanish Succession (1701 to 1714), a conflict sparked by the disputed succession to the Spanish throne after the death of Charles II of Spain. Archduke Charles, a member of the Habsburg dynasty, was one of the claimants to the Spanish throne, opposing Philip of Anjou (later Philip V of Spain), the grandson of Louis XIV of France. The war ended with the Treaty of Utrecht (1713), which recognized Philip V as the king of Spain but prohibited the unification of the French and Spanish crowns. Charles, meanwhile, inherited the title of Holy Roman Emperor in 1711 but was forced to relinquish his claim to Spain. His reign was marked by efforts to strengthen the Habsburg monarchy in Central Europe, but his failure to secure a male heir led to the War of the Austrian Succession following his death in 1740.[219]

The War of the Spanish Succession was primarily a power struggle among European monarchies over who would control the vast Spanish Empire following the death of the childless King Charles II of Spain. **The contest between the Habsburg and Bourbon dynasties reflected how political power dynamics in Europe were driven by royal ambitions rather than the needs of the people (-). The war saw heavy taxation, conscription, and significant economic hardship inflicted on the common people, who had no voice in the decisions that directly impacted their lives (-).**

The feudal system remained a dominant social structure during this period, especially in regions where the war was fought. **For the common people, their lives were tied to the land they worked on, with obligations to their lords that provided them with few opportunities for upward mobility while living in relative poverty (-).** The protracted war and the shifting alliances among the ruling elites made it increasingly evident that political power was concentrated in the hands of monarchs and nobility, who were more interested in expanding their influence than in addressing the economic and social concerns of the lower classes. Although still far from revolutions, this period began to sow the seeds of discontent among the populace. **Seeing the disregard for their well-being, some segments of society began to question the legitimacy of rulers who used power for personal gain rather than the public good (-).**

---

[218] arker, G. (1998). *The Grand Strategy of Philip II*. Yale University Press.
[219] McKay, D., & Scott, H. M. (1984). *The Rise of the Great Powers 1648-1815*. Longman.

CONFLICT

1607 to 1750 – Jamestown & Quebec in the Americas: The Jamestown Colony, established in 1607 in present-day Virginia, was the first permanent English settlement in North America. It was founded by the Virginia Company of London, a joint-stock company chartered by King James I, with the goal of expanding English influence and seeking wealth in the New World. The settlers initially faced severe challenges, including hostile relations with Indigenous tribes, a lack of food, and disease, leading to the period known as the "Starving Time" during the winter of 1609 to 1610. The colony's survival was due to the leadership of Captain John Smith and, later, the successful cultivation of tobacco, which became a lucrative cash crop under the guidance of John Rolfe.[220]

Jamestown's establishment marked the beginning of English colonization in the Americas, which would grow over the following centuries. **The colony also laid the groundwork for the development of representative government in the New World, ensuring equal representation of the new lands (+).** In 1619, the Virginia House of Burgesses was formed, becoming the first elected legislative assembly in colonial America. **However, the introduction of African slavery that same year had a profound impact on the colony's economy and social structure, establishing a labor system that would last for centuries (-).**[221]

Meanwhile, the city of Quebec was founded in 1608 by French explorer Samuel de Champlain and became the first permanent French settlement in North America. Located on the St. Lawrence River, Quebec was strategically positioned to control trade routes and serve as the capital of New France. Champlain's efforts to forge alliances with Indigenous groups, particularly the Huron and Algonquin, were crucial for the colony's survival and economic success, especially in the fur trade. Despite early hardships similar to other colonial endeavors, including harsh winters and supply shortages, Quebec grew steadily as the center of French colonial power in the region.[222]

Quebec's establishment marked the beginning of French colonization in North America, and the settlement played a key role in the fur trade, exploration, and missionary activities throughout the 17th century. The colony expanded French influence deep into the interior of North America. Quebec's founding also set the stage for centuries of conflict between the French and English over control of North

---

[220] Horn, J. (2005). *A Land as God Made It: Jamestown and the Birth of America*. Basic Books.
[221] Kelso, W. M. (2006). *Jamestown: The Buried Truth*. University of Virginia Press.
[222] Eccles, W. J. (1983). *The Canadian Frontier, 1534-1760*. Holt, Rinehart, and Winston.

America, culminating in the British capture of Quebec during the Seven Years' War in 1759, which led to British dominance in Canada.[223]

1618 to 1648 – The Thirty Years War in Europe: The Thirty Years' War was a prolonged and devastating conflict that primarily took place in the Holy Roman Empire but also involved much of Europe. The war began as a religious conflict between Catholic and Protestant states following the rise of Protestantism during the Reformation. **It was triggered by the Defenestration of Prague in 1618, where Protestant nobles in Bohemia threw Catholic officials out of a window in protest of religious persecution (-).** Over time, the war evolved into a broader political struggle for power and influence among major European powers, including Spain, France, Sweden, and the Dutch Republic, **each seeking to exploit the chaos for territorial and political gain (-).**[224]

The Peace of Westphalia in 1648 ended the Thirty Years' War, bringing about significant political and religious changes in Europe. The treaties recognized the sovereignty of over 300 German principalities, effectively weakening the Holy Roman Empire and establishing the modern concept of state sovereignty. **Additionally, the war resulted in the legalization of Calvinism alongside Lutheranism and Catholicism, reinforcing the principle of *cuius regio, eius religio* – the right of rulers to determine their states' religion (+).** The conflict left much of Central Europe devastated, with large-scale population losses and economic ruin.[225]

1707 CE – The Founding of Great Britain: The formation of Great Britain as a unified political entity began with the Acts of Union in 1707, which united the Kingdom of England and the Kingdom of Scotland into a single state known as the Kingdom of Great Britain. The union came after a long history of both conflict and cooperation between the two nations, driven by political, economic, and religious factors. Scotland had faced economic difficulties after failed colonial ventures, such as the Darien Scheme, while England sought to secure a Protestant succession and prevent any possibility of a Catholic monarch on the Scottish throne. The union was facilitated by mutual economic interests, with the English offering to relieve Scottish debt

---

[223] Greer, A. (1997). *The People of New France.* University of Toronto Press.
[224] Parker, G. (1997). *The Thirty Years' War.* Routledge.
[225] Wilson, P. H. (2009). *Europe's Tragedy: A History of the Thirty Years War.* Allen Lane.

and provide access to England's growing global trade networks.[226]

The Acts of Union created a single Parliament at Westminster and combined the two crowns, while maintaining separate legal systems and religious institutions for Scotland and England. This political unification set the stage for the development of Britain as a global power, particularly during the 18th century, when the British Empire expanded rapidly through colonization and trade.

The union was further solidified in 1801 with the Acts of Union between Great Britain and Ireland, forming the United Kingdom of Great Britain and Ireland. **While the union brought political stability and economic growth (+), it also sparked resistance in Scotland and Ireland, where many opposed the loss of independence and local authority (-).**[227]

1763 to 1783 CE: The Declaration of Independence & American Revolution: The Declaration of Independence, adopted on July 4, 1776, was a formal statement by the Thirteen American Colonies asserting their right to independence from Great Britain. **Written primarily by Thomas Jefferson and approved by the Continental Congress, the document articulated the colonies' grievances against King George III and proclaimed the inherent rights to life, liberty, and the pursuit of happiness (+).** Influenced by Enlightenment ideals, the Declaration emphasized the concept of natural rights and the right of a people to revolt against a government that no longer served their interests. **The document was a revolutionary step, as it not only declared the colonies' separation but also provided a philosophical foundation for democratic governance (+).**[228]

The adoption of the Declaration set the stage for the American Revolutionary War, a conflict in which the colonies fought for and eventually won their independence from Great Britain. The war officially began in 1775 with battles at Lexington and Concord, and while the early years were difficult for the Continental Army, key victories such as the Battle of Saratoga in 1777 and the crucial alliance with France in 1778 shifted the momentum in favor of the Americans. Under the leadership of General George Washington, the Continental Army triumphed with the surrender of British General Charles Cornwallis at Yorktown in 1781. The war formally ended with the

---

[226] Devine, T. M. (2006). *The Scottish Nation: 1700-2007*. Penguin Books.
[227] Colley, L. (2009). *Britons: Forging the Nation 1707-1837*. Yale University Press.
[228] Maier, P. (1997). *American Scripture: Making the Declaration of Independence*. Knopf.

EARLY MODERNITY (1500 TO 1800 CE)

Treaty of Paris in 1783, in which Britain recognized the independence of the United States. The revolution not only established the United States as a new nation but also had lasting global impacts, inspiring other independence movements and contributing to the spread of democratic ideas.[229]

1776 to 1787 CE – The Birth of Capitalism & Democracy: In France, Adam Smith's *The Wealth of Nations*, published in 1776, became one of the foundational texts of modern economic theory and marked the beginning of classical economics. **In this work, Smith explores the dynamics of markets, trade, and production, advocating for the idea that individuals pursuing their own self-interest inadvertently promote the public good through a mechanism he famously described as the "invisible hand" (+).**

Smith argued that free markets, characterized by competition and voluntary exchange, are more efficient than systems where the government intervenes heavily in economic activity. He also discussed the division of labor, suggesting that specialization increases productivity, as seen in his example of a pin factory.[230] The Wealth of Nations critiqued mercantilism, the dominant economic system of the time, which prioritized state control of trade and the accumulation of wealth through a favorable balance of trade. Smith instead promoted the idea that wealth comes from production and exchange, not just hoarding gold and silver.[231]

Smith's ideas laid the groundwork for laissez-faire economics, a principle that advocates minimal government intervention in economic matters (+). Laissez-faire, meaning "let do" in French, holds that economies function best when individuals and businesses are free to pursue their own economic interests with little or no government interference. This concept became central to the development of capitalist economies, particularly in the 19th century. **As capitalist economies became more prominent, the incentive for technological advances began to align more closely with economic profit rather than the advancement of human rights and community (-).** Foreseeing this, Smith did recognize that some government involvement was necessary to align such

---

[229] Middlekauff, R. (2005). *The Glorious Cause: The American Revolution, 1763-1789.* Oxford University Press.
[230] Smith, A. (1776). *The Wealth of Nations.* W. Strahan and T. Cadell.
[231] Rothschild, E. (2001). *Economic Sentiments: Adam Smith, Condorcet, and the Enlightenment.* Harvard University Press.

advancements with human flourishing, particularly in providing public goods such as infrastructure, education, and national defense (+) – services that the market might not adequately supply on its own due to their incapacity to profit economically.[232]

Meanwhile in the Americas, The United States Constitution, drafted in 1787 and ratified in 1788, became the foundational legal document of the United States, and established the framework for its federal government. Written during the Constitutional Convention in Philadelphia, the Constitution was a response to the weaknesses of the Articles of Confederation, the country's first governing document, which had proven ineffective in creating a strong national government. The Constitution created a system of checks and balances by dividing the federal government into three branches: the executive, legislative, and judicial branches. **The Constitution's first ten amendments, known as the Bill of Rights, were added in 1791 to guarantee individual liberties such as freedom of speech, religion, and the press (+), reflecting the influence of Enlightenment thinkers like John Locke.**[233]

The Constitution established a federal system of government, which balanced power between the national government and the states. It also introduced the principle of popular sovereignty, meaning that the authority of the government comes from the consent of the governed, and the rule of law, ensuring that government power is limited and defined by law. Over time, the Constitution has been amended 27 times to address changing political, social, and economic conditions. As a living document, it continues to be interpreted by the courts, most notably the Supreme Court, which plays a crucial role in interpreting its meaning. The Constitution has been a model for many other nations' legal frameworks and remains one of the most influential political documents in modern history.[234]

1789 to 1799 – The French Revolution: The French Revolution was a pivotal period of social, political, and economic upheaval in France, marking the end of the Ancien Régime and the rise of modern democratic and republican ideals. It began in 1789 with the financial

---

[232] Heilbroner, R. L. (1999). *The Worldly Philosophers: The Lives, Times, and Ideas of the Great Economic Thinkers.* Touchstone.
[233] Wood, G. S. (2009). *Empire of Liberty: A History of the Early Republic, 1789-1815.* Oxford University Press.
[234] Amar, A. R. (2005). *America's Constitution: A Biography.* Random House.

crisis and widespread discontent among the Third Estate (commoners), which led to the calling of the Estates-General and the formation of the National Assembly. The revolution was driven by Enlightenment ideas of liberty, equality, and fraternity and led to the abolition of feudal privileges, the declaration of the Rights of Man and of the Citizen, and the establishment of a constitutional monarchy. However, internal divisions and external threats, particularly from monarchies opposed to the revolution, led to radicalization.[235]

The Reign of Terror (1793 to 1794) was the most violent phase of the French Revolution, characterized by mass executions and political purges. Led by the Committee of Public Safety, dominated by Maximilien Robespierre, the Reign of Terror sought to defend the revolution from internal enemies and foreign invaders. **The use of the guillotine became a symbol of this period (-), as thousands of people, including King Louis XVI and Marie Antoinette, were executed for being perceived enemies of the revolution.** The Committee justified these actions as necessary to preserve the republic, but the widespread violence led to Robespierre's downfall and execution in 1794, signaling the end of the Reign of Terror. The revolution transformed France, leading to the rise of Napoleon Bonaparte and inspiring revolutionary movements worldwide, though it also highlighted the dangers of radicalism and political violence.[236]

Napoleon Bonaparte's rise to power in France in 1799 as First Consul and later as Emperor in 1804 showed France's shift from a revolutionary republic to a centralized empire (-). Through a series of military campaigns known as the Napoleonic Wars (1803 to 1815), Napoleon sought to expand French influence across Europe and beyond. His key victories, such as the Battle of Austerlitz in 1805 and the Battle of Jena-Auerstedt in 1806, enabled him to dominate much of continental Europe, including parts of Italy, Germany, Spain, and the Netherlands. Napoleon's ambitions extended beyond Europe, as evidenced by his expedition to Egypt in 1798, aimed at undermining British interests. **However, his attempts at world domination (-) faltered due to several key factors, including the failed invasion of Russia in 1812, which decimated his army, and his eventual defeat at the Battle of Waterloo in 1815.** These failures, combined with growing coalitions against him, led to his abdication and exile, ending his aspirations of global conquest.[237]

---

[235] Doyle, W. (2001). *The French Revolution: A Very Short Introduction.* Oxford University Press.
[236] Schama, S. (1989). *Citizens: A Chronicle of the French Revolution.* Penguin Books.
[237] Broers, M. (2014). *Napoleon: Soldier of Destiny.* Faber & Faber.

CONFLICT

III.iv THE INDUSTRIAL AND MODERN ERAS
(1800 CE TO PRESENT TIME)

The Industrial Era and modern period ushered in unprecedented technological, political, and ideological change. **The rise of technological advancements through organized industry and the shift toward urbanized societies placed new value on human labor, but also led to exploitation, spurring both oppressive policies (-) and dignity-affirming labor movements in response (+).** In response to the increasing economic costs that came with increasing quality of life, governing powers engaged in capturing resources through imperial expansions on foreign lands, driven no longer by territorial gain but by the desire to control valuable resources, establish trade routes, and assert economic and military power. The struggle for sovereignty, freedom, and autonomy for smaller economies became increasingly difficult as the world's powers grew dependent on lower-cost, out-group labor markets to maintain in-group ideologies.

As we approach modern times, we witness increased labor outsourcing to lower-cost regions as a strategy for stability in higher-cost regions, exacerbating economic gaps (-) and inequality between regions. Political structures evolved through democratic reforms and the push for human rights, spurred by Enlightenment ideals and global conflicts that tested humanity's commitment to upholding human dignity in wartime (+). The emergence of global institutions through technological advancements in communication and the push toward human rights frameworks in recent times signify an increased recognition of universal dignity. **However, modern conflicts, both ideological and political through territorial disputes, continue to reflect humanity's ongoing struggle to reconcile these ideals with the realities of political power and resource competition (-).**

1800 to 1900 – European Colonialism in Asia and Australia: European expansion in Asia and Australia began to intensify in the 19th century, with European powers seeking resources, trade dominance, and territorial control. The British Empire played a leading role, with significant actions beginning in the early 1800s. The British East India Company had already established control over large parts of India by the 18th century, but after the Indian Rebellion of 1857, the British government formally took control, establishing the British Raj in 1858.[238] During this period, Britain expanded its reach in Southeast Asia as well, establishing Singapore as a key trading hub in 1819 and later securing control over Burma in the 1880s. The Dutch Empire controlled the Dutch East Indies (modern-day Indonesia) throughout the 19th century, beginning with Dutch colonization of the islands in the 17th century but intensifying during the 1800s. The French expanded their presence in Indochina, with Cochinchina (southern Vietnam) becoming a colony in 1862, followed by the rest of Vietnam, Laos, and Cambodia, which formed French Indochina by 1887.[239]

Meanwhile, Russia expanded eastward into Central Asia during the 19th century, completing its domination of much of the region by the late 1800s. Russia's influence extended into parts of Manchuria and China in the later stages of the century, particularly with the Treaty of Tientsin (1858) and other agreements that ceded territories. **China was increasingly subject to foreign imperial influence throughout the 19th century, especially following the Opium Wars (1839 to 1842 and again from 1856 to 1860), which led to the imposition of unequal treaties granting economic and territorial concessions to European powers (-), including Britain and France.**

In Australia, British imperialism began with the establishment of the First Fleet in 1788, when Britain established the New South Wales colony as a penal colony. The British continued to expand their settlements across the continent throughout the 1800s, with Australia officially becoming a part of the British Empire, and its colonies increasing through the century. The Gold Rushes of the 1850s spurred further migration, cementing British control. **The Indigenous Aboriginal population faced extensive displacement, violence, and diseases brought by European settlers, causing significant cultural disruption and population loss (-).**[240]

The territorial expansion, economic exploitation, and cultural disruption spanning from the late 18th century to the early 20th century would lay the foundation for the economic disparities we see today (-). In Asia, this period stretched from the early 1800s with the British, French, Dutch, and Russian expansions, reaching its peak by the 1890s. In Australia, British control from 1788 into the 1800s left a lasting impact on Indigenous populations, which still persists today.

---

[238] Subrahmanyam, S. (2004). *The British in India: A study in imperialism*. Oxford University Press.
[239] Stone, D. (2010). *The colonial legacy in Asia*. Oxford University Press.
[240] Glick, T. F., & Woodward, W. (Eds.). (1992). *European expansion and the response of Indigenous peoples*. Cambridge University Press.

CONFLICT

1800 to 1830 – Central American Liberation: Central America was one such key region in the broader quest for local autonomy. Simón Bolívar (1783 to 1830), known as "El Libertador," was a Venezuelan military and political leader who played a key role in the independence movements across South America from Spanish Colonial rule. Inspired by the ideals of the Enlightenment, as well as the success of the American and French Revolutions, Bolívar led multiple military campaigns throughout the early 19th century, liberating Spanish territories that would become modern-day Venezuela, Colombia, Ecuador, Peru, and Bolivia (the latter named in his honor).

His vision extended beyond mere independence; Bolívar aimed to unite the newly liberated territories into a single nation called *Gran Colombia*. However, political infighting and regional differences thwarted this dream, leading to the eventual fragmentation of Gran Colombia. **Despite Bolívar's struggles to create a unified Latin American republic, Bolívar is remembered as a national hero throughout the continent and as a symbol of Latin American independence and unity (+).**[241]

1845 to 1848 – The Birth of Communism: Karl Marx (1818 to 1883) and Friedrich Engels (1820 to 1895) were German philosophers, economists, and political theorists who co-authored *The Communist Manifesto* in 1848, a formative text in the development of modern socialism and communism. Marx, the principal thinker, is best known for his theory of historical materialism, which argued that human history is driven by class struggles, primarily between the bourgeoisie (the capitalist class) and the proletariat (the working class). **Marx believed that capitalism, while revolutionary in its creation of wealth (+), was inherently exploitative of both the working class and the earth's natural resources (-) and would eventually be replaced by socialism, and ultimately, communism, a classless society which worked to minimize the exploitation of resources and people (+).** Engels, a close collaborator and supporter, contributed to both the development and promotion of Marx's ideas, through his own works like *The Condition of the Working Class in England* (1845), which examined the harsh realities of industrial capitalism.[242]

Together, Marx and Engels envisioned a society where the

---

[241] Lynch, J. (2006). *Simón Bolívar: A Life*. Yale University Press.
[242] Engels, F. (1845). *The Condition of the Working Class in England*.

THE INDUSTRIAL AND MODERN ERAS (1800 CE TO PRESENT TIME)

means of production – land, factories, and natural resources – were collectively owned and class distinctions were abolished (+). Their ideas laid the foundation for the international socialist movement, influencing labor unions, political parties, and revolutionary movements across the world. Marx's *Das Kapital* (1867), a critical analysis of capitalist economics, further developed their critique of capitalism, arguing that it would inevitably collapse due to its internal contradictions. Engels, after Marx's death, continued to advocate for their ideas and helped publish Marx's unfinished manuscripts. While their revolutionary predictions did not immediately happen, their work profoundly shaped 19th and 20th-century political thought, particularly in the rise of socialist and communist states such as the Soviet Union.[243]

1830 to 1910 – The Industrial Revolution: The largest leap in technology in modern history was the Industrial Revolution, which started between the 1840s and 1850s. This was a period of rapid technological advancements that significantly transformed manufacturing, transportation, and communication. **One of the most important developments was the improvement of the steam engine, which had been introduced in the late 18th century but was refined during this period by figures like George Stephenson and Isambard Kingdom Brunel (+).**[244] These innovations made the steam engine more efficient, powering not only factory machines but also steamships and locomotives, revolutionizing transportation and industrial output. **The improvement in steam technology contributed to economic growth by boosting industrial production and enabling faster transportation of goods and raw materials (+).**

In addition to the steam engine, communication was transformed with the invention of the telegraph by Samuel Morse, which became widely used in the 1840s. **The telegraph allowed messages to be transmitted across long distances almost instantaneously, significantly improving political power dynamics by facilitating faster decision-making (+) and diplomacy in business, politics, and warfare.**[245] The expansion of the railroad network also played a

---

[243] Marx, K., & Engels, F. (1848). *The Communist Manifesto*. Penguin Books.
[244] Stephenson, G. (1840). *The locomotive engine*. In *The life and works of George Stephenson* (pp. 121-145). London: Smith, Elder & Co.
[245] Morse, S. F. B. (1844). *The telegraph and its application to the commercial and political needs of the world*. New York: D. Appleton & Company.

crucial role during this time. Railroads connected distant cities, making transportation of goods and people faster and cheaper, which fueled economic growth and helped integrate local and global markets.

By the early 20th century, the pace of innovation continued to accelerate with the development of the automobile and the airplane (+). The automobile, popularized by Henry Ford's assembly line in the 1910s, revolutionized personal transportation, boosting the economy (+) and providing greater mobility for people, while reshaping cities and industries.[246] The growth of the automobile industry also influenced infrastructure development (+), such as the creation of roads and highways. Similarly, the invention of the airplane by the Wright brothers in 1903 marked the beginning of air travel, enabling faster global communication and trade, and revolutionizing both political power dynamics and economic growth.[247] These advancements, building on the foundation of earlier innovations, helped create a more interconnected world (+), fundamentally altering transportation, commerce; unbeknownst to the inventors, many of these innovations would be used for warfare and other forms of human-degrading conflict, too (-).

1831 to 1865 – The Abolition of Slavery: The abolition of slavery marked a significant ideological, political, and social transformation, particularly in the United States and the British Empire. This period was characterized by the clash between the rising ideological belief in human rights and equality (+) and the entrenched economic and political interests that benefited from slavery (-). Ideologically, the abolitionist movement gained momentum, driven by activists like William Lloyd Garrison, who founded the anti-slavery newspaper *The Liberator* in 1831, and Frederick Douglass, a former slave who became a leading voice for abolition. These advocates emphasized the inherent dignity and equality of all human beings, challenging the dehumanizing ideologies that justified slavery.

Political power dynamics played a critical role during this period, particularly in the United States. The tensions between Northern states, which were moving toward industrialization and free labor markets (+), and Southern states, which relied heavily on the plantation economy and slave labor (-) – all of which led to

---

[246] Ford, H. (1922). *My life and work*. Garden City Publishing Co.
[247] Wright, O., & Wright, W. (1903). *The Wright brothers: How they invented the airplane*. Dayton, OH: Wright Brothers Foundation.

THE INDUSTRIAL AND MODERN ERAS (1800 CE TO PRESENT TIME)

escalating human-degrading conflicts. Slavery had been a divisive issue since the nation's founding, with the southern states relying heavily on enslaved labor for their agricultural economy, particularly in the production of cotton and tobacco. The passage of the Fugitive Slave Act of 1850, which required escaped slaves to be returned to their owners, intensified abolitionist resistance and contributed to political polarization.

Technological advancements during this period, such as the printing press, played a crucial role in spreading abolitionist literature and rallying public support. Pamphlets, newspapers, and books like Harriet Beecher Stowe's *Uncle Tom's Cabin* (1852), which exposed the harsh realities of slavery, were widely disseminated, shaping public opinion and galvanizing support for the abolitionist cause.[248] **This culminated in the election of Abraham Lincoln in 1860, who was seen as a threat to the institution of slavery despite his initial moderate stance (+).**[249]

The Southern states' response was the secession that led to the American Civil War (1861 to 1865), a conflict that ultimately resulted in the end of slavery.[250] **During the war, Lincoln stressed his ideologies of freedom in an address to the United States Congress, saying, "In giving freedom to the slave, we assure freedom to the free – honorable alike in what we give, and what we preserve." (+).**[251] The Emancipation Proclamation of 1863 declared the freedom of slaves in Confederate states, and the ratification of the 13th Amendment in 1865 abolished slavery throughout the United States.[252] This marked a turning point in American history, but the fight for true equality for African Americans continues even today, though it reached its recent peak during the Civil Rights Movement of the 20th century.[253]

1850 to 1914 – Imperial Expansion; The Scramble for Africa: Throughout the second half of 19th century, European powers like Britain, France, Germany, Belgium, Portugal, and Italy were engaged in an imperial race to expand their influence around the globe. **As**

---

[248] Stowe, H. B. (1852). *Uncle Tom's Cabin*. John P. Jewett & Company.
[249] Foner, E. (1988). *Reconstruction: America's Unfinished Revolution, 1863-1877*. Harper & Row.
[250] McPherson, J. M. (1988). *Battle Cry of Freedom: The Civil War Era*. Oxford University Press.
[251] Lincoln, A. (1862). *Annual Address to Congress*. Retrieved from: https://www.loc.gov/item/scsm000136/
[252] Berlin, I. (2003). *Generations of Captivity: A History of African American Slaves*. Harvard University Press.
[253] McPherson, J. M. (1988). *Battle Cry of Freedom: The Civil War Era*. Oxford University Press.

CONFLICT

Adam Smith's economic ideas influenced the industrial markets towards a capitalist society oriented towards economic power and financial profit as the end goal (-), raw materials were increasingly important for production. **The Industrial Revolution had transformed European countries into economic and military powerhouses, creating the need for raw materials, new markets, and sources for the exploitation of cheap labor (-).** As European industries grew, there was an increasing demand for resources like rubber, minerals, and oil, which Africa was rich in.

The Berlin Conference of 1884 formalized the process. **In 1885, convened by German Chancellor Otto von Bismarck, European powers negotiated the division of Africa without regard to Indigenous populations (-).**[254] **Motivated by a mix of economic interests (particularly access to raw materials), strategic concerns, and a belief in European superiority thanks to a misunderstanding in Darwin's theories, the Scramble for Africa resulted in deeper subjugation and exploitation of African peoples (-), with few regions, such as Ethiopia and Liberia, remaining independent.** The lasting impact of European colonialism in Africa included the arbitrary drawing of borders, which contributed to ethnic and cultural conflicts, economic underdevelopment, and the disruption of African societies.

As a result of the Berlin Conference, African lands were carved for European Empire control. The British Empire received rights to Egypt, Sudan, Nigeria, Kenya, South Africa, and Rhodesia (modern Zimbabwe and Zambia). France established a large colonial empire in West Africa and North Africa, with key colonies like Algeria, Senegal, Mali, Côte d'Ivoire, and Tunisia. Germany managed to secure significant territories in East Africa (Tanzania), South-West Africa (Namibia), Cameroon, and Togo. King Leopold II of Belgium acquired the Congo Free State as his personal possession, separate from the Belgian government. **The exploitation of the Congo's resources, especially rubber, led to atrocities and widespread suffering**

---

[254] Pakenham, T. (1991). *The Scramble for Africa: White Man's Conquest of the Dark Continent from 1876 to 1912*. Random House.

among the local population (-). Portugal, one of the earliest colonial powers in Africa, controlled territories like Angola and Mozambique, maintaining its grip on these regions well into the 20th century. Italy sought to build its empire in the Horn of Africa, colonizing Eritrea, Somalia, and attempting to conquer Ethiopia.

The impact of arbitrary division of a continent led to political fragmentation (-), economic exploitation (-), social and cultural disruption (-), resistance, rebellion, and dissolution of established ethical values among African cultures (-). Today, many African countries remain underdeveloped and divided among cultures as a result of the scramble for Africa in the 19th century.

1854 to 1910 – Japan's rise through Imperialism: In the mid-19th century, Japan faced a new threat when Commodore Matthew Perry of the United States Navy arrived in 1853 and forced Japan to open its ports to foreign trade through the Treaty of Kanagawa in 1854. While the United States did not colonize Japan, this event marked the beginning of significant foreign influence, causing Japan to end its policy of seclusion. The Western powers, particularly the United States, Britain, and Russia, began to exert pressure on Japan for trade and territorial concessions, but Japan resisted outright colonization.

Forced interaction with the West exposed Japan's weakness in comparison to imperial powers, leading to the realization that the country needed to modernize rapidly to protect its sovereignty and compete on the world stage. **Japan's rise to imperialism in the late 1800s was driven by a combination of ideological developments (+), economic instability (-), and political power dynamics (-), which were shaped by both internal and external factors.**

Japan underwent the Meiji Restoration (1868), a period marked by significant ideological developments focused on the need for modernization and industrialization. The Japanese government embraced Western technology, education, and military reforms while attempting to maintain traditional elements of governance, leading to economic growth and military strength. This modernization was crucial to Japan's ability to project power and pursue imperial ambitions. **Economic instability in Japan also contributed to this rise; Japan's growing population and limited natural resources made it increasingly dependent on external territories for raw materials and markets, forcing a change in traditional values (-).**

CONFLICT

By the 1890s, Japan had successfully established itself as an imperial power with the victory in the First Sino-Japanese War (1894 to 1895), which gave it control over Taiwan and increased its influence in Korea. **The political power dynamics within East Asia shifted towards imperialism (-) as Japan emerged as a new competitor to the declining Chinese empire.** Japan's imperial ambitions continued with the annexation of Korea in 1910 and the expansion of its military and economic control over Northeast China and other parts of China in the early 20th century. **The drive for imperialism was driven by the need to secure resources, strategic positioning, and the perceived need to be recognized as a major world power to avoid external colonial rule (-).**

1867 to 1914 - The Austro-Hungarian Empire: Meanwhile in middle Europe, the unification of Hungary and Austria was formed through a dual monarchy under the rule of Emperor Franz Joseph I. The empire was formed following the Austro-Hungarian Compromise of 1867, which came after Austria's defeat in the Austro-Prussian War of 1866. This defeat weakened Austria's position in Europe and led to internal demands for greater autonomy, particularly from Hungary. The internal conflicts consumed much of Austria-Hungary's political and military focus, leaving it out of the Scramble for Africa.

To resolve internal tensions, the empire was reorganized into two equal entities – Austria and Hungary – each with its own parliament and government, but sharing a common monarch, foreign policy, and military (+). The compromise gave Hungary significant autonomy, but other ethnic groups within the empire, such as Czechs, Slovaks, Serbs, and Croats, continued to push for more rights, creating lasting internal divisions (-).[255]

The Austro-Hungarian Empire was a multi-ethnic state, comprising over a dozen distinct nationalities, which made governance challenging. The empire's leaders struggled to balance the competing demands of various ethnic groups, many of whom sought greater political representation or independence. **Cities like Vienna and Budapest became cultural and intellectual hubs, contributing to the arts, music, and sciences (+). However, the empire's political stability remained fragile, with nationalist movements gaining strength among Slavic populations, particularly in the Balkans,**

---

[255] Kann, R. A. (1977). *A History of the Habsburg Empire: 1526–1918*. University of California Press.

THE INDUSTRIAL AND MODERN ERAS (1800 CE TO PRESENT TIME)

driving division and disunity (-).[256] Despite these tensions, the empire experienced a period of economic growth and modernization during the late 19th century, but ultimately were not as involved with imperial expansion due to internal struggles.

Austria-Hungary's aggressive foreign policy in the Balkans, especially its annexation of Bosnia and Herzegovina in 1908, heightened tensions with Serbia and Russia. These tensions culminated June 28, 1914, when Archduke Franz Ferdinand and his wife were assassinated while visiting Sarajevo, the capital of Bosnia. The assassin was Gavrilo Princip, a member of a secret Serbian nationalist organization called the Black Hand.

The assassination was driven by the misconception that eliminating the heir to the throne would destabilize the empire (-), forcing the need for Slavic unification (+). The empire, a patchwork of over a dozen Slavic ethnic groups, was held together by a fragile balance of power that revolved around the dual monarchy of Austria and Hungary. **Austria-Hungary's subsequent harsh response to Serbia's assassination was an attempt to reassert control and unity, but instead triggered a series of alliances and escalations that led to the outbreak of World War I (-).**

1893 to Present – The Women's Suffrage Movement: The women's suffrage movement has been a transformative chapter in global history that intersected with the factors of ideological developments, political power dynamics, and technological advancements. **At its core, this movement has been driven by the ideological shift toward recognizing equality and human rights (+), challenging longstanding beliefs about women's roles in society.** Countries like New Zealand led the way in 1893 by becoming the first to grant women the right to vote.[257] This ideological push gained momentum in the early 20th century as social reformers and activists advocated for women's political rights, sparking similar movements in other nations.

Political power dynamics played a critical role in either advancing or delaying suffrage rights. For example, in the United Kingdom, the political landscape shifted during and after World War I, leading to the Representation of the People Act of 1918, which allowed women over the age of 30 who met certain property qualifications to vote. This was

---

[256] Bérenger, J. (1994). *A History of the Habsburg Empire, 1700–1918*. Longman.
[257] Brookes, B. (2017). *A History of New Zealand Women*. Bridget Williams Books.

expanded in 1928 to include all women over 21, reflecting a broader ideological acceptance of gender equality. In the United States, the passage of the 19th Amendment in 1920 was the result of decades of advocacy and political negotiation by suffragettes, who strategically aligned their cause with the democratic ideals of the nation.[258] However, in countries like France and Switzerland, deeply ingrained political and social structures delayed suffrage until after World War II and as late as 1971, respectively.

Technological advancements also played a supporting role in amplifying the message of the women's suffrage movement. The development of the printing press and later communication technologies, such as newspapers and radio, allowed activists to reach a broader audience and mobilize support.

Despite progress in many regions, the struggle for full political participation continued, as seen in Saudi Arabia, where women were only granted the right to vote in municipal elections in 2015.[259] **While legal voting rights exist universally, practical barriers – such as cultural norms, political instability, and logistical challenges – impede women's full participation in the electoral process in certain regions even today (-).**

1912 to 1916 – The End of Dynasties in China: After the fall of the Qing Dynasty in 1912, Sun Yat-sen was initially declared the provisional president of the newly established Republic of China. **His rise to power was the result of a long process of ideological developments advocating for modernization and the overthrow of imperial rule (+), particularly through his Three Principles of the People – nationalism, democracy, and the people's livelihood (+).**[260]

Sun Yat-sen's leadership followed the Xinhai Revolution, which marked the collapse of the Qing Dynasty after widespread discontent among intellectuals, reformers, and the general population. However, Sun's presidency was short-lived. Faced with the fragmented nature of Chinese politics and a lack of military support, he was forced to step down in favor of Yuan Shikai in March 1912, who became the president of the Republic of China.

Yuan, a former Qing general with substantial military power, was

---

[258] Flexner, E., & Fitzpatrick, E. (1996). *Century of Struggle: The Woman's Rights Movement in the United States.* Harvard University Press.
[259] Doumato, E. A. (2010). *Women and the State in Saudi Arabia.* Indiana University Press.
[260] Fairbank, J. K. (1992). *China: A new history.* Belknap Press.

able to secure the presidency with the backing of the military and political elites, establishing control over the country. **This move reflected political power dynamics that leveraged politics over the people (-), as Yuan's support base was primarily in the military, which held significant sway over China's political landscape at the time.** While Sun had envisioned a democratic republic, Yuan's leadership marked a shift toward authoritarian rule. In 1915, Yuan declared himself emperor, attempting to restore the monarchy, but this move met widespread opposition, contributing to his eventual downfall and death in 1916. **His attempt to consolidate power further destabilized China, leading to the Warlord Era (1916 to 1928), where regional military leaders controlled various parts of the country, further demonstrating how the political power dynamics (-) of the time kept China from achieving unity and stability in its early years as a republic.**

1914 to 1918 − The First World War: The First World War was the result of a complex web of political, military, and social tensions that had been building in Europe for nearly a century. **One of the most significant long-term causes was the rise of nationalism (-), particularly in the multi-ethnic empires of Austria-Hungary and the Ottoman Empire, where various ethnic groups sought independence.** Nationalist movements also heightened tensions between rival European powers, especially between France and Germany, who were still recovering from the Franco-Prussian War of 1870. **Nationalism's influence on ideological developments, technological advancements, and political power dynamics was detrimental in the 19th century because it fostered division among cultures, dehumanization of out-groups in Africa and Asia, and violence through unnecessary material competition (-).**

At the same time, imperialism played a crucial role, as **European nations competed for colonies and resources around the world, exacerbating rivalries (-), particularly between Britain, Germany, and France.**[261] Militarism also contributed to the outbreak of war. By the early 20th century, many European powers had adopted aggressive military policies by increasing the size of their armies and

---

[261] Clark, C. (2012). *The Sleepwalkers: How Europe Went to War in 1914*. Penguin Books.

modernizing their weapons. **This arms race, particularly between Germany and Britain, was accompanied by elaborate military alliances designed to provide security (+) but which ultimately bound nations to mutual defense agreements (-).** The most significant of these alliances were the Triple Alliance of Germany, Austria-Hungary, and Italy, and the Triple Entente of Britain, France, and Russia. These alliances created a volatile environment in which a conflict involving one country could quickly draw in others, making a larger war inevitable.[262]

The immediate spark for the war came from the assassination Archduke Franz Ferdinand of Austria-Hungary. **Austria-Hungary blamed Serbia for the assassination and issued an ultimatum, leading to a series of diplomatic failures (-).** With Germany's support, Austria-Hungary declared war on Serbia on July 28, 1914. Russia, allied with Serbia, mobilized in response, prompting Germany to declare war on Russia, and then France. When Germany invaded Belgium as part of its strategy to quickly defeat France, Britain entered the war in defense of Belgian neutrality. Germany invited allies abroad to join the war after they continually sought to suffocate the allies on the European mainland by using U-boat submarines to destroy merchant vessels carrying supplies and resources from allies abroad. Within months, much of Europe was engulfed in a conflict that would spread across the globe and become one of the deadliest wars in history.[263] In a short span, soldiers from Canada, Australia, New Zealand, India, Brazil, Mexico, the United States, and other countries from every continent on the globe had joined the war.

World War I lasted until November 11, 1918, spanning just over four years. It resulted in an estimated 15-20 million deaths, including both military personnel and civilians, with another 21 million wounded. **The causes of war were complex, involving militarism (-), private alliances (-), imperialism (-), and national interests over human rights (-), all of which created a tense and volatile environment in Europe.** Additionally, advancements in weaponry, such as machine

---

[262] Fromkin, D. (2007). *Europe's Last Summer: Who Started the Great War in 1914?*. Vintage Books.
[263] Keegan, J. (1998). *The First World War*. Alfred A. Knopf.

THE INDUSTRIAL AND MODERN ERAS (1800 CE TO PRESENT TIME)

guns, tanks, and chemical warfare, escalated the destruction and loss of life during the conflict.

The Austria-Hungary Empire's subsequent involvement in World War I, alongside the German Empire, led to its collapse. By the end of the war in 1918, the Austria-Hungary Empire was dissolved, and its territory was divided into several independent nations, including Austria, Hungary, Czechoslovakia, and parts of Yugoslavia. The fall of the Austro-Hungarian Empire marked the end of centuries of Habsburg rule in Central Europe and redrew the political map of the region.[264]

Following World War I, several treaties were signed to reshape Europe and the broader international order. **The Treaty of Versailles (1919) imposed harsh terms on Germany, including territorial losses, military restrictions, and heavy reparations (-). The Treaty of Trianon (1920) similarly dismantled the Austro-Hungarian Empire, significantly reducing Hungary's territory and population by nearly two-thirds, creating foreseeable cultural and political divides across newly drawn borders (-).**[265] Other treaties addressed specific countries: the Treaty of Saint-Germain (1919) created new states from the Austro-Hungarian Empire and placed restrictions on Austria. The Treaty of Neuilly (1919) forced Bulgaria to cede territory and pay reparations. The Treaty of Sèvres (1920) dismantled the Ottoman Empire but was later replaced by the Treaty of Lausanne (1923), which solidified modern-day Türkiye's borders and ended the conflict between Türkiye and the Allies. In addition, the Treaty of Rapallo (1922) marked an important agreement between Germany and Soviet Russia, establishing diplomatic and economic relations.

These treaties were aimed at resolving the political vacuum left by the collapse of empires and establishing new nation-states, with ideological developments that promoted self-determination and national sovereignty (+). However, many of the provisions created political power dynamics that fostered lasting resentment (-), inequality through unresolved territorial

---

[264] Taylor, A. J. P. (1948). *The Habsburg Monarchy 1809-1918: A History of the Austrian Empire and Austria-Hungary*. Penguin Books.
[265] Macartney, C. A. (1962). *Hungary and her successors: The treaty of Trianon and its consequences*. Macmillan.

disputes over borders (-), and economic instability through reparations and punitive terms (-), contributing to the conditions that led to World War II. The harsh terms imposed on defeated nations and the failure to address the aspirations of various ethnic and political groups led to a sense of injustice and a desire for revenge, which undermined efforts for lasting peace.

1918 to 1919 – The Spanish Flu: Following World War I, the Spanish flu pandemic, lasting from 1918 to 1919, became one of the deadliest global health crises in history, infecting an estimated one-third of the world's population and causing the deaths of at least 50 million people. The pandemic spread rapidly due to the movement of troops and the disruption of global infrastructure during and after the war.

Unlike previous flu outbreaks, the Spanish flu disproportionately affected young, healthy adults, rather than just the young or elderly. The scale of the pandemic was exacerbated by wartime conditions, including overcrowded military camps, poor sanitation, and weakened immune systems from the physical toll of the war.[266] In many countries, the flu's impact was intensified by politics, as governments initially downplayed or censored reports of the virus to avoid demoralizing their populations. **The Spanish flu was a stark reminder of the vulnerability of humanity in the face of global conflict, as the pandemic amid the war undermined public health and human life (-), further deepening the physical and psychological scars left by the war.**

1919 to 1937 – Instability and China: Following the First World War – a war in which China allied with the British and the French after declaring war against Germany in 1917 – China found itself in the middle of the Warlord Era at home. Despite China's support for the allies by providing raw materials and sending laborers to dig trenches in France, China was negatively affected by the Treaty of Versailles.

Instead of recognizing China's territory that had been governed by Germany, the Treaty of Versailles handed control of the region of the Shandong Peninsula to Japan, a decision that

---

[266] Barry, J. M. (2004). *The great influenza: The story of the deadliest pandemic in history*. Viking.

caused widespread outrage in China and led to the May Fourth Movement in 1919, a large-scale student protest that called for greater national unity, reform, and rejection of the unequal treaties with foreign powers (-).[267]

When the treaty gave Japan claim of the Shandong Peninsula, it only reinforced Japan's era of Imperial conquest and the West's dependence on Japan to continue supporting western ideologies of global expansion and the exploitation of foreign resources (-). In turn, not giving the land to China was a public rebuke of the Chinese people, who were in the midst of internal political turmoil with widespread unrest and a fragmented government. This move paved the way for the rise of Chinese nationalism and the eventual growth of the Chinese Communist Party (CCP).

Political power dynamics during this period were characterized by the tension between the Kuomintang (KMT) and the Chinese Communist Party (CCP), which had initially cooperated with the KMT in the First United Front (1924 to 1927) to fight warlords and imperialist Japanese forces. After the Warlord Era ended in the late 1920s, China experienced significant political and social changes as the KMT, led by Chiang Kai-shek, sought to consolidate power and unify the country after years of fragmentation. **In 1927, Chiang Kai-shek broke with the communists, initiating a violent purge of communist forces in a series of events known as the Shanghai Massacre (-). This marked the beginning of the Chinese Civil War between the KMT and CCP, with the CCP retreating to rural areas and adopting guerrilla warfare tactics to challenge KMT authority (-).** To make matters worse, Japan's increasing presence in China during the 1930s, particularly with the Manchurian Incident in 1931 and the subsequent establishment of the puppet state of Manchukuo, reflected economic instability and growing tensions between China and Japan.

This period was marked by the Nanjing Decade (1927 to 1937), during which the KMT, with Chiang at its helm, established a centralized government, rebuilding China after the political chaos of the Warlord Era. The KMT's victory over regional warlords and the creation of a nominally unified China were significant achievements, but the country still faced deep internal challenges as it coped with ramifications of civil war and the threat of imperialism.

---

[267] Wang, J. (2014). *The Shandong problem and the Chinese response to the Treaty of Versailles.* In J. D. Lary (Ed.), *China's foreign relations in the twentieth century* (pp. 35-57). University of California Press.

CONFLICT

1922 – The Emergence of The Soviet Union: The Soviet Union, officially known as the Union of Soviet Socialist Republics (USSR), was formally established on December 30, 1922. It emerged after the Russian Revolution of 1917. **The Russian Revolution occurred because of the deep social and economic inequalities (-) that had built up over centuries, the autocratic nature of the Tsarist government, and the lasting impacts of World War I.**[268] The failure of the Tsarist regime to adapt to modern demands, combined with the influence of revolutionary ideas, created a situation ripe for change. The February and October Revolutions ultimately dismantled the old system and paved the way for the rise of the Soviet Union under Bolshevik rule, a Marxist political party led by Vladimir Lenin.

The revolution led to the Russian Civil War (1917 to 1922) between the Bolshevik Red Army and various anti-Bolshevik forces, known as the White Army. Between 7 to 12 million Russians died as a result of the Russian civil war, most of which due to combat, disease, famine, and harsh conditions. **The Russian civil war also saw mass executions (-), reprisals, and the establishment of the Soviet state's brutal methods of political repression (-), especially during the period known as the Red Terror.**

After the Bolshevik victory, the Russian Soviet Federative Socialist Republic (RSFSR) was the largest of the newly formed Soviet Republics. In December 1922, the RSFSR, along with the Ukrainian, Belarusian, and Transcaucasian Soviet Republics, formally united to create the Soviet Union, a federation of Socialist Republics under a centralized government controlled by the Communist Party.[269] **Influenced by Marxist ideals, the economic theory advocated for the establishment of a classless society in which the means of production are controlled by the welfare of the workers (+), and not purely focused on economic profit of businessmen (-).** In practice, the Bolsheviks sought to overthrow the capitalist system and replace it with a socialist state controlled by the working class, though in reality, the Soviet government was highly centralized and controlled

---

[268] Pipes, R. (1990). *The Russian Revolution*. Vintage Books.
[269] Rounding, V. (1993). *The Russian Revolution, 1900–1927*. St. Martin's Press.

THE INDUSTRIAL AND MODERN ERAS (1800 CE TO PRESENT TIME)

by the Communist Party. **Over time, especially under Joseph Stalin's rule, the principles of Marxism were heavily modified to fit the political and economic needs of the Soviet state, leading to a more authoritarian system (-).** The Soviet Union existed until its dissolution on December 26, 1991.

1929 to 1939 – The Great Depression in the United States: Following nearly a decade of economic flourishing in the 1920s, known as the "Roaring Twenties," the United States experienced the catastrophic collapse of its stock market on October 29, 1929, a day famously known as Black Tuesday.[270] The stock market crash was the result of speculative investments, inflated stock prices, and a lack of regulatory oversight, which ultimately caused a panic among investors. As stocks plummeted, banks failed, businesses closed, and millions of Americans lost their savings, leading to widespread unemployment and poverty. **The Great Depression in the United States, which began in 1929 and lasted throughout the 1930s, was caused by a combination of economic instability (-), over-speculation in the stock market, banking failures, and widespread agricultural hardship. The political power dynamics at the time, marked by a lack of government intervention and ineffective responses under President Herbert Hoover, worsened the crisis as millions of Americans faced widespread economic disparity (-).**

The effects of the Depression were severe, with unemployment reaching 25%, widespread poverty, and a collapse of the banking system. **The economic instability (-) led to significant social unrest, prompting many people to lose faith in the existing economic and political systems.** In response, President Franklin D. Roosevelt introduced the New Deal in 1933, aiming to provide immediate relief, recovery, and reform.[271] **These measures sought to stimulate the economy (+) through public works programs, social security, and banking reforms, ultimately reshaping the**

---

[270] Bernstein, M. (2001). *The Great Depression: Delayed Recovery and Economic Change in America, 1929-1939.* Cambridge University Press.
[271] Roosevelt, F. D. (1933). *Fireside chat on the New Deal.* Retrieved from https://www.archives.gov/exhibits/american_originals/fdr.html

role of the government in economic affairs. The ideological developments surrounding government intervention in the economy had lasting effects on American economic policy and societal norms, to include the standardization of a 44-hour work week through the Fair Labor Standards Act of 1938, which was eventually reduced to 40 hours. Full economic recovery did not come until World War II, which stimulated industrial production and reduced unemployment.

1935 to 1945 CE – The Second World War: In Germany in the 1930s, a man named **Adolf Hitler came to power, promising the German people to restore national pride and undo the humiliating terms of World War I's Treaty of Versailles, including rearmament and regaining of lost territory (-).** He also promised to bring economic recovery by creating jobs and reviving industry, which resonated during the economic instability of the Great Depression. **Additionally, Hitler promised to restore order and stability by ending political chaos, while promoting the idea of a racially pure nation through his focus on Aryan supremacy (-).**[272] His promises of military strength and territorial expansion (Lebensraum) appealed to nationalistic sentiments, paving the way for his totalitarian rule.

On September 1, 1939, Germany invaded Poland to reclaim territory lost under the Treaty of Versailles, expand eastward for "Lebensraum," and implement Nazi racial ideology. The invasion was facilitated by the Molotov-Ribbentrop Pact with the Soviet Union, which divided Eastern Europe in a way that allowed for the attack to happen without the Soviet Union getting involved. The attack itself was justified by the staged Gleiwitz Incident, in which German operatives, posing as Polish saboteurs, attacked a German radio station, giving Hitler a pretext to claim that Poland had provoked the war. This act marked the start of World War II.

In response, Britain and France declared war on Germany on September 3, 1939, marking the official start of the war. World War II

---

[272] Hitler, A. (1933). *Mein Kampf* (R. Manheim, Trans.). Houghton Mifflin. (Original work published 1925).

THE INDUSTRIAL AND MODERN ERAS (1800 CE TO PRESENT TIME)

quickly became a global conflict involving most of the world's nations, including the major powers divided into two opposing alliances: the Allies (led by Poland, United Kingdom, France, Soviet Union, United States, and China) and the Axis Powers (led by Nazi Germany, Imperial Japan, and Fascist Italy).

With the war raging in Europe, Japan saw opportunity for imperial dominance in the Pacific (-), culminating in the attack on Pearl Harbor in 1941, which brought the United States into the conflict.[273] The war was fought across Europe, Africa, and the Pacific, with key events such as the Battle of Stalingrad (1942 to 1943), the Normandy Invasion (D-Day, 1944), and the Battle of Midway (1942) marking pivotal turning points.

The war concluded in 1945 with the total defeat of the Axis Powers. Germany surrendered in May after the fall of Berlin, and Japan surrendered in August following the dropping of atomic bombs on Hiroshima and Nagasaki by the United States.

The human toll was staggering, with an estimated 70 to 85 million people dead, including six million Jews who perished in the Holocaust (-). The war reshaped the global political landscape, leading to the emergence of the United States and the Soviet Union as superpowers and the start of the Cold War.[274] Additionally, the war resulted in the formation of the United Nations in 1945, an international body aimed at preventing future conflicts, and decolonization movements that followed in the aftermath of the war as former colonies sought independence.

1937 to 1949 – Continued Chinese Tension: The Second Sino-Japanese War (1937 to 1945) further complicated the political landscape in China, leading to a temporary cooperation between the KMT and CCP to fight the Japanese invaders. This alliance, known as the Second United Front (1937 to 1945), was fragile and short-lived, as the internal conflict between the KMT and CCP remained simmering.

During the Second United Front of the KMT and CCP, ideological

---
[273] Keegan, J. (1989). *The Second World War*. Viking Penguin.
[274] Overy, R. (2013). *The Bombing War: Europe 1939-1945*. Allen Lane.

developments influenced the political direction of both the KMT and CCP. **The KMT promoted nationalism, modernization, and a Chinese version of Western-style democracy (+), while the CCP, under Mao Zedong, emphasized Marxist-Leninist principles, advocating for land reform and class struggle, particularly among the rural population (-).** Despite the KMT's efforts to modernize China, including the development of infrastructure and education, the country remained deeply divided, and its governance was weakened by corruption and inefficiency, which undermined its ability to effectively govern and resist foreign powers.

By 1937, the Second Sino-Japanese War had engulfed China, and the focus shifted to resisting Japanese aggression. **The war with Japan exacerbated existing political and social tensions (-), ultimately contributing to the resumption of the Chinese Civil War after the Japanese surrender in 1945.** The KMT, weakened by the war and plagued by internal corruption, faced a resurgent CCP, which had gained significant support in the countryside. This laid the groundwork for the final phase of the Chinese Civil War (1945 to 1949).

The KMT, with its capital in Chongqing, controlled the majority of China's urban centers, while the CCP, which had built a stronghold in rural areas, focused on winning the support of the peasantry through land reforms and promises of equality.[275]

Despite initial advantages in terms of labor and international support, particularly from the United States, the KMT struggled with corruption, economic mismanagement, and low morale (-). The CCP, on the other hand, effectively employed guerrilla warfare tactics and garnered support through successful reforms in the countryside to appease the people. In 1949, after a series of decisive military defeats, the KMT forces retreated to the island of Taiwan, where they established a government-in-exile. On October 1, 1949, Mao Zedong declared the establishment of the People's Republic of China (PRC) in Beijing, marking the communist victory. The conflict left deep scars in Chinese society, setting the stage for the PRC's

---

[275] Fenby, J. (2003). *Chiang Kai Shek: China's Generalissimo and the Nation He Lost.* Carroll & Graf Publishers.

THE INDUSTRIAL AND MODERN ERAS (1800 CE TO PRESENT TIME)

dominance of mainland China and the KMT's continued governance of Taiwan, which remains a politically sensitive issue to this day.[276]

1945 to 1948 – The Founding of the State of Israel: The establishment of the State of Israel in 1948 was a direct consequence of the upheavals following World War II, shaped by a combination of historical, religious, and political factors. **Following the Holocaust conducted by the Nazi party of Germany, there was increasing international support for a Jewish homeland, particularly from the United States and Western European powers, who were deeply moved by the genocide and sought to provide a safe haven for Jewish families (+).** The political power dynamics after WWII, along with the declining influence of British colonial rule in the Middle East, set the stage for the creation of the State of Israel. Britain had governed Palestine under a League of Nations mandate since 1920, but tensions between the Jewish and Arab populations, fueled by conflicting national aspirations, led Britain to withdraw from the region and turn the matter over to the United Nations.

The religious significance of the land, dating back to the Prophet Abraham, had nearly uncompromising significance for Muslims, Jews, and Christians. With over 4,000 years of religious tension, the United Nations voted that the best way to ease tensions was to partition the land into separate Jewish and Arab states in 1947, with Jerusalem designated as an international city for all religions.[277]

The Zionist movement celebrated the partition plan, which legitimized their decades-long campaign for a Jewish homeland. However, the Arab states and Palestinian Arabs rejected the UN plan, leading to violence between the Jewish and Arab populations.

Prior to the founding of the State of Israel, Jews had not governed the region around Jerusalem since the fall of the Kingdom of Judah to the Babylonian Empire in 586 BCE (see chapter III, section ii). **When the State of Israel was declared on May 14, 1948, the surrounding Arab people – hundreds of thousands of whom were displaced to**

---

[276] Zarrow, P. (2005). *China in War and Revolution, 1895-1949*. Routledge.
[277] United Nations. (1947). *Resolution 181 (II): Future government of Palestine*. Retrieved from https://www.un.org/en/ga/search/view_doc.asp?symbol=A/RES/181(II)

CONFLICT

resettle Jewish victims of the holocaust – immediately invaded the state of Israel, triggering the first Arab-Israeli war on May 15, 1948 (-). Despite being vastly outnumbered, the newly formed Israeli Defense Forces, trained with the latest military technology from WWII, successfully repelled the invaders and expanded the territory under Israeli control. **The ideologies and political power dynamics of the region shifted dramatically, as Israel became a focal point of conflict between the Jewish and Arab populations, and between the broader West and the Arab world.**

Under the 1949 Armistice Agreements following the Arab-Israeli war, the western part of Jerusalem came under Israeli control, while the eastern part, including the Old City and significant religious sites like the Temple Mount, was controlled by Jordan. This division ended in 1967 during the Six-Day War, when Israel captured East Jerusalem and declared the city to be under its administration.

The region surrounding Jerusalem has been, and will continue to be, of profound religious significance to Judaism, Christianity, and Islam. For Jews, it is the site of the ancient Temple Mount, central to their religious and cultural identity.[278] For Christians, it is considered sacred because it is where Christians believe Jesus was born, lived, preached, was crucified, and resurrected.[279] For Muslims, it is home to the Al-Aqsa Mosque, one of Islam's holiest sites.[280] This ongoing conflict, rooted in both religious and political aspirations, remains a central feature of the Israeli-Palestinian dispute today.

The founding of Israel in 1948 marked a turning point in the history of the Middle East, igniting ideological conflicts and territorial disputes that continue to shape the region. It was the culmination of Jewish historical ties to the land of Israel but also the beginning of a protracted conflict with the Arab world, whose nations saw the establishment of Israel as an infringement on Palestinian Arab rights.

---

[278] Goodnick, M. (2008). *The Temple Mount: History, archaeology, and the politics of Jerusalem.* Cambridge University Press.
[279] Sakenfeld, K. D. (2009). *The history of Palestine in Christian thought.* Oxford University Press.
[280] Khalidi, R. (2006). *The Iron Cage: The Story of the Palestinian Struggle for Statehood.* Beacon Press.

THE INDUSTRIAL AND MODERN ERAS (1800 CE TO PRESENT TIME)

1945 to 1948 – The United Nations' Universal Declaration of Human Rights: The formation of the United Nations (UN) in 1945 was a response to the devastating consequences of World War II, with the goal of preventing future conflicts, fostering international cooperation, and promoting peace and security. **The political power dynamics during and after the war – with the Allies seeking to maintain influence and control over the post-war order (-) – played a key role in the establishment of the UN.** The structure of the organization was designed to reflect the power balance, with the Security Council dominated by the United States, the Soviet Union, KMT China, France, and the United Kingdom as permanent members, each holding veto power. **The ideological development of collective security and multilateral diplomacy helped shape the UN's founding principles, aimed at ensuring that no single country could dominate world affairs (+),** as the Axis powers had done in the lead-up to the war.

In 1948, just three years after the UN was formed, the **Universal Declaration of Human Rights (UDHR) was drafted by the UN General Assembly as part of its commitment to protecting the inherent dignity and equal rights of all individuals (+).** The drafting process was deeply influenced by the war's human atrocities, including the Holocaust, which underscored the need for international legal standards to protect human rights. The ideological developments of the period, driven by a shared belief in human rights, equality, and freedom, were fundamental in the creation of the UDHR. **The Declaration was drafted by the Commission on Human Rights, chaired by Eleanor Roosevelt, and its adoption marked a significant step in the evolution of global human rights (+).** While the UDHR was non-binding, it set a moral standard that would influence later treaties and conventions.

The countries involved in drafting and adopting the UDHR were in agreement, but there were notable abstentions and disagreements. After much healthy conflict through diplomacy and debate, the UDHR was adopted on December 10, 1948. Several key principles include the right to life, liberty, and security of person (Article 3), the right to equality before the law (Article 7), and the right to education (Article 26). It also emphasizes the right to work and fair wages (Article 23) and the right to participate in government (Article 21). **The UDHR asserts that all people are entitled to these rights without discrimination, regardless of nationality, ethnicity, or religion (+).**[281]

The Declaration was signed by 48 countries in total, with eight countries abstaining from the vote. The Soviet Union and several of its satellite states, for example, abstained from the vote due to the inclusion of provisions related to freedom of speech and the press, which clashed with communist ideologies.[282] Saudi Arabia also abstained, citing concerns over the Declaration's stance on gender equality, particularly in regard to women's rights, which conflicted with the country's ideologies and legal system at the time. In contrast, amid their civil war, China was represented by the Republic of China (ROC), which was led by the KMT under Chiang Kai-shek. The Chinese Communist Party (CCP) of the People's Republic of China (PRC), which would take control of China less than a year later, was not involved in the signing of the UDHR. China's transition to Communist rule under the CCP would later influence China's stance on human rights in global discussions.

The UN came together as a product of the ideological shift towards international cooperation and the desire to prevent the horrors of global conflict, while the UDHR reflected a growing consensus around universal human rights (+). The political power dynamics at the time, shaped by the influence of the victorious Allied powers, played a key role in determining which countries were involved and what values were prioritized. Despite the consensus, there were tensions and disagreements over the specific provisions of the Declaration, which reflected the diversity of political ideologies and cultural norms around the world.

---

[281] Roosevelt, E. (1948). *The Universal Declaration of Human Rights*. United Nations. Retrieved from https://www.un.org/en/universal-declaration-human-rights/
[282] Donelly, J. (2003). *Universal human rights in theory and practice* (2nd ed.). Cornell University Press.

1946 to 1970 – Decolonization of past Imperial Colonies: The decolonization movement after World War II was a transformative period that spanned roughly from 1945 to the 1970s, during which dozens of countries in Asia, Africa, and the Caribbean gained independence from European colonial rule. This shift was driven by a combination of political power dynamics, ideological developments, and the consequences of technological and economic changes brought about by the war.[283] The devastation of World War II left many European powers, such as Britain and France, economically weakened and less capable of maintaining control over their colonies. At the same time, the rise of the United States and the Soviet Union as superpowers introduced a new global political landscape that was less tolerant of colonialism.[284]

Ideologically, there was a growing recognition of the principles of self-determination and human rights (+), reinforced by documents like the United Nations Charter (1945) and the UDHR (1948). Anti-colonial movements were further bolstered by leaders like Mahatma Gandhi in India, Kwame Nkrumah in Ghana, and Ho Chi Minh in Vietnam, who inspired their people to fight for independence through nonviolent resistance.

The impact of political power dynamics was also evident as former colonial powers faced mounting pressure both from within their colonies and from the international community. For instance, the independence of India and Pakistan in 1947 marked a critical turning point, demonstrating that colonial rule could be successfully challenged. In Africa, the 1960s saw a wave of decolonization, with nearly 20 countries gaining independence that decade, culminating in the independence of Algeria in 1962 after a brutal war against French rule.[285] The process was not always peaceful; many regions, such as Vietnam, Algeria, and Kenya, experienced violent human-degrading conflicts as colonized nations came together in the struggle to gain their freedom from out-group powers.

---

[283] Hargreaves, J. D. (1996). *Decolonization in Africa*. Longman.
[284] Smith, T. (1978). *The Pattern of Imperialism: The United States, Great Britain, and the Late Industrializing World Since 1815*. Cambridge University Press.
[285] Fanon, F. (1963). *The Wretched of the Earth*. Grove Press.

Despite the political successes of decolonization, the newly independent states often faced challenges in achieving economic stability and social identity. **The withdrawal of colonial administrations left many nations with underdeveloped infrastructure and economies overly reliant on the export of raw materials (-). These challenges were compounded by the ideological and political legacies of colonial rule, leading to internal conflicts such as cultural disparities, military coups, and struggles over national identity, often leading to corruption (-).** The effects of this era continue to shape global geopolitics and developing societies today.

1949 – The North Atlantic Treaty Organization (NATO): The North Atlantic Treaty Organization (NATO) was created as a response to the growing threat posed by the Soviet Union and the spread of communism in Europe after World War II. It was founded on April 4, 1949, by 12 founding members: the United States, Canada, and 10 Western European countries, including the United Kingdom, France, Belgium, the Netherlands, Luxembourg, Norway, Denmark, Italy, Portugal, and Iceland.

The formation of NATO was largely influenced by the political power dynamics of the time, which was characterized by a division of Europe into Soviet-controlled Eastern Europe and democratic Western Europe. The alliance's central aim was to provide collective defense, under Article 5, which states that an attack on one member is considered an attack on all members. This principle was a direct response to the fear of Soviet expansionism and the need for a unified defense strategy among Western democracies.

1950 to 1991 – The Space Race amid a Cold War: The Cold War was a period of intense geopolitical tension between the United States and its allies, representing the capitalist, democratic West, and the Soviet Union and its allies, representing the communist East. **This ideological conflict was a direct result of the post-World War II world, where the two superpowers emerged as the dominant global forces (-).** The West aimed to spread democracy and capitalism, while the Soviet Union sought to expand communism and

THE INDUSTRIAL AND MODERN ERAS (1800 CE TO PRESENT TIME)

establish a sphere of influence over Eastern Europe and beyond. This struggle for ideological and political dominance was cast over most international affairs during the second half of the 20th century.

The Cold War was marked by ideological developments that shaped both domestic and foreign policies in the West and the USSR. For example, the United States promoted liberal democracy, individual freedoms, and a free-market economy, while the Soviet Union advocated for a centralized economy and state control, with a focus on the working class and collective governance. These differences in ideology led to confrontations in various forms, such as the space race and the arms race, to prove superior technological capability.

The Space Race, which occurred between the late 1950s and 1975, was a key element of the Cold War rivalry between the United States and the Soviet Union, with each superpower striving to outcompete the other in space exploration. **The political power dynamics of the time were compelled to take part in the competition to demonstrate the superiority of their economic system (-).** The race began after the Soviet Union launched Sputnik 1 in 1957, marking the first successful satellite. This achievement prompted the U.S. to accelerate its space program, culminating in President John F. Kennedy's 1961 pledge to land a man on the moon within the decade. In 1969, the U.S. achieved this goal with the Apollo 11 mission, when Neil Armstrong became the first human to walk on the moon, solidifying Western dominance in space exploration.[286]

Meanwhile, the nuclear arms race was another significant aspect of the Cold War, with both superpowers developing and stockpiling nuclear weapons. **The idea of forcing diplomacy by maintaining the capacity for overwhelming military force, including nuclear weapons, aligned with U.S. strategies of deterrence, such as the policy of Mutually Assured Destruction (MAD) during the Cold War (-).** The deterrence concept relied on the idea that nuclear powers would avoid direct conflict, knowing that any aggressive actions would lead to devastating nuclear retaliation. Adopting these policies forced nations throughout the world to feel the need to belong under a nuclear umbrella in order to feel protected.

By 1960, the Soviet Union had built over 500 nuclear warheads, while the United States had an even larger stockpile of about 1,000. By the early 1970s, the U.S. and the USSR had amassed tens of thousands of nuclear warheads, with the U.S. holding approximately 31,000 and

---

[286] Chaikin, A. (1994). *A Man on the Moon: The Voyages of the Apollo Astronauts*. Viking Press.

the Soviet Union around 40,000. **The nuclear arms race and the Space Race were linked by the same underlying rivalry for technological and political superiority, each serving as a symbol of military and ideological power (-).** The economic strain from the race to develop both space technology and nuclear arsenals led to challenges for both nations, with the Soviet Union facing economic instability and resource limitations (-).

Despite the absence of direct military conflict between the superpowers, the Cold War led to numerous proxy wars (-), including the Korean War (1950 to 1953), the Vietnam War (1955 to 1975), and various conflicts in Africa, Latin America, and the Middle East. These wars were often fought by local forces backed by one of the superpowers, with both sides seeking to expand their ideological influence in different regions of the world. Military forces between the USSR and the United States did not fight directly with each other, knowing that the consequences could be nuclear retaliation.

The international economic instability (-) and ideological confusion (-) in cultures caused by these prolonged conflicts, combined with the financial strain of the arms race, eventually led to the decline of the Soviet Union and many of its puppet states.[287] By the late 1980s, under Mikhail Gorbachev, the Soviet Union began to experience reforms, including openness and economic restructuring, which paved the way for the eventual collapse of the Soviet system in 1991, marking the end of the Cold War. The ideological and political battle between the U.S. and the USSR fundamentally reshaped the international order, with the U.S. emerging as the world's sole superpower.

The effects of the Cold War are still prominent today, as the threat of nuclear war remains a fundamental aspect of strategic deterrence to world wars for military superpowers today. **Although deaths as a result of war have significantly decreased since the Cold War and the nuclear arms race, the threat of mutually assured destruction continues to loom over diplomacy and the very institutions that work to maintain peace. As such, deterrence through power has been a lingering blockade to genuine acknowledgment of universal human dignity through diplomacy and equality (-).**

1950 to Present – Modern Religious Practice: Moving past the second world war, new ideologies began to modernize religious

---

[287] Nove, A. (1992). *An economic history of the USSR: 1917-1991* (2nd ed.). Penguin Books.

practice. **As the international community grew more interconnected, increased dialogue between world religions occurred, and the growth of religious pluralism, alongside the rise of human rights discussions tied to religious values began to take shape (+).**[288]

In 1986, a meeting of world religions took place in Assisi, Italy. Known as the World Day of Prayer for Peace, major leaders in twelve world religions – Christianity, Islam, Judaism, Buddhism, Hinduism, Shintoism, Jainism, Zoroastrianism, Sikhism, Bahá'í Faith, Indigenous religions from Native America, and Traditional African religion leaders – met to pray for the inherent human dignity of all people. This was the first time an interfaith event had ever taken place on such a scale. **The event demonstrated that despite doctrinal and ideological differences, these religions could unite in their commitment to peace and mutual respect (+).** Today, groups such as the Parliament of The World's Religions host international gatherings to allow religions to have dialogue on modern-day issues and how to address such issues with respect to human rights.[289] **In doing so, religious leaders have set an example for how political power dynamics can be respected despite ideological differences (+).**

1954 to 1968 – The Civil Rights Movement in the U.S.: The Civil Rights Movement in the United States was a pivotal social and political campaign aimed at ending racial segregation, discrimination, and inequality, primarily focusing on the rights of African Americans. This movement gained momentum in the mid-20th century, particularly from 1954 to 1968, although its roots stretch back to earlier decades of organized resistance against systemic racism following the end of slavery.[290] The Civil Rights movement was characterized by widespread nonviolent protests, legal challenges, and civil disobedience, which sought to dismantle the legal and social structures that enforced racial segregation in the South.

One of the earliest and most significant milestones was the *Brown v. Board of Education of Topeka* Supreme Court decision in 1954, which declared the segregation of public schools unconstitutional (+).[291] This ruling provided a legal foundation for

---

[288] Knitter, P. F. (2008). *Introducing Theologies of Religions*. Orbis Books.
[289] Parliament of the World's Religions. (n.d.). *Our mission*. https://parliamentofreligions.org/our-work/mission/
[290] Fairclough, A. (2001). *Better Day Coming: Blacks and Equality, 1890-2000*. Penguin Books.
[291] Klarman, M. J. (2004). *From Jim Crow to Civil Rights: The Supreme Court and the Struggle for Racial Equality*. Oxford University Press.

further actions challenging racial discrimination. **In 1955, the Montgomery Bus Boycott, led by figures like Rosa Parks and Dr. Martin Luther King Jr., marked the beginning of widespread, organized nonviolent resistance (+).** The boycott, which lasted over a year, eventually led to a Supreme Court ruling that desegregated the public transportation system.[292]

Throughout the 1960s, the movement saw significant legislative victories, such as the *Civil Rights Act of 1964*, which prohibited discrimination in public places, and the *Voting Rights Act of 1965*, which aimed to eliminate barriers preventing African Americans from voting. The movement's achievements were driven by the collective efforts of various organizations, including numerous grassroots activists. **Despite facing violence and opposition, the Civil Rights Movement left a lasting legacy on American society, advancing ideals of free speech, equality, justice, and human rights (+).**

1970 to Present – The Digital Revolution: The Digital Revolution, which began in the latter half of the 20th century, refers to the rapid shift from mechanical and analog technologies to digital systems powered by computers, the internet, and mobile devices. This transformation was driven by advances in semiconductor technology, data storage, and telecommunications, which laid the groundwork for the information age.[293] It represents a profound technological advancement that reshaped industries, economies, and societies by enabling unprecedented levels of connectivity and information sharing.

From a technological advancement perspective, the Digital Revolution enhanced access to information, democratized communication, and accelerated innovation (+). For example, the advent of the internet in the late 20th century and the subsequent development of search engines, social media platforms, and mobile apps revolutionized how people access information and interact.[294] This has empowered individuals with tools to connect globally, promote social causes, and advance human rights by giving marginalized communities a platform to voice their concerns. **Additionally, technological advancements in areas like AI, big data, and cloud computing have significantly improved healthcare and education (+).**

---

[292] Branch, T. (1988). *Parting the Waters: America in the King Years, 1954-1963*. Simon & Schuster.

[293] Castells, M. (2010). *The Rise of the Network Society: The Information Age: Economy, Society, and Culture*. Wiley-Blackwell.

[294] Negroponte, N. (1995). *Being Digital*. Alfred A. Knopf.

However, the Digital Revolution also introduced significant negative political power dynamics, including challenges related to privacy, surveillance, and misuse of information (-). The rise of social media platforms has allowed governments and corporations to collect massive amounts of data on individuals, raising concerns about surveillance and the erosion of privacy rights. Additionally, the spread of misinformation and fake news has influenced political processes, contributing to polarization, and undermining democratic institutions. **Ideologically, while the internet has been hailed as a tool for freedom and empowerment, it has also been used to spread extremist ideologies, cyberbullying, and hate speech (-), highlighting the dual potential of technological progress.**

Overall, while the Digital Revolution has provided substantial benefits, its impact on human rights is complex, with both positive and negative consequences. The challenge moving forward is to align digital technological advancements with ideologies that prioritize ethical behavior, rights to privacy, and equitable access, ensuring that these tools serve to enhance rather than degrade the human person.

1979 to Present – The Middle East: The Middle East in the 20th century underwent significant transformation, shaped by post-colonialism, the Cold War and the continuing struggle for resources and political influence. The end of the Cold War in the late 1980s and early 1990s marked a shift in international power dynamics, as the United States emerged as the sole superpower, shifting focus to regional conflicts and the maintenance of strategic control, particularly in the Middle East. **The political power dynamics of the region had been defined for much of the 20th century by the aftermath of the Ottoman Empire's collapse following World War I, which had left a legacy of artificial borders drawn by British and French colonial powers (-).** These borders often failed to account for the diverse ethnic, religious, and tribal populations, leading to internal divisions and political instability.

In the post-colonial era, the Middle East experienced a rise in nationalism and demands for independence. As former colonies gained autonomy throughout the mid-20th century, new political ideologies emerged, including pan-Arabism and Islamic fundamentalism. **The Enlightenment ideals of self-determination spread across the region (+), but the quest for independence was hindered by its strategic importance, particularly international interest in its vast natural resources (i.e., oil reserves) (-).** This led to the Middle East being caught in the Cold War's ideological struggle, with the United States and the Soviet Union vying for influence by providing military equipment to suppress opposing ideologies.

During the Yom Kippur War in 1973, the U.S. airlifted over 22,000 tons of supplies to Israel, while the Soviets provided approximately 12,500 to 15,000 tons to Egypt and Syria.[295] Later, in 1979, the Soviet Union invaded Afghanistan to support a communist government facing internal resistance, while the United States supported Afghan mujahedeen fighters, including future Taliban leaders, as part of its strategy to counter Soviet expansion. The Afghan war ended in 1989 with the Soviet withdrawal, but Afghanistan was left in a state of chaos, leading to the eventual rise of the Taliban.

Following the Cold War, the Middle East became increasingly defined by economic interests – especially related to oil and energy security – as resource competition (-) played a central role in conflicts such as the Gulf War (1990 to 1991). After Iraq's invasion of Kuwait, the U.S. and a coalition of Western and Arab states intervened to protect oil supplies and maintain regional stability. The Gulf War marked the beginning of a series of military interventions that would continue into the 21st century. **The 1990s also saw the rise of Islamic extremism, partly as a response to Western intervention in the region, culminating in the September 11, 2001, attacks, and the subsequent War on Terror (-).** This led to the U.S.-led invasions of Afghanistan and Iraq, both of which were justified by the need to eliminate terrorist groups and weapons of mass destruction (WMDs), none of which were found.[296]

The aftermath of these interventions has had lasting consequences for the region. **Economic instability (-) in the wake of the Iraq War, coupled with the rise of the Islamic State of Iraq and Syria (ISIS), and ongoing sectarian violence continues to shape the geopolitics of the Middle East. Western interventionism has amplified political tensions in the middle east, leading to internal strife, the rise of extremism, and resource competition (-).** The involvement of external powers, including the United States, Russia and regional powers like Iran and Türkiye, further continue to complicate the situation. **Despite the global push for human rights and stability, the Middle East's political landscape remains**

---

[295] Quandt, W. B. (2005). *Peace Process: American Diplomacy and the Arab-Israeli Conflict since 1967*. Brookings Institution Press.

[296] Blix, H., & ElBaradei, M. (2004). *Report of the Iraq Survey Group*. Central Intelligence Agency. Retrieved from https://www.cia.gov/library/reports/general-reports-1/iraq_wmd_2004/

THE INDUSTRIAL AND MODERN ERAS (1800 CE TO PRESENT TIME)

subdued in human-degrading conflict due to cultural fragmentation, with ideological conflicts between secular and religious forces, and between competing visions of ideological influence (-). The region's ongoing struggle reflects humanity's challenge to balance the ideals of independence, self-determination, and resource control with the realities of global power struggle.

Present time – Challenges by Continent: As we arrive from our exploration of conflict to the modern day, it is worth a summary of where the world stands by continent, to help lead into the next part of this book about how conflict affects us today on a global scale.

Africa has made significant strides in recent years, yet it still faces major challenges with respect to human rights. **Ideological development has been marked by a renewed push for human rights in many nations, such as Kenya and Ghana (+); however, political power dynamics remain a concern, with some regions experiencing ongoing conflicts, especially parts of Eastern Africa that receive external influence promoting struggles for power (-). Technological advancements are on the rise, particularly in areas like mobile banking and digital communication, empowering communities that were previously underserved (+). However, the lack of infrastructure and persistent corruption hinders the equitable distribution of these benefits (-).** Africa's trajectory toward ensuring human rights is complicated by economic inequalities, political instability, cultural divides, and climate change impacts (-), but there is hope in the growing civil society movements that emphasize accountability and justice (+).

Asia presents a diverse landscape when it comes to human rights and the factors influencing it. **Ideologically, many countries are caught between traditional values and modernizing pressures, as seen in the contrasting dynamics between countries like Japan and China (-).** The rapid technological advancements, particularly in East Asia, are driving economic growth and transforming societies (+), but they are also creating tensions around privacy, surveillance, and freedom of expression (-). **Political power dynamics remain a significant factor, especially in regions like the South China Sea, where territorial disputes continue to strain international relations (-).** While Southeast Asia has seen gains in achieving equality and human rights (+), countries such as Myanmar are struggling with authoritarianism and inequality (-). **The continent's economic prowess provides opportunities for improving human rights (+),**

but this progress is often uneven, with marginalized communities facing exclusion (-).

Europe, since the World Wars, has been a stronghold of human rights, democracy, and technological innovation (+). Ideological developments in recent years have focused on inclusivity and social justice, particularly with respect to immigration, gender equality, and climate change (+). **However, political power dynamics have been turbulent, with the rise of populist movements challenging established democratic norms in countries like Hungary, Germany, France, and Poland (-). Technologically, Europe remains at the forefront, particularly in green technologies and AI regulation (+). The continent is grappling with the balance between technological progress and ethical considerations, aiming to protect human rights while fostering innovation (+).** Despite its progress, Europe faces challenges related to social cohesion, economic disparities, and the integration of refugees, which tests its commitment to upholding human rights.

North America has worked diligently to protect the progressive freedoms that were desired by its European settlers centuries ago; however, **the ideological divide between progressive and conservative values, particularly in the United States continues to undermine authentic attempts at achieving universal human rights (-).** Issues such as racial inequality, immigration, and the protection of civil liberties are at the forefront of ideological debates. **Technological advancements continue to drive economic growth, with the technology sector in the United States leading in AI, biotechnology, and clean energy (+). However, wealth gaps have only grown, and political polarization has intensified, hindering governance and public trust in institutions (-).** Canada, by contrast, maintains a more stable political climate, with a focus on inclusivity and social welfare through transparent institutions, but suffers economically. **While North America remains a global leader in innovation and democratic values (+), it faces challenges in ensuring that technological benefits are equitably distributed and that political divisions do not erode the social fabric (-).**

South America has made progress in promoting human rights, but it is still marred by economic instability and political corruption. **Ideologically, there is a growing emphasis on social justice and Indigenous rights, particularly in countries like Bolivia and Colombia (+).** However, political power dynamics remain turbulent, with recent protests in countries such as Chile and Brazil highlighting the demand for reforms; meanwhile, mass emigration in Venezuela underpins the turbulent economy for the country and the effects it has on its neighbors (-). **Technological advancements are slowly being adopted, but economic disparities limit access to digital infrastructure, which hampers development (-).** The region faces challenges related to poverty, violence, and environmental degradation, particularly in the Amazon rainforest (-). Despite these difficulties, there is hope in the grassroots movements advocating greater transparency, equality, and environmental protection (+).

Oceania, including Australia and the Pacific Islands, is navigating a complex landscape in terms of human rights. Ideologically, there is a strong focus on Indigenous rights, climate action, and social inclusivity (+). **Australia leads in technological advancements in sectors like renewable energy and healthcare (+), but political debates often revolve around immigration policies and the treatment of asylum seekers (-).** The Pacific Island nations are particularly vulnerable to climate change, which threatens their livelihoods and exacerbates social inequalities by limiting the physical protections of those who have less wealth (-). **Political power dynamics in Oceania are influenced by external powers like China and the United States, which seek to solidify their influence in the region (-).** While Oceania enjoys stability, the challenge remains to address the social and environmental issues that impact the dignity of its diverse populations (+/-).

Antarctica remains largely uninhabited, but **its geopolitical significance is growing as countries compete for access to its resources (-). Ideologically, Antarctica is governed by the Antarctic Treaty System, which emphasizes scientific cooperation and prohibits military activity (+).** However, technological advancements in exploration and research are unlocking new possibilities, raising concerns about the potential exploitation of natural resources (-). Political power dynamics are subtle but present, as countries like China, Russia, and U.S. seek to expand their presence in the region (-). **The focus on preserving the continent's environment and ensuring that it remains a space dedicated to peaceful research is crucial for maintaining human rights on a global scale (+), particularly in the face of climate change.** Antarctica serves as a reminder of the importance of international cooperation in addressing global challenges in a united manner.

III.v CLOSING THOUGHTS: THE CYCLE OF CONFLICT

The last 5,300+ years have shown progressive ways to achieve peace, but they have also exposed the human-degrading conflicts we must avoid if we hope to continue growing in freedom and responsibility as a human race. This raises a vital question: **What distinguishes humanity's advancements – those that improve freedoms and responsibilities without causing lasting harm – from those which come at the cost of human-degrading conflict?**

Using the three factors laid out in Chapter I, we assessed history in this Chapter to understand the influence that these factors have had over time. We observed how Ideological Developments and Political Power Dynamics were closely intertwined. Whenever a new ideology was introduced, political power dynamics and economic systems took the idea into consideration.

We noticed that any ideological shift disrupts systems as new ideas are absorbed and digested into one's own understanding and viewpoint. For positive ideological developments, this individual change in perception is required before witnessing stable, dignity-enhancing systems. For ideological developments that are conducted in a human-degrading manner, we historically see a similar pause in reaction before a public viewpoint is established. Evolution shows us that we take a pause in our actions to avoid potentially life-threatening conflict, to orient our understanding, and to avoid the possibility of being wrong. If this is the case, then why do we still engage in conflict?

Historically, it seems that, out of necessity, conflicting viewpoints on ideologies come to an intersection in which groups will use all means politically, economically, and technologically – not to prove that the conflicting ideology is wrong – but to reinforce that one's own ideology is right. If an ideology or system is under threat, it is forced to defend itself by all means possible. This is how life itself has been wired to survive through billions of years of evolution. The need to be right often presents itself through supremacy, pride, power, and competition. If not addressed with understanding and diplomacy, then out-group human-degrading conflict often ensues as a justified act to eliminate greater human-degrading conflict.

Before proceeding, it is essential to emphasize a fundamental truth: **Ideological developments that promote cooperation, ethical behavior, human rights, and equality shape our world in a positive way.** Nearly all nations and historical figures have sought these ideological developments from their perspective, and we have seen the repeating cycle of human-degrading conflict towards out-groups in order to defend in-group ideological developments. **This only reinforces that humanity has an inherent desire to do good towards their in-group.**

We have observed that, once an in-group establishes a positive set of ideologies, they incorporate such ideas (theories) into their political and economic systems by attempting to put them into practice. In observing history, reality often falls short of theoretical ideologies.

As a result, we witness well-intended political and economic systems forced to seek out technological advancements that are required simply to sustain the very systems that were created to support the original theoretical ideology. Hence, we find ourselves in a cyclical, continuous competition amongst out-groups to outperform the other's way of life. This brings us to the *Cycle of Conflict*, a framework for better understanding of how these factors interact over time. The *Cycle of Conflict* is broken into four quadrants:

Quadrant One – Ideological Developments: Ideological developments form the foundation for humanity's evolutionary progress. In this phase, new ideas and beliefs unite groups under common values, driving systemic change. Ideologies shape political and economic systems and create the need for technological advancements to bring these theories into practice.

Quadrant Two – Foundational Political Power Dynamics: Once ideological frameworks are established, political systems emerge to implement them. Effective political structures translate ideologies into actionable policies that promote social welfare and benefit the group as a whole. When successful, these systems provide a stable foundation for continued progress towards human flourishing.

Quadrant Three – Technological Advancements: The progress of political power dynamics is often demonstrated through technological advancements, highlighting the successes within the establishment of a political system and inherently demonstrating the quality of the ideological system it represents. While technology has the potential to reduce conflict by alleviating basic human struggles, it rarely achieves this without supportive ideologies and equitable political systems that can manage the power that comes with technological advancement.

When technological advancements occur outside established norms or disregard human rights, they can exacerbate inequalities, deepen social divisions, and destabilize political power structures. Rapid technological changes – introduced without thoughtful motivation or through frameworks that fail to prioritize equity and dignity – have historically magnified disparities and misled existing power structures. These disruptions often divide societies and foster degrading conflict.

The delicate balance of power of technological advancements shows us how technology can influence political power dynamics in two primary ways: either by intensifying divisions, leading to the magnified marginalization of out-groups; or, by providing the necessary steppingstones to continually address disparities and enhance society through a cycle of in-group growth. If the latter occurs, then the cycle will go back to Quadrant Two so that foundational in-group political power dynamics can continue to adapt a framework for growth within the context of the group's ideologies. If the former occurs, then technological advancements will destabilize the system beyond the capacity of internal resolution, and the *Cycle of Conflict* will progress to Quadrant Four.

Quadrant Four – Unstable Political Power Dynamics: As technological advancements magnify inequalities and fall out of line with ideological theories and political systems, human inequality increases – often through the unintended promotion of superiority, exclusion of inferior groups, or oppression of any opposition – leading to the breakdown of social cohesion and escalation of extreme political power dynamics.

At this stage, human-degrading conflicts become increasingly pronounced until some form of intervention resets the cycle back to refining ideologies in Quadrant One. Historically, out-group intervention occurs through either diplomatic means or through physical force (i.e., war), which forces an opposing ideology into reevaluation of their prevailing ideologies and power structures.

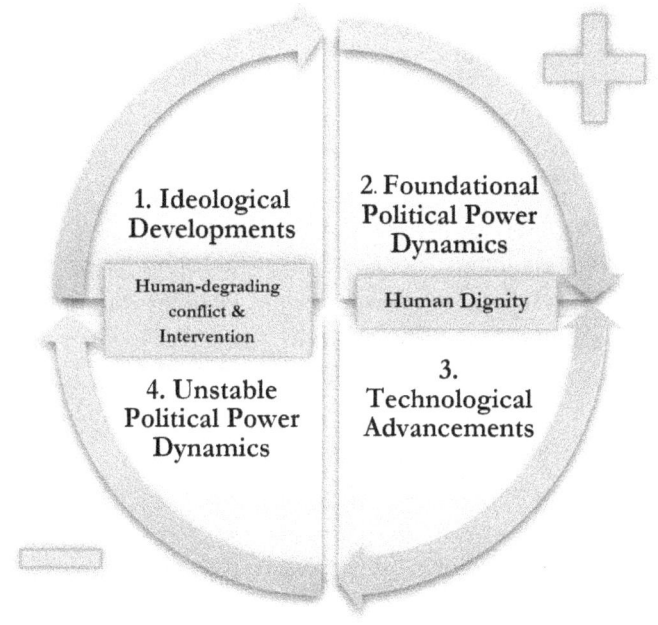

The Cycle of Conflict

With the *Cycle of Conflict*, we can begin to understand the cyclical nature in Ideological developments, Technological Advancements, and Political Power Dynamics, and how they influence conflict within societies in a complex way. The consequences of this cycle, if conducted without thought or intervention, lead to destructive human suffering that can bring an end to civilizations. Some civilizations, however, have found ways to effectively manage in-group growth to maximize their potential through technology.

As mentioned at the beginning of Part I of this book, two critical insights shape the role of conflict:

1. **Humanity's Inherent Desire for Good** reminds us that ideological developments, however diverse, often emerge from a genuine intent to benefit the in-group. Yet this well-meaning intent is rarely thoughtfully extended beyond those who share the same ideological alignment.

2. **Conformity's Role in Conflict** highlights how pressures to conform sustain these ideologies within the in-group, creating divisions and tensions with out-groups. These dynamics are often amplified by unstable political, economic, or technological forces, leading to human-degrading conflict.

Over time, however, as universal human rights gain international recognition, the boundaries of what constitutes an "in-group" have expanded. In our increasingly interconnected digital information era, shared ideals are more widely acknowledged, offering opportunities to foster global collaboration (+). Yet the same forces that unite us can also reveal unstable power dynamics (-), making it crucial to intervene in the *Cycle of Conflict* to prevent further division.

In Part Two, we will examine how these patterns manifest in our modern world and explore how understanding the *Cycle of Conflict* can guide us toward more equitable and sustainable progress.

THE CYCLE OF CONFLICT

CONFLICT

PART TWO

HOW THE *CYCLE OF CONFLICT* AFFECTS US TODAY

IV

PERCEPTIONS, PERSPECTIVES, & PSYCHOLOGY

In the first part of this book, we took a deep dive into history to understand how we arrived at the present moment, uncovering how human experiences fall into recurring *Cycles of Conflict*. Now, as we turn our focus to the present, it is time to consider how we fit into the *Cycles of Conflict* unfolding today and, more importantly, how we might influence their outcomes by intervening in order to reduce human-degrading conflict.

However, unlike our historical analysis, where we could adopt a more holistic perspective on known facts of history, our understanding of current events is inherently limited. Today, we must rely on our lived experiences and the voices that surround us to discern where we stand within these ongoing cycles. These voices – often echoing stories and ideologies of the past – are saturated with perceptions and perspectives that aim to shape our understanding of the world. Whether intentional or not, they deeply influence our perception of reality, framing how we see the world and shaping the psychological makeup we carry into our daily lives. Depending on how we interpret these voices, we may either align with them, as understood through the in-group homogeneity effect, or oppose them, becoming susceptible to the out-group homogeneity effect.

At the heart of this dynamic is perception – the initial sensory interpretation of our experiences. As these perceptions accumulate, they shape our perspectives, which are our attitudes toward the world. These perspectives, in turn, influence our psychological framework and

IV. PERSPECTIVES, PERCEPTIONS, & PSYCHOLOGY

affect our overall well-being. This framework often acts as a filter, selectively focusing on information that confirms our existing worldview – whether consciously or unconsciously – as a coping mechanism inherent to our evolutionary survival.

In Part Two of this book, we will explore how our understanding of the world has been profoundly shaped by the past. While we will strive to minimize biases in this examination, the science underlying our discussion acknowledges that biases are, in fact, inevitable. Chapter IV will introduce this section by helping us recognize and understand these biases, paving the way for deeper insights into how we can navigate the complexities of today's conflicts with greater awareness.

IV.i PERCEPTION IS NOT ALWAYS REALITY

We have all heard the phrase, "perception is reality." Our perception is really what we take in from the world around us through our senses. However, as we will come to find, through the technological advances of the 21st century, our perceptions no longer align directly with reality. Increasingly, our perceptions are filtered through digital communication and media rather than through firsthand experiences. How does this tie into conflict?

The late neuroscientist Emile Bruneau spent extensive time studying human behavior, particularly in the context of inter-group conflict. In his research, he made a critical distinction between dehumanization – the act of viewing others as less than human – and simple dislike toward those who are different. Bruneau's team conducted studies on metadehumaniztion – the idea that when an in-group perceives itself as being dehumanized by an out-group, it often retaliates by dehumanizing that out-group in return.[297]

Bruneau's research shows that perceptions of those who are different can eventually fuel out-group aggression and perpetuate ongoing violence by slowly extending to generational hatred and systemic dehumanization. When groups begin to ideologically view other groups in different ways, in-groups will naturally define their own ideologies as superior to those of other groups. This quickly accelerates inter-group conflict, which often leads power struggles and competition. This in turn influences the political power dynamics within a society away from an in-group focus (Quadrant two) and towards unstable power dynamics (Quadrant Four), as reinforced in the *Cycle of Conflict*.

In today's world, we rarely witness reality firsthand. When reality was witnessed firsthand in the same physical world, perceptions evolved to keep us safe, to detect immediate threats, and to make quick judgments for survival. For millennia, humans relied on direct sensory input to inform their decisions. It was not until recently, with the invention of digital media, that indirect sensory data began to dominate our lives. Instead of physical interaction, our perceptions of conflict are primarily shaped through sensory processes (visual and auditory) that are increasingly mediated by digital platforms. The shift from

---

[297] Kteily, N., Hodson, G., & Bruneau, E. (2016). They see us as less than human: Meta-dehumanization predicts intergroup conflict via reciprocal dehumanization. *Journal of Personality and Social Psychology, 110*(3), 343–370.

physical to digital perception accounts for less than 0.05% of the time humanity has been on its evolutionary path. Further studies may suggest that 0.05% of our evolutionary timeline is not enough for our senses to adapt to the vast amount of mediated digital information we now consume. As a result, we may be overly vulnerable to these indirect digital experiences.

As our perceptions of out-groups around us become increasingly available through digital media, their influence on our in-group ideologies can create unstable political power dynamics. As history has shown, conflicting viewpoints on ideologies come to an intersection in which groups will use all means politically, economically, and technologically – not to prove that the conflicting ideology is wrong – but to reinforce that one's own ideology is right. This forces the need for competition, increased political power, and eventually leads to the forced adaptation of one ideology over another either through intervention or through some form of human-degrading conflict.

Sun Tzu, author of *The Art of War*, was one of the first great minds to document humanity's understanding of perception, and more importantly, humanity's vulnerability to deception.[298] In it, he highlights how all warfare is based on deception – the idea that if you can lead your enemy to perceive a situation incorrectly, you can influence their decisions and force them into making mistakes. By understanding perception's influence on inter-group conflict, we can begin to understand how easily we can be deceived and drawn into unnecessary human-degrading conflict.

We are, in many ways, a vulnerable species. Our survival instincts have rightly led us to trust in-group figures with our safety. However, as the world becomes intertwined, so do our sensory inputs through mediated information, often creating conflicting viewpoints and questions in our minds. In the next section, we will discuss how our perceptions in the digital era shape the perspectives we hold about the world we live in. In understanding this relationship, we will learn more about how each group coexists with each other, each amid their own *Cycle of Conflict*.

---

[298] Sun Tzu. (1910). *The art of war* (L. Giles, Trans.). Luzac & Co. (Original work published ca. 5th century BCE)

IV.ii PERSPECTIVE IS UNDERSTANDING
HOW WE SEE EACHOTHER

Perspective is the lens through which individuals or groups interpret the world around them, shaped by sensory input, cultural context, and ideological frameworks. In today's world of intertwined sensory inputs, we often trust authority figures to inform our perspectives rather than forming them independently based on our own perceptions. As perceptual data becomes more accessible through indirect means (i.e., digital media), our perspectives of the world have grown more complex. Yet, the world was not always this way.

From the beginning of humanity until roughly 5,000 years ago, individual in-groups shared similar views of the world around them thanks to accurate evolutionary sensory processing. Using their senses, people created a picture of their immediate environment, often limited to what was physically near them. This shared sensory data allowed groups to form a collective perspective, leading to shared intellectual knowledge that easily aligned with their cultural norms. In turn, this sparked ideological developments that initiated the first stage of the *Cycle of Conflict*. As distinct groups interacted, their ideological developments may have differed slightly, leading to early stages of Quadrant Four of the *Cycle of Conflict*.

Using an example to better understand how we go from Quadrant One to Quadrant Four, imagine two independent groups – "A" and "B". Although Group A and Group B live among other groups, their circle of influence (i.e., sensory inputs informing their perceptions) is only informed by their surroundings and, to an extent, by each other.

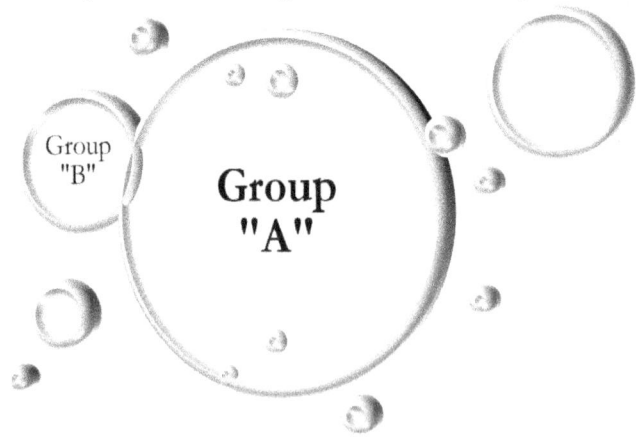

IV. PERSPECTIVES, PERCEPTIONS, & PSYCHOLOGY

Groups A and B independently seek in-group empathy, collaboration, and equitable treatment (Quadrant One of the *Cycle of Conflict*). In turn, they take actionable steps towards societal progress by providing shelter, agriculture, infrastructure, and education (Quadrant Two). All seems well until Group A pursues technological advancements requiring resources that, while beneficial to their own development, could threaten Group B's progress (Quadrant Three). If leaders in Group A feel justified to acquire the resources that threaten Group B, the *Cycle of Conflict* suggests that the next step will go one of two ways: either the two groups will find a mutual ideological agreement through conflict resolution and diplomatic political power dynamics (back to Quadrant Two); or, the cycle will reset to Quadrant One through a series of destabilizing political power dynamics and human-degrading conflicts (Quadrant Four). History has shown that, due to our internal biases, Group A's perspective will almost always find a way to justify why they need the resources more than Group B, even if Group B does not agree.

Today, the same processes unfold, but in the digital era, physical sensory data is bombarded with noise and distraction. This digital noise can distort our sensory inputs, even in our own Group, leading to fragmented perspectives within the same physical space. While some of this noise can be beneficial, especially when credible sources of information are being broadcast freely and responsibly, this is not always the case. In the digital age, our perceptions no longer inform our perspective via geographical circles of influence; rather, they have expanded into digital spaces.

Continuing with the "Group A and B" example, this time, place yourself in the position of a member in Group A. In the digital context, once Group A justifies doing something that can potentially impact the welfare of another group, then Group B – and countless others – are instantly aware. Additional groups ("C," "D," "E," etc.) weigh in, creating a "three-dimensional" intertwinement of perspectives.

Meanwhile, our evolutionary "two-dimensional" mindset remains focused on geographic circles of influence to inform our perspectives. As a member of Group A, we learn through digital means that someone across the world (i.e, Group F), who shares few ideological beliefs, is influencing our *Cycle of Conflict*. In turn, we feel instinctually threatened and determined to show that our ideologies justify our actions towards technological advancement (Quadrant Three). This creates heavily biased – often misinformed and misunderstood –

perspectives of the other out-groups weighing in on our individual *Cycle of Conflict*. This creates a continuous state of instability, leading to a desire to justify one's ideology through power and superiority.

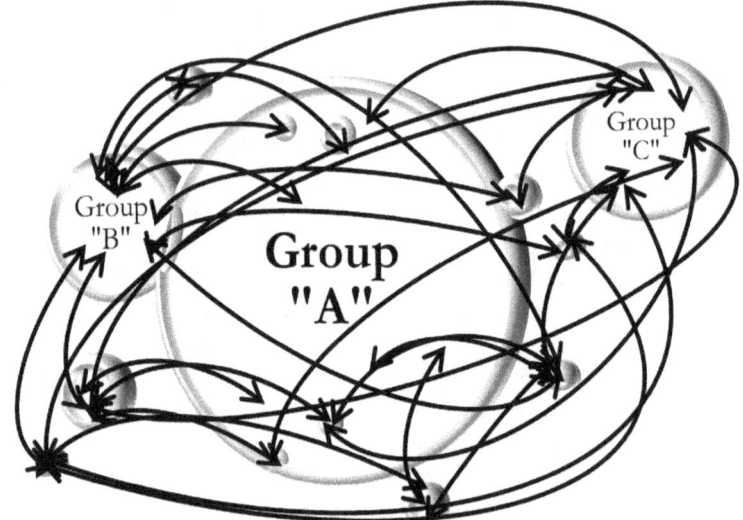

The way in which the digital landscape has, in a way, interconnected humanity into a vast in-group provides extraordinary opportunity; however, millions of years of differing out-group perspectives and ideologies, defined by geopolitical factors, continue to dominate our perspective and drive division within in-group decision making. For this reason, sub-groups existing beyond the geopolitical landscape of humanity (i.e., cultures, religions, political parties, etc…) now have the opportunity to evolve through the iterative *Cycle of Conflict* in a slightly more accelerated way than groups still defined by geography (i.e., Nations).

As a result, human-degrading conflict becomes an everyday event in the digital realm, often detached from core ideologies in the physical realm. In turn, ideologies are compared rather than genuinely practiced, and our senses grow numb from the constant exposure to digital trauma of misunderstood ideologies being put into practice. Sadly, this can lead individuals within sub-groups of humanity to avoid conflict in the physical world rather than seeking the resolutions needed to sustain universal human rights.

As we navigate the complexities of both the digital and physical world, the *Cycle of Conflict* serves as a reminder – not just a guide – of where we need to be within the *Cycle* to genuinely uphold ideologies which support human rights. We can no longer outright avoid conflict

IV. PERSPECTIVES, PERCEPTIONS, & PSYCHOLOGY

(as was done 70,000 years ago via physical migration) nor can we facilitate geopolitical diplomacy in a "two-dimensional" space (as was done prior to the digital era). Without a unifying factor to orient all groups toward universal human rights, conflict will continue to be increasingly complex, and our appreciation for others will be reduced to physically isolated interactions.

Psychologically, the implications of an increasingly digitally connected world amid an increasingly noisy, disconnected physical world are new and challenging. When we begin to understand how the noise of the digital space bleeds into the physical space and fogs our perspectives, we can begin to see why groups and individuals are unknowingly falling into various stages of the *Cycle of Conflict* – or worse – choosing to abandon it entirely. We will discuss these implications next.

CONFLICT

IV.iii PSYCHOLOGY: THE GOODNESS PARADOX

As we reflect on our origins, we begin to realize that pain is omnipresent and seems to have always been so. Yet, throughout human history, goodness has prevailed. If we look closely, we can see that where there is pain and suffering, good people tend to take a stand against it. In-groups formed through misguided collusion may fail to see the good; however, when more people are involved, there is usually at least one person – or perhaps one sub-group – who speaks up for what is right and good. The beauty of the digital era is that more voices are heard, potentially amplifying those who advocate for goodness.

Richard Wrangham coined the term, *The Goodness Paradox*, referring to the puzzling coexistence of our capacity for both extreme violence and profound kindness. This tension has shaped human behavior for millennia, rooted in billions of years of cellular evolution. Wrangham writes, "A great oddity about humanity is our moral range, from unspeakable viciousness to heartbreaking generosity. From a biological perspective, such diversity presents an unsolved problem. If we evolved to be good, why are we also so vile? Or if we evolved to be wicked, how come we can also be so benign?"[299]

Understanding human DNA and the behavioral traits we inherited from our ancestors allows us to begin unraveling the mystery of humanity's 'goodness paradox.' How can we reconcile our capacity for both selflessness and cruelty?

Religious ideologies and philosophies have worked to reconcile this question with guides to moral behavior (i.e. Christianity's seven virtues and seven deadly sins, Buddhism's Five Precepts and the Eightfold path, Hinduism's Yamas and Niyamas, Islam's Five Pillars and Islamic Virtues, Judaism's Ten Commandments and Ethical teachings of the Torah, Confucianism's Five Constant Virtues, Taoism's Three Treasures, the Greek's Four Cardinal Virtues, Stoicism's four stoic virtues, Sikhism's Five Thieves versus the Five Virtues, Zoroastrianism's three core principles, Native American's concept of harmony with the natural world, etc…). While an entire series of books could be dedicated to exploring these guides, we will focus here on their commonality: a shared emphasis on values like compassion, honesty, humility, self-control, and dignity.

These guides promote ethical behavior, social harmony, and personal spiritual growth, demonstrating a universal recognition of the

---

[299] Richard Wrangham, *The Goodness Paradox: The Strange Relationship Between Virtue and Violence in Human Evolution* (Pantheon, 2019), 2.

IV. PERSPECTIVES, PERCEPTIONS, & PSYCHOLOGY

need for a moral framework within the confines of human rights. This raises a crucial question: if goodness is inherent across all cultures, what drives us to choose one path over another? And can we ever fully understand the roots of such profound moral duality?

By examining these questions through the lens of equality, we can better understand not only where we have succeeded in recent history, but also where we have faltered – and how we can prevent further harm to the human person to ensure a more just and compassionate future.

Human tendencies to dehumanize others based on differences like language, appearance, sex, and race are deeply rooted in both evolutionary and social psychology. As we well know by now, humans categorize themselves into groups, leading to "us" vs. "them" thinking. This often results in in-group favoritism and out-group degradation, where those who are different are seen as less human or trustworthy. Differences such as language or skin color become more pronounced, fueling prejudice and stereotyping. These biases are reinforced by cultural influences that associate specific traits with social values.

The *Goodness Paradox* is deeply intertwined with the psychological mechanisms that govern human behavior. At its core, human morality and its dualities stem from our evolutionary journey and the way our brains are wired to respond to social and environmental pressures. Evolutionary psychology suggests that the same traits that enable kindness and altruism within groups also predispose humans to conflict and aggression when dealing with outsiders. This duality likely evolved as a survival mechanism, allowing early humans to cooperate effectively within their groups while defending against external threats.

One of the key psychological mechanisms at play is empathy, which acts as a driving force for kindness and altruism. Empathy allows individuals to understand and share the feelings of others, fostering cooperation and social harmony. However, studies suggest that empathy is often biased toward in-group members.[300] This bias can lead to selective compassion, where individuals extend care and kindness to those within their group while remaining indifferent or even hostile toward out-group members.

Additionally, cognitive biases like the fundamental attribution error and the out-group homogeneity effect influence how we perceive the goodness of our actions compared to the vile acts of others. These biases lead us to oversimplify out-group behaviors and assign negative traits to those who are different, reinforcing stereotypes and justifying

---

[300] Cikara, M., Bruneau, E., & Saxe, R. (2011). Us and them: Intergroup failures of empathy. *Current Directions in Psychological Science, 20*(3), 149-153.

dehumanization. In-groups tend to attribute others' behavior to internal traits while underestimating external situational influences.[301] As a result, even individuals with a capacity for profound kindness may participate in or condone actions that harm out-group members when these biases are left unchecked.

The *availability heuristic* – a psychological tendency to judge the frequency or likelihood of events based on how easily examples come to mind – can skew our understanding of morality and plays a key role in shaping our perceptions of the frequency of goodness or wickedness.[302] For instance, the prevalence of negative news in the digital age often amplifies perceptions of violence and cruelty of out-groups, overshadowing acts of kindness and generosity. This creates a paradoxical world where we are constantly bombarded with images of human suffering, even as charitable efforts flourish in the background.

Neuroscience further sheds light on this paradox. Studies have shown that the same neural networks associated with empathy and compassion are also involved in processing aggression and conflict.[303] This overlap suggests that the capacity for both good and evil is biologically ingrained, with environmental and social factors determining which path individuals or groups choose to follow.

Despite these psychological mechanisms to try to understand this paradox, humanity's ability to create systems of ethical thought and behavior demonstrates an adaptive capacity for self-reflection and moral growth. Moral frameworks across cultures share common values, such as fairness, compassion, and justice, which provide tools to counteract biases and promote human goodness. These frameworks are essential for transcending the evolutionary predispositions that drive in-group favoritism and out-group hostility.

The digital era presents unique challenges and opportunities for moral development. On one hand, it amplifies voices advocating compassion and justice, allowing individuals from diverse backgrounds to unite for common causes. On the other hand, the same digital platforms can fuel tribalism, misinformation, and dehumanization by reinforcing echo chambers and intensifying ideological divides.[304]

The solution lies in leveraging psychological insights to build empathy beyond the geopolitical in-group. Educational initiatives, cross-cultural dialogues, and transparent communication can help

---

[301] Ross, L. (1977). The intuitive psychologist and his shortcomings: Distortions in the attribution process. In L. Berkowitz (Ed.), *Advances in experimental social psychology* (Vol. 10, pp. 173–220). Academic Press.
[302] Kahneman, D. (2011). *Thinking, fast and slow*. Farrar, Straus and Giroux.
[303] de Waal, F. B. M. (2009). *The age of empathy: Nature's lessons for a kinder society*. Harmony Books.
[304] Tajfel & Turner, *Social Identity Theory*, 1979.

individuals recognize and counteract their biases. By emphasizing shared human dignity, we can foster an inclusive moral framework that aligns with the universal values found in religious and philosophical traditions.

Despite the challenges posed by the Goodness Paradox, humanity's capacity for self-reflection and adaptation offers hope for increased equity in humanity. By recognizing the psychological and evolutionary mechanisms that drive both kindness and cruelty, we can actively work to counteract biases that fuel conflict and division. Moral frameworks across cultures and traditions provide valuable tools for fostering empathy, justice, and dignity, which are essential for overcoming our predispositions toward in-group favoritism and out-group hostility.

In the digital era, the stakes are higher than ever in establishing humanity as one in-group. The interconnectedness of our world offers unprecedented opportunities for collaboration and mutual understanding, but it also amplifies the risks of tribalism and misinformation. To navigate these complexities, we must prioritize education, cross-cultural communication, and transparent dialogue. By emphasizing shared human dignity and universal values, we can build a more inclusive and compassionate society.

Ultimately, addressing the psychology of conflict requires collective action. As individuals, communities, and nations, we now know that we have the power to choose kindness over cruelty, inclusion over exclusion, and understanding over division. The path forward lies in leveraging our shared humanity to create a future where goodness prevails – not as a fleeting response to suffering, but as the foundation for lasting peace and progress.

IV.iv THE SOURCE OF DIGNITY
WHY CONFLICT IF WE ARE WIRED TO EVOLVE TOGETHER?

As we reflect on human history, we see a paradox: while we have made remarkable evolutionary leaps in cooperation, we also witness moments when extreme discontent of others' ideologies threatens to destroy that progress, catalyzing human-degrading conflict. **This again raises a fundamental question: if we are wired to evolve together, why do we still engage in conflict?**

Each human being possesses a unique dignity among nature, defined by the innate characteristics that we come to recognize in everyone. These characteristics – free will, moral virtues, and intellect – enable self-determination and the achievement of complex goals. They are expressed through our capacity for moral growth, our choices, and our ability to shape our own path in life to create a positive influence on the lives of those around us. This individual dignity connects us with others, forming communities capable of achieving greater goals through collaboration. So, we ask again, why do we experience human-degrading conflict in this cooperative framework?

The evolution of humanity reflects a profound shift from individual survival to collective well-being. Enabled by early Technological Advancements such as agriculture, electricity, or digital communication, we have laid the groundwork for communal welfare and social complexity. Initially, dignity was linked to individual status within small groups, but as human societies grew, Ideological Developments introduced shared values that promoted mutual respect and cooperation. These norms, particularly within settled societies, transformed dignity into a collective good, essential to societal stability.

As societies grew and became more complex, the notion of dignity expanded to encompass a broader sense of shared identity and communal welfare. Larger, interdependent communities began emphasizing mutual respect, fairness, and collaboration – qualities crucial for social cohesion and stability.[305] Technological Advancements reinforced these shifts, favoring communal welfare and enabling more robust social structures.

Research suggests that as human groups transitioned from nomadic tribes to settled agricultural societies, moral norms became integral to

---

[305] Boehm, C. (1999). *Hierarchy in the Forest: The Evolution of Egalitarian Behavior.* Harvard University Press.

reducing forms of human-degrading conflict and fostering harmony.[306] Ideological Developments illustrate how dignity evolved not only as a personal trait but also as a collective value – demonstrated through empathy, collaboration, and equitable treatment – that underscored the inherent worth of individuals.[307] However, as societies grew larger and more interconnected, beyond geographical relationships, complex goals began to interfere with one another.

Throughout history, humanity has organized itself into in-group tribes, civilizations, empires, nations, and alliances to address these increasingly complex relationships and goals. Yet, humanity has rarely been *willingly* organized into a single group. Power dynamics often led groups to prioritize their ideologies over others, creating alliances that prevented voluntary unity. As ideological developments reinforced perceptions of superiority or exclusivity, human-degrading conflict remained inevitable.

Research has shown that the out-group homogeneity effect is more pronounced when people have minimal contact with the out-group. Lack of exposure increases the reliance on generalized stereotypes, which can contribute to dehumanization.[308] However, the digital world offers unprecedented opportunities for connecting humanity, reducing the out-group homogeneity effect, and fostering greater understanding of the value that each of us provide. As noted, this opportunity must be approached freely, with a sincere recognition of the responsibility in building unity and equity over division and hierarchy.

When individuals recognize one another as members in the same dignified humanity, human-degrading conflict is rare. Instead of division, conflict often becomes a force for growth and cooperation. This transformation relies on the recognition of shared dignity – a concept rooted in Ideological Developments that prioritize moral growth and empathy. Shared dignity requires international recognition of every individual's complex wants, needs, and desires, as well as responsible leadership grounded in respect and compassion.

Failing to do so by categorizing out-group members, individuals are prone to dehumanization, diminishing the humanity of others and reinforcing in-group societal hierarchies. Empathy, by contrast, requires seeing others as unique individuals with diverse perspectives

---

[306] Richerson, P. J., & Boyd, R. (2005). *Not by Genes Alone: How Culture Transformed Human Evolution.* University of Chicago Press.

[307] Tomasello, M. (2019). *Becoming Human: A Theory of Ontogeny.* Harvard University Press.

[308] Ostrom, T. M., & Sedikides, C. (1992). Out-group homogeneity effects in natural and minimal groups: The mediating role of differential memory for in-group and out-group behavior. *Personality and Social Psychology Bulletin, 18*(3), 302-309.

and experiences that can benefit one's own experience.

As we have witnessed, conflict at the individual level often finds resolution through the recognition of shared dignity. However, as societies have evolved, conflict has expanded beyond individuals and small communities to encompass entire groups and nations, often losing the humanity that these groups enshrine. When nations go to war, individuals within each nation often have no direct contact with those in the opposing nation, exacerbating dehumanization in the worst ways.

In the digital era, technological advancements have the potential to transform these dynamics. By increasing exposure and fostering understanding across cultural and national boundaries, AI and digital platforms will reduce out-group biases and promote empathy. Over time, this could shift the out-group mindset toward an international "in-group" founded on shared dignity. As humanity becomes more interconnected, we stand at a unique crossroads in history – where our collective choices can enable a universal recognition of human dignity.

The chapters ahead will outline humanity's evolutionary journey from an out-group mindset to this potential future of shared dignity. By learning from history, we can embrace the tools of the modern age to create a world that values every individual, not as part of a fragmented system of groups, but as part of a united humanity.

IV.v CLOSING THOUGHTS

Today, the digital world is so engaging that it allows us to feel as though we are perceiving events firsthand, even if they are occurring on the other side of the world or originate from fictional messages. These digital sources shape our perspectives and opinions as if we had direct, unfiltered experiences. However, these perspectives – increasingly developed through news, social media, the internet, or television – often prioritize one ideology over another. The result?

We become internally divided despite being a part of a single humanity. As the goodness paradox becomes more evident in our everyday lives, we witness unnecessary political power escalated to human-degrading conflict. The division begins to surface in simple, everyday encounters – like seeing someone wearing a shirt that represents something we dislike, whether it be a sports team, a political party, a philosophical idea, or national symbol. In that moment, we instinctively categorize them into an out-group. Yet we are always left with the free will of a choice: to see people as individuals with equal human dignity or as members of a group that differs from our values.

Humanity's evolutionary journey – shaped through ideological developments, political power dynamics, and technological advancements – has created a social system that celebrates the goodness and exceptionality of those within our circles. Although good, this system often makes it difficult to recognize the goodness and exceptionality of those who think or act differently. By thriving on the competition of ideas, we have inadvertently created an environment where it is challenging to see shared human dignity without being reminded of the small things that divide us.

Political power, inherently built to implement ideologies, often seeks to strengthen its position by seeking in-group support to justify its actions. To draw power and influence from the in-group, it becomes necessary to distinguish oneself from the rest of humanity, often by embracing a sense of exceptionalism. This reliance on political power to drive progress has created a system where power comes with the great responsibility of supporting the in-group it represents.

History has shown repeatedly that such responsibility and power is often too much for one person – or one group – to bear. This "overdose" of power frequently manifests itself in rash decisions to engage in unnecessary human-degrading conflict. The burden of power raises an important question: How do we avoid the overdose of power in order to maintain the dignity of humanity? We will discuss this next.

CONFLICT

V

POWER AS AN ADDICTION

Historically, political power has been the primary tool for groups to reinforce ideologies and maintain order. When wielded responsibly, power can be a force for good – promoting stability, justice, and progress. However, unchecked power has often led to corruption, destabilization, and human-degrading conflict. Like a drug, power is intoxicating and addictive, requiring care, self-awareness, and ethical restraint to avoid its destructive consequences.

In today's world, we increasingly witness disagreements escalating into human-degrading conflict. Something as trivial as a snide remark towards another person implies a position of power over the other, and any encouragement of such behavior perpetuates human-degrading conflict. These moments mirror the larger struggles humanity faces in managing power dynamics responsibly, underscoring how even subtle power imbalances can erode relationships and human dignity.

Humanity has an inherent desire to do good; over time, humanity has developed ideological concepts to reinforce positive behavior and discourage harmful actions. These ideologies are often "written in blood" – born from the pain of past human-degrading conflict. History shows that we only address harm once it becomes impossible to ignore, underscoring our inability to predict what we have yet to experience.

Despite our best intentions, we still struggle with following the rules we create. This chapter will examine the complex role of power in conflict, exploring how it can both fuel and resolve tensions. Most importantly, we will discuss the critical role of community in surrounding those with power, ensuring it is exercised responsibly, ethically, and with accountability.

CONFLICT

V.i THE DEVELOPMENT OF UNCHECKED POWER

The cognitive revolution marked a turning point in human history, introducing advanced thinking that significantly accelerated humanity's development. Over the past few millennia, ideological developments, political power dynamics, and technological advancements have transformed human societies, enabling unparalleled progress.[309] Tools and innovations allowed one person to perform the work of many, and formal education cultivated specialized knowledge, laying the foundation for the distinct cultures and belief systems we see today.

However, early leaders of the Neolithic period had little understanding of how rapid technological and ideological progress would create conflicts on such a large scale. Their focus remained on the positive development of civilizations for the good of the humanity that surrounded them, yet their limited evolutionary capacity to manage power laid the groundwork for unchecked authority. This paved way for group dynamics entering into the earliest forms of written history.

History reveals how centralized power often resulted in "overdoses" of authority. From the conquests of Alexander the Great to the rise of global misinformation networks today, the common thread is humanity's inability to restrain power when concentrated in the hands of a few. Centralized power that prioritizes in-group growth over general human dignity, historically lays the groundwork for competition that can result in complex human-degrading conflict. Such actions highlight the dangers of societal structures that concentrate power in the hands of a single individual or a small group.[310]

In witnessing history, the accepted level of human suffering has only increased despite efforts to prevent it. Although we must certainly hold powerful individuals accountable in the eyes of history for their human-degrading actions, we must also recognize that the power they wielded was not theirs alone. Rather, it was developed through an enabling societal structure that fed power to these individuals.

Power emerges from societal systems that empower a few members to be responsible for the acts of the many. Civil society, based on hierarchical structures, has existed for less than 2% of human evolution – only 300 to 400 generations. Such rapid development has outpaced humanity's evolutionary ability to responsibly wield power.

Human biological evolution is remarkably slow. Changes in

---

[309] Smithsonian Museum of Natural History, *Human origins*.
[310] Scarre, C. (2013). *The Human Past: World Prehistory and the Development of Human Societies* (3rd ed.). Thames & Hudson.

V. POWER AS AN ADDICTION

response to environmental pressures take thousands, if not tens of thousands, of years.[311] With each human generation spanning 20 to 25 years, evolutionary responses can take well over 400 generations. Thus, humanity is not equipped to adapt quickly to the challenges posed by centralized power. This challenge has left humanity vulnerable to the dangers of unchecked authority.

Unchecked power, which often lasts only a generation or two before intervention makes way for a new ideology, has historically been a fleeting threat. However, the stakes are higher than ever. Modern technological advancements have exponentially increased individual capabilities to destabilize political power dynamics, creating the potential for irreversible human-degrading conflict. Nuclear weapons, AI, and global misinformation networks are just a few examples of how modern power dynamics can spiral out of control.

Today, humanity stands at a critical juncture. The concentration of unchecked power has brought us to a point where the consequences of abuse could be catastrophic. To avoid an irreversible "overdose," we must evolve quickly – we must recognize that we have a problem and find reasonable ways to work against such power. In doing so, we can begin rethinking how power is distributed, exercised, and restrained in a rapidly advancing world. If unchecked power is an addiction humanity cannot yet manage, how do we begin to address it in an era of unprecedented global challenges? We will discuss ideas for this, next.

---

[311] Boyd, R., & Silk, J. B. (1997). *How humans evolved*. W. W. Norton & Company.

V.ii THE FIRST STEP TO OVERCOMING ADDICTION

The first step to overcoming addiction is to recognize that we have an addiction in the first place.[312] Humanity, throughout history, has demonstrated an addiction to power. This addiction manifests in the hierarchical structures that we construct, which, while enabling progress, often place a disproportionate amount of authority in the hands of a few. Over time, these structures repeatedly show their fragility, as the accumulation of unchecked power corrupts, overwhelming individuals with responsibilities far beyond natural capacity. This inevitably leads to unstable political power structures.

Addiction thrives on denial. In recovery, denial is the greatest barrier, often preventing individuals from confronting the harm they perpetuate. Similarly, humanity has been slow to acknowledge the destructive consequences of concentrated power. Consider the fall of the Roman Empire, where unchecked imperial authority created a cycle of instability and corruption, or more recent corporate scandals, where opaque leadership allowed abuse and exploitation to flourish. These examples reveal a pattern: when power is too centralized, accountability erodes, and the structure crumbles under its weight.

Recognizing our addiction to power and hierarchical structures is not an act of blame but a responsibility to understand and address our limitations. In the medical world, mutual-help groups for addiction recovery have shown that accountability and community are crucial for recognition of one's responsibility.[313] These groups thrive on principles of transparency, shared responsibility, and mutual respect – principles that could be transformative if applied to power dynamics. Hierarchical systems, while enabling progress, often become corrupted because the responsibility they place on individuals exceeds natural human capacities. In the same way that mutual-help groups create environments of trust and accountability for individuals, international frameworks or forums for leaders could foster collective responsibility and transparency. Fostering transparency and mutual respect, akin to the accountability fostered in mutual-help groups – where dignity and trust are foundational – would create an environment for leaders to work together in managing their political power dynamics. So, what are some actionable steps we can take?

---

[312] American Psychiatric Association. (2013). *Diagnostic and statistical manual of mental disorders* (5th ed.). Arlington, VA: American Psychiatric Publishing.
[313] Kelly, J. F., & White, W. L. (2011). *Addiction recovery management: Theory, research, and practice.* Humana Press.

V. POWER AS AN ADDICTION

Imagine a world where leaders participate in forums akin to mutual-help recovery groups, candidly discussing the pressures they face, the mistakes they have made, and the lessons they have learned. Such gatherings would not only humanize those in power but also build systems of trust between leaders, their teams, and the public. Transparency would become a cornerstone, breaking the cycle of secrecy and isolation that often accompanies positions of authority.

This transparency, however, must be reciprocal. In return for openness from leaders, the public must commit to fostering a respectful environment when engaging with those in leadership roles. Mutual respect ensures that leaders and citizens alike see each other as human beings, acknowledging both the weight of responsibility and the shared goal of a better society which fosters equality and dignity.

The solution is not to dismantle hierarchies entirely but to reimagine them as systems of shared leadership. Rather than relying on rigid, vertical hierarchies, we can begin to see a flattened hierarchy which provides support at all levels – up and down. Leadership, particularly political leadership, could be reframed as a form of servant leadership, where political power is subordinate to the people it serves.

Mutual-help groups teach us that recovery from addiction is not about erasing the past but about transforming harmful patterns into constructive ones. Similarly, leadership models that rotate responsibilities, emphasize consensus, and prioritize accountability could shift humanity away from power structures that are corrupt, toward structures that uphold power through equality and dignity.

The first step to overcoming power addiction is simple yet profound: admitting that no single individual can, or should, bear the burden of absolute power. This recognition invites us to embrace shared responsibility and cooperative leadership, creating a future where humanity values collaboration over control. It is only by addressing our collective addiction to power that we can begin to build systems where power serves the many, rather than consuming the few.

Admittedly, these ideas may seem idealistic, and one might argue, 'If it worked, we would have done this already.' The truth is that implementing a cooperative structure as described above is extremely difficult – not because the world is simply full of bad people, but because we are wired by evolution to trust ourselves over others. Thus, a flattened hierarchy will immediately find disagreement at all levels of, reinforcing the need for a more traditional vertical hierarchy. But what if we knew how to disagree in ways that encouraged trust, empathy, dialogue, and growth rather than distrust and hate for one another?

V.iii MINIMIZING OTHERS' BELIEFS TO FEEL COMFORTABLE WITH OUR OWN

Often, when we encounter disagreement, our minds instinctively scan for reasons why we are right to enforce our own ideology. This reaction, rooted in our evolutionary history, is a survival mechanism – a mental shortcut designed to protect our worldview, which we perceive as an extension of our identity and security. Today we call such reactions confirmation bias, ingroup bias, or cognitive dissonance reduction.[314] While this instinct once served us well in small, tightly knit groups, it now creates challenges in a globalized, interconnected world.

As we stand at a juncture between an opportunity for global peace or continued human-degrading conflict, it is crucial to examine how these instincts influence our actions today. Despite knowing, as Gandhi warned, that "an eye for an eye makes the whole world blind," we continue behave in ways that perpetuate cycles of mistrust and hostility. From geopolitical conflicts to interpersonal disagreements online, we often minimize or dismiss others' beliefs to preserve our own sense of comfort and correctness. For humanity, this is expected, given that we instinctually avoid out-group interaction or unfamiliar dialogue as a means to minimize life-threatening conflict.

This tendency, though natural, prevents genuine dialogue and understanding, which becomes detrimental in an increasingly connected world. By avoiding or internally invalidating opposing perspectives, we deny ourselves the opportunity to gain experience and growth. Instead of building connection, we reinforce division, making cooperation and mutual respect required for human dignity impossible. The result is not just the perpetuation of small-scale conflicts but the amplification of systemic issues that escalate into larger, more destructive forms of human-degrading conflict.

Recognizing this instinct is the first step toward enabling the mutual help and cooperation that we discussed in the previous section. If we are to move toward global peace, we must learn to challenge our reflexive need to be "right" and instead cultivate empathy, curiosity, and humility. These qualities are not just moral virtues but practical tools for conflict resolution, fostering environments where trust and dialogue can thrive in upholding equality and dignity.

---

[314] Festinger, L. (1957). *A theory of cognitive dissonance*. Stanford University Press.

V.iv CLOSING THOUGHTS

To reduce human-degrading conflict, we must enable dialogue, empathy, and trust. This requires us to disable the addictive power structures that have even caused well-intended figures to slip into actionable human-degrading conflict.

Understanding power as an addiction not only frames power in a relatable way, but also highlights the responsibility and accountability that necessarily come with the power that freedom provides through our inherent dignity. Power, especially when it impacts the lives of others, must never be taken lightly. Nor should it rest in the hands of a single person, nation, or ideology. Instead, power must be shared continually through open dialogue, fostering the equitable integration of ideas and resources across humanity.

If we fail to address power in this way, we will perpetuate human-degrading behaviors and outcomes. By centering ourselves on the principle of universal human dignity, we can better appreciate the intrinsic value of humanity and recognize the urgent need for actionable steps to confront the modern threats to our survival.

The next chapter will explore specific threats to humanity and propose actionable steps to address them, offering a path forward to prevent Quadrant Four of the *Cycle of Conflict* by creating systems that uphold dignity for all.

VI

GLOBAL CHALLENGES: THREATS TO OUR SURVIVAL

Humanity faces unprecedented challenges that threaten our survival by undermining the value of our shared dignity. Given their critical nature, these issues are deeply embedded in our political power dynamics, making them sensitive topics for many. From environmental changes and resource scarcity to geopolitical instability and technological misuse, these threats are deeply intertwined with the dynamics we have highlighted in the *Cycle of Conflict*.

Where do these challenges fit within the *Cycle of Conflict*? Are they merely symptoms of deeper divisions, or do they function as catalysts for further human-degrading conflict? And if we come to understand human dignity as a universal value, would these threats be diminished?

This chapter will explore these critical questions, delving into the role of global challenges that have perpetuated conflict and examining the political power dynamics that hinder humanity's ability to address these threats in a unified way. The solutions are within our reach – only if we recognize the urgency of acting together as a single humanity.

VI. GLOBAL CHALLENGES: THREATS TO OUR SURVIVAL

VI.i ENVIRONMENTAL CHANGES

As we mentioned in Chapter I, environmental challenges we face are defined as external forces beyond short term control. Whether or not they were caused by human activities may remain a debate, but the facts are clear: there has been a 1.1°C (2°F) rise in global temperatures since the late 19th century, with significant impacts on weather patterns, sea levels, and ecosystems.[315] In response to environmental change, the United Nations formed the *Paris Agreement*, an inclusive document ordered towards limiting humanity's negative impact on environmental changes.[316]

As humanity acknowledges these changes, resulting dynamics have created resource conflicts, climate migration, inequity through indirect accountability, political polarization, economic instability in regions most affected, and new forms of colonialism to address the changing landscape. We will peel back these concerns to better understand how human dignity can remain a solution to the factors being influenced by environmental change.

One prominent example of the effects of environmental change is **increased resource conflicts**, particularly through disputes over freshwater and Arctic resources. The melting of glaciers and reduced freshwater availability have increased tensions between nations sharing water resources, such as the ongoing disputes over the Indus River Basin between India and Pakistan. Reduced flows of fresh water have heightened mistrust and competition between these countries.[317] Similarly, Arctic ice melting has escalated competition among nations like Russia, Canada, China, and the United States for untapped oil, gas, and mineral resources. This rivalry has led to increased militarization and geopolitical posturing in the region, threatening long-term cooperation.[318]

Climate migration and the rise of nationalism further underscore the negative impacts of environmental change on political power dynamics. Forced displacement due to rising sea levels and extreme weather events has affected millions, particularly in vulnerable regions such as Bangladesh and Pacific Island nations. Host countries often struggle to accommodate climate refugees, resulting in heightened

---

[315] National Aeronautics and Space Administration (NASA). (n.d.). Global climate change: Evidence. NASA's Goddard Institute for Space Studies. https://science.nasa.gov/climate-change/evidence/
[316] United Nations. (2015). *Paris Agreement*. Retrieved from https://unfccc.int/sites/default/files/english_paris_agreement.pdf
[317] Singh, A. (2021). Water disputes between India and Pakistan: A climate change perspective. *Water International*, 46(4), 409–427.
[318] Pincus, R., & Ali, S. H. (2016). Have you heard of Arctic geopolitics? *Foreign Affairs*, 95(4), 117–128.

nationalist and prejudiced sentiments.[319] Furthermore, restrictive immigration policies in Europe and North America have raised human rights concerns and contributed to regional instability, as governments attempt to curb the influx of climate migrants.[320]

Inequities in climate responsibilities highlight the divide between developed and developing nations. Many developing countries, which are disproportionately affected by climate change, argue that industrialized nations are largely responsible for greenhouse gas emissions but fail to provide sufficient financial or technological support for mitigation and adaptation. The slow progress of the *Green Climate Fund*, established to assist developing countries, has deepened mistrust and exacerbated tensions between the Global North and South.[321] Additionally, disagreements over carbon markets and emissions reduction commitments have led to conflicts, as seen during the Paris Agreement negotiations, where wealthier nations faced criticism for not meeting financial pledges.[322]

The militarization of climate responses represents another concerning trend. Many countries now view climate change as a national security threat, prioritizing defense-driven strategies over cooperative solutions. For instance, the U.S. Department of Defense has labeled climate change as a "threat multiplier,"[323] prompting investments in military infrastructure to address climate-related risks, rather than investing in global mitigation efforts.[324]

Political gridlock and polarization also hinder effective climate action. In several nations, climate change has become a divisive political issue, with partisan divides obstructing comprehensive policy responses. The United States, for example, has faced legislative gridlock on critical climate policies, such as carbon pricing, due to strong opposition from fossil fuel lobbies and entrenched political power dynamics.[325] Similarly, the *Yellow Vest Movement* in France exemplifies the populist backlash against policies like carbon taxes, where citizens protested the perceived economic burden of climate

---

[319] McAdam, J. (2011). *Climate Change, Forced Migration, and International Law*. Oxford University Press.
[320] Betts, A. (2013). *Survival Migration: Failed Governance and the Crisis of Displacement*. Cornell University Press.
[321] Pauw, P., Klein, R. J. T., Menzel, C., & Theuer, S. L. (2020). *Post-Paris: Reconciling climate finance targets and instruments*. Springer Nature.
[322] Rajamani, L. (2016). The 2015 Paris Agreement: Interplay between hard, soft and non-obligations. *Journal of Environmental Law, 28*(2), 337–358.
[323] U.S. Department of Defense. (2014). *2014 Climate Change Adaptation Roadmap*. https://www.acq.osd.mil/eie/Downloads/CCARprint_wForward_e.pdf
[324] Schwartz, P., & Randall, D. (2003). *An abrupt climate change scenario and its implications for United States national security*. Pentagon Report.
[325] Dunlap, R. E. (2014). Climate change and partisan polarization in the US Congress. *Climatic Change, 124*(3), 451–466.

VI. GLOBAL CHALLENGES: THREATS TO OUR SURVIVAL

initiatives on lower-income groups.[326]

Economic instability driven by climate change complicates these issues further. The global shift toward renewable energy has created tensions between fossil fuel-dependent economies, such as Saudi Arabia and Russia, and nations advancing green energy policies. This shift has resulted in price wars and conflicts over energy dominance, as seen during the oil price wars of the early 2020s.[327] Additionally, climate-induced changes to agricultural patterns have disrupted global food supplies, sparking trade restrictions, price volatility, and disputes over agricultural exports. For example, export bans during droughts have strained relations between nations reliant on food imports.[328]

Finally, **climate colonialism** highlights how wealthier nations and corporations exploit developing countries for resources essential to green technologies, such as rare earth minerals, while leaving these nations to bear the environmental and social costs. This dynamic has fueled resentment and allegations of neo-colonialism, as vulnerable regions grapple with the disproportionate burden of climate change and global economic inequities.[329] China's extensive involvement in Africa's extraction of critical minerals, particularly rare earth elements, has sparked discussions about neo-colonialism, "debt-trap" diplomacy, and environmental exploitation. China has provided significant loans to African nations, totaling $182.28 billion between 2000 and 2023, to fund large-scale infrastructure projects such as roads, railways, and power plants, which has raised concerns about debt sustainability and sovereignty for recipient countries.[330] Due to corruption in many of these countries, the loans often fail to go towards the intended projects. In return, these agreements often leave African nations to contend with significant environmental degradation, financial indebtedness, and social inequity.

As a threat to our survival and a clear catalyst for human conflict, environmental changes must be addressed with human dignity and the respect for life at the forefront. The examples of current-day conflict with respect to environmental challenges demonstrate that political power dynamics remain divisive by region,

---

[326] Gössling, S., Humpe, A., & Bausch, T. (2019). Yellow Vests and climate change: Societal resistance in a politically divided France. *Journal of Sustainable*
[327] Overland, I. (2020). The geopolitics of renewable energy: Debunking four emerging myths. *Energy Research & Social Science, 68,* 101549.
[328] von Braun, J. (2019). Global food systems under climate change. *Science, 365*(6457), 507–509.
[329] Bassey, N. (2016). *To Cook a Continent: Destructive Extraction and the Climate Crisis in Africa.* Pambazuka Press.
[330] Boston University. (2024). *Chinese loans to Africa database: 2000-2023.* Global Development Policy Center.

despite symbolic unity through the Paris Agreements. Similar to the UDHR, the world must come together to acknowledge universal standards in order to prevent human-degrading conflict. This means fostering equitable solutions that prioritize collaboration over competition and ensuring that vulnerable populations are protected through the recognition of universal human dignity.

Addressing climate-induced challenges requires a global commitment to sustainable practices, transparent governance, and investment in resilient infrastructure that benefits all nations, not just the wealthiest. By emphasizing fairness in resource allocation, supporting climate migrants with compassion, and eliminating exploitative practices such as climate colonialism, humanity can transform environmental challenges into opportunities for unity and progress. The continued human-degrading conflict surrounding these challenges presents a clear and present danger not only to the long-term sustainment of humanity but also to the delicate balance of the Earth and other vital forms of life that cohabitate Earth with us. Ultimately, by embedding human dignity into climate action, we have the potential to build a more just and harmonious world for future generations.

VI. GLOBAL CHALLENGES: THREATS TO OUR SURVIVAL

VI.ii WORLD-ENDING WAR

As the world becomes more interconnected, differences in political power dynamics become increasingly relevant. Humanity's largest atrocities from war have occurred within the last century – an astonishingly brief period, representing only the last 0.05% of human existence. While the World Wars may feel distant, their legacy continues to shape global political and military strategies, particularly through the concept of *deterrence* – a strategic military policy designed to prevent an adversary from taking undesirable actions, such as aggression or human-degrading conflict, by convincing them that the costs or consequences of such actions will outweigh any potential benefits. With increasingly human-degrading military threats looming over humanity, how can we ensure that they are mitigated to prevent history from repeating itself?

In the aftermath of the Second World War, humanity made significant efforts to prevent such atrocities from recurring. Institutions like the *United Nations* and agreements such as the *Geneva Conventions* were established to promote peace and protect human rights. Through these strides, international progress towards peace was made.

Today, we have international councils and organizations such as the *United Nations Security Council, Human Rights Council, International Court of Justice, International Criminal Court, the European Union, African Union, Organization of the American States, Association of Southeast Asian Nations, The Commonwealth, The North Atlantic Treaty Organization, The International Committee of the Red Cross, The World Trade Organization, The International Monetary Fund, The G20,* and more.

While these councils and organizations are designed to promote peace and cooperation, their structures and policies can create perceptions of inequality or elitism. Further, international policies from these councils and organizations are quick to isolate countries through sanctions, military alliances, and global trade agreements, which can influence extremism and power in isolated countries. When paired with modern military weapons, to include nuclear weapons, the threat of an isolated country finding itself amid unstable political power dynamics can rapidly increase into irreversible human-degrading conflict.

To reduce the risk of isolated powers taking irreversible action, one of the most prominent post-war strategies has been deterrence through military force, particularly nuclear deterrence. Advocates argue that the prospect of mutually assured destruction has significantly reduced the likelihood of large-scale global wars. The principle of Mutually Assured Destruction (MAD – as noted in Chapter III in the Cold War-era), posits that the catastrophic consequences of nuclear conflict function as a strong disincentive for direct confrontation between nuclear-armed states.[331] While this may contribute to relative peace among these powers, it comes at a significant moral and societal cost.

Nuclear deterrence reinforces a system of forced inequality through implied superiority and overwhelming power. Only a handful of nations possess nuclear weapons, and their strategic monopoly creates a hierarchy that marginalizes non-nuclear states, forcibly subordinating their ideologies in the international order. This dynamic often exacerbates tensions, as nations without nuclear capabilities may feel compelled to align with nuclear powers for protection or, conversely, strive to develop their own nuclear programs to counter perceived life-threatening ideologies or vulnerabilities.[332] This struggle perpetuates instability and increases the magnitude of the *Cycle of Conflict* between nuclear "haves" and "have-nots," fostering resentment and undermining the principle of equality and human dignity.

Since the advent of nuclear weapons, large-scale conflicts have occurred within the territories of non-nuclear nations, highlighting the immoral tendency of nuclear "haves" to displace physical conflict onto "have-not" nations. In effect, nuclear deterrence has created implicit "fighting zones" and "non-fighting zones," where the burden of conflict is disproportionately borne onto non-nuclear states. Lacking clear international policies to support refugees or those displaced by war as conflicts begin to arise, people in "have-not" nations are often caught in the crossfire as nuclear "haves" wield their military-diplomatic influence on foreign lands. That is not to say that this is the only reason for the conflicts in non-nuclear regions of the world; often, the root causes of non-nuclear conflicts in non-nuclear nations are complex and multifaceted.

The policy of nuclear deterrence carries significant ethical implications, as the threat of total annihilation places humanity's future in the hands of a few decision-makers, concentrating immense power in an unelected elite class of international humanity. This dynamic perpetuates fear, mistrust, and competition among cultures rather than fostering cooperation and mutual recognition of human dignity and respect. It also imposes a moral cost on all of humanity, as the mere

---

[331] Freedman, L. (2003). *The Evolution of Nuclear Strategy* (3rd ed.). Palgrave Macmillan.
[332] Sagan, S. D. (1996). Why do states build nuclear weapons?: Three models in search of a bomb. *International Security, 21*(3), 54–86.

VI. GLOBAL CHALLENGES: THREATS TO OUR SURVIVAL

existence of nuclear weapons implies that their use – even if emotionally charged or accidental – remains a possibility and therefore an acceptance of mass human-degrading conflict.

Although nuclear deterrence may have tampered down the idea of a world-ending war, it has also locked humanity into a system of perpetual human-degrading conflict. To ensure these threats are mitigated, global advocacy for disarmament and equitable international security have taken place. Since the peak of the MAD policies during the cold war, nuclear weapons have slowly faded away, but they are still a significant tool in the arsenal of power-wielding nations. In 1986, the total number of nuclear warheads worldwide was approximately 70,300. By early 2024, this number had declined to an estimated 12,100, marking a reduction of over 80%.[333] Further efforts such as the *Treaty on the Prohibition of Nuclear Weapons* represent a step toward challenging the narrative of deterrence and promoting a vision of security that does not rely on the implicit threat of offensive destruction.[334]

While nuclear deterrence may remain one of the few mechanisms capable of threatening humanity into avoiding another World War for generations to come, the threat of its use through MAD policies arguably poses a larger moral threat.

The growing emphasis on equality and human dignity offers hope for a future that prioritizes cooperative security over destructive power. Advancements in technology can now limit the ability of bad actors to inflict harm without the need of resorting to nuclear means.

International councils and organizations must redouble their efforts to build justice systems that uphold and enforce human rights for all nations, regardless of their nuclear status or alliances. By embracing these principles, humanity can move away from a reliance on deterrence and subjugation, transitioning to a world where peace, equality, and mutual respect – through the recognition of human dignity – serve as the foundations of global stability.

---

[333] Federation of American Scientists. (2024). *Status of world nuclear forces*. Retrieved from https://fas.org/initiative/status-world-nuclear-forces

[334] United Nations. (2017). *Treaty on the Prohibition of Nuclear Weapons*. Retrieved from https://treaties.un.org

CONFLICT

VI.iii BUREAUCRATIC ORGANIZATIONS

The existence of bureaucracy dates back to the beginning of civilization, evolving alongside humanity's need for structure and order. While bureaucracy itself may never directly cause out-group human-degrading conflict, its mechanisms often contribute to a subtler but equally troubling form of degradation: the erosion of individual purpose and value in work. At some point, when humans have achieved their basic needs, the work they perform must have a meaning beyond something tangible. In large institutions, the necessity of repetitive, impersonal, or tangibly-purposeless tasks can alienate individuals from the intrinsic dignity of their labor, reducing their work to a mere function rather than a meaningful expression of their humanity.

Philosopher Karol Wojtyla, in *The Acting Person*, emphasized that human dignity is inherently tied to meaningful action.[335] For Wojtyla, work is not simply a means of survival or productivity – it is a fundamental way through which individuals realize their personhood through human dignity and contribute to the greater good of humanity. When bureaucracy strips work of its personal significance, it risks reducing individuals to "cogs in a machine," disconnected from their capacity for self-determination and moral agency. This is a profound affront to human dignity.

The lack of purpose found in some forms of work within bureaucratic systems reflects a deeper crisis of understanding of purpose in modern institutions. Individuals are not merely defined by their roles but by their intentional actions and the values they embody through their work. Bureaucracy, when unchecked, undermines this dynamic by prioritizing efficiency and process over the flourishing of the human person. This creates inequality, often left unchecked by satisfying impersonal work with a sense of achievement through extrinsic motivations alone (i.e., monetary reward).

Participation in work is essential for preserving human dignity in collective settings. It entails not only contributing to a shared purpose

---

[335] Wojtyla, K. (1979). *The acting person*. D. Reidel Publishing Company.

but also engaging authentically with others in a way that respects their personhood. Bureaucracies that fail to foster genuine participation through intrinsic motivations risk alienating individuals from their communities, reinforcing a sense of isolation and insignificance.

To address these challenges, institutions must strive to align their structures with the inherent dignity of the human person. This means reimagining bureaucratic work as an opportunity for individuals to express their creativity, exercise moral responsibility, and form direct links in which they can see how they contribute to the ideologies and goals of the organization to benefit the common good. By doing so, organizations can become not merely systems of bureaucratic order, but arenas for meaningful human action that aligns with human dignity.

With respect to the *Cycle of Conflict*, bureaucratic work is itself a form of human-degrading conflict, resulting from a political power dynamic that has slowly turned from its original ideologies to prioritizing power and economic benefit over human dignity. In a world increasingly dominated by large institutions motivated by money, the challenge lies in transforming work towards the ideologies of an organization which aligns with the overall good of society in some manner. To make this a reality, economies and political policies must also find ways to reward the creation of meaningful work that achieves continued recognition of human dignity and value in work.

Through technological advancement, many of the bureaucratic roles that society fulfills today can soon be filled by technology so that humanity may center their human work towards tasks which have human value and purpose. As Wojtyla reminds us, the value of work is not measured solely by its outcome but by its capacity to affirm and uplift the dignity of those who perform it. By finding a direct incentive for work that provides value and meaning, rather than simple job creation and economic growth, societies will begin to see positive changes in the treatment of individuals within humanity – a treatment of others oriented towards human dignity. Recognizing this truth is essential for creating institutions that serve humanity, rather than simply subsume it.

CONFLICT

VI.iv NATURE'S INSTINCT TO EVOLVE

In Part I of this book, we explored how life within nature evolved over hundreds of millennia, culminating in the emergence of humans. Throughout this evolutionary timeline, survival was driven by one fundamental force: competition. Species of all kinds developed survival instincts, striving to dominate their physical environments to secure resources needed to live, reproduce, and thrive. Today, we witness this same competitive drive within humanity. Whether we consciously acknowledge it or not, we instinctually prioritize the in-groups we belong to – our family, local community, country, or even humanity as a whole – seeking to protect and perpetuate their survival over others.

This prioritization is rooted in our evolutionary survival instincts and remains deeply embedded in our psychology. At its core, nature defaults to protect the innermost group to which it belongs, instinctively protecting those closest to them. Psychologically for humans, this protection can expand outward if we find reasoning to do so. For example, one might justify the protection of their community as inherently supporting the well-being of their family, but this justification requires some recognition of shared values within the community. Similarly, if we trust our community, we might extend this justification to protecting broader groups, such as a nation. If we trust our nation, we may even embrace the idea of protecting humanity as a whole, seeing this as inclusive of all smaller groups with shared value.

This concept aligns with Abraham Maslow's *Hierarchy of Needs* and the psychological model of *Social Identity Theory*, which posits that individuals derive part of their identity and self-esteem from the groups to which they belong.[336] However, we know from Chapter IV that these group-based affiliations also create out-group boundaries that complicate our appreciation for shared value. Our evolutionary instincts, while beneficial in smaller-scale settings, make it challenging to acknowledge and reinforce human dignity on a global scale.

When trust between groups is absent – whether between communities, nations, or cultures – our evolutionary instincts exacerbate divisions. We default to questioning the intentions of those we cannot relate to or trust, reinforcing an "us versus them" mentality. This lack of trust is the greatest barrier to expanding our circle of influence to include all of humanity. Until we evolve beyond these survival-driven instincts as a species, we will continue to struggle with

---

[336] Tajfel & Turner, *Social Identity Theory*, 1979.

fostering universal trust and prioritizing human dignity across cultural and national boundaries.

Acknowledging our evolutionary inheritance within the *Cycle of Conflict* is critical to understanding the challenges of global unity and the limitations at our current state in evolution. Each time a form of human-degrading conflict occurs, the *Social Identity Theory* is reinforced, solidifying instinctual divides between groups. By recognizing these instincts in our ideologies and political power dynamics, we can consciously begin to counteract them.

Fostering trust and empathy across groups requires deliberate effort and systemic change. Once we can consciously begin to counteract our evolutionary instincts that force us into human-degrading conflict, humanity move toward a more inclusive understanding of dignity – one that transcends both the physical and abstract boundaries created by in-group favoritism.

VI.v CLOSING THOUGHTS

We possess the capacity to resolve the challenges we face in the present moment by recognizing who we are as an evolutionary species. In many ways, we become our own greatest obstacle when we fail to recognize the inherent unity of our shared humanity. Whether confronting environmental crises, the looming threat of world-ending war, bureaucratic inefficiencies, or the instincts ingrained in us by evolution, we hold within ourselves the ability to transcend these barriers through the recognition of universal human dignity.

Our unique intellectual and moral capacities set us apart in the natural world. Unlike other species, we are capable of self-reflection and deliberate action to accomplish complex goals. We can look within ourselves, evaluate the consequences of our choices, and freely decide who we want to be. Furthermore, we have the rare ability to recognize when unchecked power becomes destructive – not only to others but to ourselves – and then give up that power for the greater good.

Nature's instinct is to dominate, to overpower the life around it in a relentless drive for survival. We have inherited this instinct, and over time, we have evolved to expect human-degrading conflict as an inevitable part of life. On a family scale, this manifests in the need for parents to create a safe environment for their children, one that shields them from external threats. On a community scale, leaders are expected to provide infrastructure, medical accessibility, and protective services like police and fire departments to ensure the survival of their people. On a national scale, military powers rise to provide mutually assured destruction as a means of deterrence from out-groups. **These efforts, while certainly protective and in line with evolution, often arise from a place of fear and as a means of passively hedging human-degrading conflict at the expense of human dignity.**

But what if we decided to actively work against human-degrading conflict by promoting human dignity? What if we could move beyond the evolutionary instincts that drive us to divide and defend? What if we could live not as fragmented groups, but as one unified people?

These questions challenge us to imagine a world where human dignity is universally recognized and actively upheld. A world where we channel our intellectual and moral capacities not toward protective instinct, but toward building bridges of trust, empathy, and respect. Such a vision may seem idealistic, but it is attainable. It begins with acknowledging that our greatest strength lies not in overpowering one another, but in choosing to live in harmony as one human family.

VI. GLOBAL CHALLENGES: THREATS TO OUR SURVIVAL

CONFLICT

PART THREE

A VISION FOR A UNIFIED HUMANITY

VII

BASIC REQUIREMENTS FOR UNITY

If we hope to attain some form of universal human dignity, it is fair to say that we need an established, inclusive system of international unity to go with it. Until we achieve universal human dignity, the persistence of human-degrading conflict will remain a defining feature of our world. Therefore, it is necessary to lay out a clear roadmap for attaining this unity.

International unity does not imply uniformity or a loss of cultural identity; rather, it requires systems that enable peaceful coexistence and mutual respect. Each nation, culture, and individual bring unique values and perspectives that, when harmonized, strengthen our shared humanity. The challenge lies in creating frameworks that transcend short-term national interests and individual greed, fostering a collective commitment to the greater good. Endeavors such as these require not only institutional reforms, but transformations in how we view ourselves – no longer as isolated entities seeking out survival but as interconnected parts of the same ecosystem seeking to thrive as one.

Achieving this unity demands addressing the root causes of negative action within the *Cycle of Conflict*. Ideological narratives must celebrate diversity while discouraging extremism. Education must remain accessible and adaptable, equipping future generations with the tools to understand the past in order to navigate complex global challenges collaboratively. Political systems must prioritize freedom, equity, responsibility, and transparency. Economic systems must promote businesses that support dignified ideological values, rather

VII. BASIC REQUIREMENTS FOR UNITY

than pursuing forms of human-degrading capitalist growth as their primary end. Similarly, technology and communication must be harnessed to bridge gaps rather than deepen divides.

This chapter will walk through each of these topics, providing a framework for a unified humanity. Before investigating the critical areas, we must first distinguish between differing concepts of social unity. Although many forms, we will go in depth on the concepts of Globalism versus Internationalism. Globalism has gained prominence in the digital era, and while it may feel like a step toward unity, we need to carefully examine why Globalism may be a step in the wrong direction in terms of evolutionary progress amid respect for diversity.[337]

---

[337] Boyd & Silk, 1997

VII.i ACHIEVING STEADFAST INTERNATIONALISM AMID GLOBALISM'S RISE

While humanity has made strides toward unity beyond national borders, we have yet to achieve meaningful international cooperation that respects diversity and advocates for diplomatic solutions aligned with the ideological, political, and cultural sensitivities of sovereign nations.

Regionalism, for instance, has functioned as a steppingstone toward broader internationalism by fostering collaboration within manageable geographic units (i.e., the European Union). However, its focus on regional integration lacks the global scope needed to address challenges related to universal human dignity.

Transnationalism has emphasized the role of non-state actors in addressing issues that transcend government boundaries, such as global health crises or environmental sustainability (i.e., Amnesty International). Yet, it lacks a framework to reconcile the differing political structures necessary for widespread change.

Cosmopolitanism closely aligns with human dignity through its emphasis on shared humanity and moral obligations that take precedent over national or regional loyalties (i.e., The United Nations). However, it often overlooks the ideological, political, and cultural nuances that are meaningful to individuals and communities, which can inadvertently lead to division.

Each of these frameworks has provided valuable tools to identify commonalities that support human dignity. However, humanity now must decide that, if we wish to address the threats addressed in Part Two, then we must function as a united whole of sovereign nations – bridging our cultural, political, and religious differences, while at the same time respecting and preserving them.

Globalism, in its pursuit of integration, often challenges national sovereignty by prioritizing a unified system over the independence of individual nations (i.e., the World Trade Organization). While it fosters interconnectedness, it can come at the expense of cultural and political self-determination.

Internationalism, on the other hand, emphasizes cooperation while preserving national sovereignty, culture, and collective action. This framework envisions a unified world composed of sovereign nations, seeking universal diplomacy as an alternative to human-degrading conflict. Internationalism upholds the dignity of nations and individuals alike, promoting unity through diversity.

VII. BASIC REQUIREMENTS FOR UNITY

While we live in a predominantly international world today, we continue to fall short of willingly adhering to internationalism's ideals. For instance, the International Criminal Court enforces international law, yet participation remains voluntary, reflecting the principle of sovereign choice. This freedom ensures that internationalism respects the dignity and autonomy of nations while requiring nations and their citizens to recognize their shared responsibility to improve humanity. If executed effectively, internationalism builds a unifying system that enhances sovereignty and individual freedoms rather than undermining them.

The rise of globalism challenges us to reimagine international cooperation in a way that respects sovereignty while addressing the realities of our interconnected and conflict-driven world. While globalism enforces international laws to promote ideologies that may lack universal consensus, steadfast internationalism offers a path forward that embraces unity through diversity and prioritizes the dignity and freedom of all people. The challenge lies in ensuring that national sovereignty and individual freedom remain aligned with the dignity of the human person.

How did we come to recognize the need for sovereignty? After World War I, the League of Nations was devised to promote peace through international cooperation while balancing national sovereignty.[338] However, punitive measures in the Treaty of Versailles undermined human dignity, sowing resentment and contributing to the outbreak of World War II. These shortcomings revealed the necessity of recognizing sovereignty and human dignity while seeking to achieve collective peace.

At the conclusion of World War II, the United Nations was created to prevent human-degrading conflict by promoting internationally recognized rules and principles. Article Two of the Charter enshrines the principle of sovereign equality, saying, "The Organization is based on the principle of the sovereign equality of its members."[339] This principle acknowledges that human dignity is best preserved when nations are treated as equal partners rather than subordinates in a global order.

Despite setbacks such as the Cold War, initiatives like the UDHR and the Paris Agreement demonstrate the potential of sovereign

---

[338] League of Nations. (1924). *The Covenant of the League of Nations.* Retrieved from https://www.un.org/en/about-us/un-charter/league-of-nations

[339] United Nations. (1945). *Charter of the United Nations.* Retrieved from https://www.un.org/en/about-us/un-charter

collective action to uphold dignity and address global issues. However, when international initiatives lack universal adherence, nations often assert political power to defend ideologies they perceive as under threat. These struggles highlight both the fragility of internationalism and its necessity for preserving universal human dignity in a world of sovereign nations.

To uphold human dignity in this context, deliberate action is required. To begin, we must show respect by treating each other equally. The following sections will outline steps to strengthen international cooperation, protect national sovereignty, and resist the erosion of autonomy in the face of rising global power.

VII.ii IDEOLOGICAL NARRATIVES AND EDUCATION

Internationalism cannot thrive without a shared understanding of world history, the value of freedom, the importance of mutual respect, and the ideological narratives that have shaped humanity across time. Education within all nations plays a vital role in fostering this understanding, creating a foundation for cooperation rooted in dignity and responsibility.

Without a scholastic approach to these ideas, ideological narratives from cultures and nations other than our own often become relegated to "out-group" thinking. Lack of education reinforces division and misunderstanding, as people fail to see the universal human aspirations underlying out-group narratives – aspirations that often aim to uphold dignity, justice, and equity. When stripped of historical and cultural context, foreign ideologies are too easily dismissed as alien or incompatible with our own, rather than being seen as contributions to humanity's collective journey toward a better world.

Education is not merely the transmission of facts and ideas, but the cultivation of critical thinking and empathy. It allows individuals to recognize that every ideological narrative, whether rooted in religion, philosophy, or politics, represents an attempt to understand the human condition and address the challenges of human coexistence. By engaging with these narratives, we develop the tools to see the dignity inherent in every person, every nation, and every "out-group" we encounter. Through education, we are offered a window to a world beyond our "in-group" norms so that we can play a larger role in supporting humanity.

While it is our inherent freedom to interpret history and narratives as we wish, it is also our responsibility to do so thoughtfully and with an openness to understanding perspectives beyond our own. By educating individuals on the diversity of ideological guides and their historical significance, we lay the groundwork for mutual respect and responsible action. This, in turn, helps bridge the ideological divides that hinder internationalism and supports a vision of global unity that values human dignity above all.

Education, therefore, is not just a tool for academic advancement but a moral imperative. It equips individuals with the knowledge and perspective necessary to navigate a complex, interconnected world responsibly, ensuring that internationalism is built on a foundation of shared understanding and respect for sovereignty and autonomy. As ideological narratives influence the ways we interpret history, justice, and human dignity, they inform the future political systems we create to govern ourselves.

By fostering a deeper understanding of these narratives, education lays the groundwork for political structures that reflect shared values and uphold the dignity of all people through the societal structures in which we live. In the next section, we will examine how political systems shape – and are shaped by – these ideological foundations, exploring their role in creating a world where freedom and responsibility coexist in balance.

VII. BASIC REQUIREMENTS FOR UNITY

VII.iii POLITICAL SYSTEMS

Political systems define the structures through which societies govern themselves, allocate power, and ensure – or fail to ensure – an accountable societal structure. These systems shape how decisions are made, how laws are enforced, and how individuals and groups interact with authority. From democracies to authoritarian regimes, political systems represent humanity's diverse attempts to balance power, freedom, and responsibility.

One common misconception is that political systems inherently dictate the economic systems that accompany them (i.e. democracy is tied to capitalism, authoritarianism is tied to communism). However, history shows that political structures are highly adaptable, often blending with various economic models to meet societal needs. For example, democracies have successfully integrated socialistic policies, such as universal healthcare and welfare programs, while maintaining the freedoms and protections central to democratic ideals. Similarly, Authoritarian regimes, such as the Chinese Communist Party (CCP), have embraced capitalist principles to fuel economic growth and consolidate power. This is exemplified by the CCP's economic reforms in 1978, which incorporated market-oriented strategies, and continues today with the throttling of market autonomy. The regime allows certain capitalist activities but maintains strict control over the economy to ensure alignment with state objectives.

While political systems are not tied to specific economic frameworks, they profoundly influence the social and cultural environments in which those frameworks operate. For instance, a democratic system prioritizes freedom of expression and equitable representation, creating space for diverse economic policies to emerge through public discourse and consensus-building. In contrast, an authoritarian system centralizes decision-making, often limiting public participation in economic choices while prioritizing the regime's stability and goals.

The relationship between political systems and human dignity is complex, as we found in the *Cycle of Conflict*. At their best, political systems promote justice, protect individual freedoms, and foster societal well-being. At their worst, they concentrate power in ways that marginalize, oppress, or exploit out-group behavior. Democracies, for example, have mechanisms to safeguard minority rights, though they are not immune to populism or systemic inequities. Authoritarian regimes may ensure stability but often do so at the expense of personal freedom and participatory governance.

Key questions arise as we analyze political systems through the lens of human dignity. To what extent do they protect freedoms such as speech, assembly, and self-determination? How do they address power imbalances within and between societies? Can political systems adapt to changing social and technological landscapes without eroding fundamental human rights? These questions underscore the importance of designing governance structures that not only preserve sovereignty but also prioritize justice, equity, and the inherent dignity of all individuals.

The best political systems to address internationalism are those that balance sovereignty with global cooperation, fostering structures that respect the diversity of nations while promoting shared goals. Systems rooted in democratic principles – where transparency, accountability, the voice of the people, and the rule of law are prioritized – tend to create an environment conducive to international partnerships. These systems empower nations to participate in collective decision-making while protecting their unique cultural and political identities. However, for internationalism to thrive, political systems must also evolve to address global challenges such as climate change, world-ending wars, bureaucratic deadweight, and technological advancements as we discussed earlier in Chapter VI. This requires not only national governance that upholds human dignity but also a commitment to international frameworks that champion equality, justice, adaptability, and the responsible use freedom through sovereignty for all.

By responsibly aligning political systems with the principles of cooperation and respect – with human dignity as the foundation – we can forge a path toward a more unified and dignified international community. While political systems define how power is distributed and governance is structured within nations, their interaction with economic systems can profoundly shape societal outcomes. These intersections will be explored further in the next section.

VII. BASIC REQUIREMENTS FOR UNITY

VII.iv ECONOMIC SYSTEMS

Economic systems define how societies allocate resources, produce goods and services, and distribute wealth. They reflect the priorities, values, and social contracts of a given population, shaping not only the material realities of individuals but also the opportunities available to them. From free-market capitalism to centrally planned economies, mixed economies to cooperative systems, the diversity of economic models reflects humanity's ongoing attempts to balance efficiency, equity, and sustainability.

Capitalism, a system rooted in private ownership and market-driven decision-making, emphasizes individual initiative and innovation. By incentivizing competition, capitalism has spurred technological advancements, increased productivity, and raised living standards for many. However, it has also faced criticism for fostering economic inequality and prioritizing profit over public welfare. Left unchecked, capitalism can exacerbate disparities, concentrate wealth in the hands of a few, and undermine social cohesion.

Socialism, in contrast, focuses on collective ownership and centralized planning, aiming to distribute resources more equitably. In theory, socialism addresses the pitfalls of capitalism by prioritizing social welfare, reducing income inequality, and ensuring access to basic needs such as healthcare and education. However, centralized control can lead to inefficiencies, stifled innovation, misguided goals, and challenges in responding to rapidly changing economic environments.

Hybrid systems, such as those in Scandinavian countries, have sought to balance socialism's emphasis on equity with capitalism's dynamism, creating mixed economies that leverage the strengths of both models.

Most nations today operate within mixed economies that combine elements of both capitalism and socialism. These systems recognize that neither extreme offers a complete solution to societal needs. Mixed economies allow private enterprises to drive innovation while implementing government interventions to address market failures, regulate industries, and provide social safety nets. This approach has proven effective in addressing complex challenges such as poverty, climate change, and economic shocks.

At their core, economic systems within internationalism must be measured by how well they uphold individual freedoms and human dignity. Systems that prioritize equitable access to resources and technology, opportunities for humanity's upward mobility, and protections against exploitation align most closely with the values of internationalism. Conversely, systems that concentrate wealth, marginalize vulnerable populations, or prioritize growth at the expense of sustainability, risk undermining international cooperation and shared prosperity.

Economic systems also play a critical role in fostering or hindering internationalism. Market-driven economies can encourage global trade and innovation but may also exploit weaker economies, perpetuating cycles of dependency and inequality. Centrally planned or protectionist economies, while safeguarding domestic priorities, can isolate nations from the collaborative potential of internationalism. The most effective economic systems are those that integrate fair trade practices, sustainable development goals, and mechanisms to reduce global disparities, creating a foundation for mutual benefit and shared progress.

By understanding the strengths and limitations of various economic models, we can identify pathways that promote not only national prosperity but also global harmony. The challenge lies in designing economic systems that harness innovation and efficiency while prioritizing equity and sustainability, ensuring a dignified future for all.

VII. BASIC REQUIREMENTS FOR UNITY

VII.v TECHNOLOGY AND COMMUNICATION

Technological advancement has dramatically accelerated human evolution in countless ways. In the context of international unity, it has revolutionized global communication, enabling instantaneous dialogue across continents, cultures, and languages. This shift represents a monumental change, particularly in its potential to facilitate effective diplomacy needed with internationalism. In a world where, historically, miscommunication or the absence of dialogue contributed to cycles of human-degrading conflict, technology now provides an opportunity to bridge divides and foster cooperation – not only at the political level but at individual levels. Thanks to technology, we can share ideas and values in ways tailored to resonate with others, transcending linguistic and cultural barriers.

This book itself is a testament to the role of technology in communication and collaboration. From accessing reliable sources and translating them, to leveraging AI for idea refinement and ensuring compliance with copyright and trademark laws, technology has been an indispensable tool in its creation. Beyond that, digital tools have made it possible to format, market, and distribute this work with unprecedented speed – delivering it to your eReader or local bookstore in a matter of hours. Such capabilities underscore the unparalleled connectivity and communicative power technology affords us today.

But with this technological power comes responsibility. How can we harness technology to foster respectful and effective communication, promoting internationalism rooted in dignity? How can we ensure that international order and law are framed through the lens of universal human dignity, rather than manipulation or exploitation? These are critical questions we must confront in an era where technology shapes nearly every aspect of our interactions.

While technology offers incredible opportunities, it also brings challenges, such as the spread of misinformation and the intentional distortion of facts. These threats demonstrate how freedom, without responsibility, can undermine the very unity we strive to achieve. Education and ethical stewardship are essential to ensuring technology serves humanity rather than divides it. Failure to use technology responsibly reflects a lack of respect for others and a disregard for the dignity inherent in all people.

To unite respectfully as one humanity, we must embrace technology as a tool for understanding and connection, while fostering a culture of accountability and truth. Only then can we navigate the complexities of global communication and use these advances to build a world rooted in mutual respect, shared values, and human dignity.

VII. BASIC REQUIREMENTS FOR UNITY

VII.vi CLOSING THOUGHTS

Humanity has yet to reach a moment in history where it can truly unite as one. While we have made significant strides in fostering understanding and collaboration, the persistent challenges of cultural divides, political disparities, economic inequalities, and technological misuse remind us how far we have to go. If we aspire to end human-degrading conflict, we must prioritize understanding one another, embracing the complexities of our differences as a foundation for unity.

Achieving this unity requires deliberate effort and commitment across all dimensions explored in this chapter. We must harness the power of education to cultivate empathy and respect for diverse ideological narratives. Political systems must evolve to balance sovereignty with cooperation, enabling nations to address global challenges while preserving cultural and national identities. Economic systems must prioritize equity and sustainability, ensuring that no society is left behind in the pursuit of shared prosperity. Finally, technology must be wielded responsibly, serving as a tool for connection, sustainability, and truth rather than division and manipulation.

The road to unity will never be without obstacles. However, steadfast internationalism offers a path forward – one that respects the sovereignty of nations while emphasizing the collective responsibility to uphold human dignity through our inherent freedoms. By integrating freedom with responsibility in every facet of human interaction, we can create systems and structures that allow humanity to thrive together under a shared international order.

The journey toward unity is not about erasing differences but about finding strength in diversity. By working together to bridge cultural, political, and ideological divides, we can build a world where human dignity is not a privilege but a universal right. Let us strive for a future where humanity moves forward not as fragmented nations or isolated groups but as a humanity united by our inherent dignity, shared values, and the pursuit of peace.

VIII

LEVERAGING TECHNOLOGY TO AID HUMAN DIGNITY

As humanity stands on the brink of an unprecedented technological revolution, the tools we create have the power to shape our societies in profound ways. From AI, AGI, and automation to biotechnology and advanced communication systems – technology offers a dual potential: it can uplift and empower, fostering greater equity, access, and dignity, or it can deepen divisions, amplifying inequalities and eroding human worth. The trajectory we choose depends not on the tools themselves, but on the principles guiding their use. This chapter explores how we must harness technology as a force for good, embedding human dignity into the heart of innovation to ensure progress serves humanity rather than diminishes or subdues it.

VIII. LEVERAGING TECHNOLOGY TO AID HUMAN DIGNITY

VIII.i THE EVOLVED USE OF TECHNOLOGY

Throughout history, humanity has continually evolved its use of technology, reshaping the way we interact with the world and each other. From the rudimentary tools of sticks and stones to the complexities of AI and the aspirations of AGI, technology reflects humanity's drive to innovate, adapt, and overcome challenges. At its core, technology has always been an extension of human ingenuity, addressing needs and solving problems in increasingly sophisticated ways.

Early technological advancements, such as the creation of tools for hunting and farming, allowed humans to survive and thrive in unforgiving environments. The development of materials like metal and the use of mathematics and science propelled societies into eras of construction, navigation, and exploration. Medicine extended lifespans and improved quality of life, while transportation and communication technologies bridged distances, enabling collaboration on unprecedented scales. Each breakthrough has contributed to humanity's growth, yet each has also introduced challenges – new power dynamics, resource dependencies, and ethical dilemmas.

Today, technological advancement can be broadly categorized into two primary forms: physical technology and digital technology. Physical technology refers to tangible innovations such as machinery, infrastructure, and devices we use in our daily lives – tools that directly interact with the physical world. Digital technology, on the other hand, encompasses intangible systems like software, networks, and data platforms, which increasingly govern how we interact with one another and make decisions. The rise of digital technology, especially, has blurred boundaries and accelerated change, influencing nearly every aspect of modern life as outlined in Chapter IV.

With the rise of capitalism, innovation in both physical and digital technologies have become a primary driver of economic mobility, offering pathways from poverty to wealth. However, this economic focus has also influenced political structures, often prioritizing technological advancement over ideological development. This prioritization has spurred significant progress but also created challenges, such as the inequities that arise when access to technology is unevenly distributed or when political systems fail to adapt to its rapid pace.

As technological advancements accelerate, our perception of these changes often lags behind their actual impact. Without sufficient understanding, we risk leveraging these tools in ways that exacerbate instability in our political systems and conflict rather than promoting human dignity. The instability identified in Quadrant Four of the *Cycle of Conflict* shows that, while technological advancements do not immediately disrupt ideological developments, they tend to destabilize political systems in the short term, leading to human-degrading conflict rather than fostering the adaptation necessary to advance dignity.

To use technology responsibly, we must recognize its forms and implications, balancing its potential for wealth creation and progress with the need for ethical stewardship and equal opportunity. Only by doing so can we guide technological advancements toward advancing humanity as a whole, ensuring they serve as tools of unity and equity rather than division and instability. This foundational understanding of technology's evolution will guide our exploration into its modern manifestations in digital and intelligent systems.

VIII.ii PHYSICAL TECHNOLOGY

Since the beginning of the agricultural revolution nearly 12,000 years ago, we have been dealing with a rapid evolution of physical technology. Up to this point, we had been using elementary tools to live lives within our small groups. As we began to understand how to use technology to benefit larger groups, civilizations grew at a rapid pace. With growth, came power. With power came the greed and destabilized political power dynamics that led to human-degrading conflict on mass scales, leading to nearly every great civilization's fall to date.

How have we learned from this? Are we implementing ideologies or political power dynamics to inhibit physical technology from creating greed or human-degrading conflict?

Unfortunately, due to our slow evolutionary processes, we have done little to address this. Today, tools are still invented for a specific purpose, often backed by a political or ideological initiative in mind. As tools are created, their invention often does not stop at their initial purpose. Anyone in a position of power can utilize nearly any piece of technology today. We trust humanity's inherent goodness to not be addicted with power, yet we have learned that humanity lacks the evolutionary ability to *not* be addicted or corrupted by power.

Take for example, the airplane. The Wright brothers, after their first successful flight in 1903, had felt they had created technology that would forever improve peace by improving transportation and exploration; however, when they flew and realized its capabilities for reconnaissance, they went to the military with an idea. In doing so, the airplane became militarized in WWI. Soon after reconnaissance pilots realized they could fly directly over the enemy to identify locations and targets, they also realized they could use the airplane to drop things on the enemy. They started by dropping bricks, rocks, steel darts, and hand grenades. This eventually led to carrying bombs. Soon, flyers would begin using handguns to shoot at ground targets or other aircraft.

In an interview during his later years, Orville Wright expressed, "We dared to hope we had invented something that would bring lasting peace to the earth. But we were wrong... I don't have any regrets about my part in the invention of the airplane, though no one could deplore more than I do the destruction it has caused."[340]

---

[340] Wright, O. (1943, April 17). Interview with the New York Times.

The intended use of technology, once it has been created, cannot be for an individual person to decide, even if they have wealth or political influence. Allowing such power for one person leads to the corruption of good things. We consistently find our troubled history encountering new forms of human-degrading conflict thanks to new forms of technology that are being used for unintended purposes.

How can we mitigate this in a world where we have determined that individual freedom, transparency, accountability, the voice of the people, and the rule of law are prioritized? Can we actually allow individual freedom if we limit access to such technologies?

Freedom must be the foundation for any society which recognizes the inherent value and dignity of the human person. Therefore, individual freedom must walk in line with responsibility. As we discussed in the last chapter, the source of such responsibility is the universally accessible education necessary for an informed society.

As we begin to understand the dilemma we face, we also begin to see the deeper issue with digital technology, which has the ability to achieve some level of intelligence in and of itself, mitigating the need for the human education and intelligence that is required for certain aspects of life. We will discuss this next.

VIII.iii DIGITAL TECHNOLOGY

Less than five generations ago, digital technology did not exist, until it was brought to life through the Zuse Z3 programmable computer in 1943.[341] Today, digital technology surrounds us nearly everywhere we go from the moment life begins. It acts as the brains of our wearable devices on our wrists, in our ears, on our fingers, and sometimes even inside of us. Even before birth, medical advancements use analog signals converted into digital readouts to monitor fetal development. Thanks to medical advancements aided by technology, the global under-five mortality rate has significantly declined over recent decades, dropping from 93 deaths per 1,000 live births in 1990 to 37 in 2022.[342] These technologies demonstrate how digital innovation, even in its evolutionary infancy, has transformed human life and health for the better.

The exponential rise of digital technology marks a significant departure from the slower, incremental changes of physical technology.[343] While physical tools like the wheel or the steam engine advanced humanity's evolution over centuries, digital innovations such as microprocessors, the internet, and AI have developed at an exponential pace. These leaps create profound impacts on how we live, work, and interact – impacts that are difficult to fully comprehend as they continue to unfold.

While the lessons of physical technology can offer guidance, the challenges of adapting to digital advancements are uniquely urgent. Physical tools advanced over centuries, giving time for political, economic, and cultural systems to adapt. The digital age, however, moves much quicker, leaving adaptation often struggling to catch up. This has created gaps in regulation, ethical considerations, and societal understanding. For instance, the industrial revolution introduced mechanized manufacturing that reshaped labor and economies while creating social upheaval, from unsafe working conditions to income inequality. Similarly, digital technologies have opened opportunities for wealth creation but also risks, such as increasing economic disparity and destabilizing traditional ideological and political dynamics.

The advent of AI has only accelerated this transformation. AI systems now power decision-making processes, influence markets, and

---

[341] Rojas, R. (Ed.). (2000). *The Architecture of Konrad Zuse's Early Computers*. Springer.
[342] World Health Organization. (2023). *Global progress in tackling maternal and newborn deaths stalls since 2015*. Retrieved from https://www.who.int/news/item/09-05-2023-global-progress-in-tackling-maternal-and-newborn-deaths-stalls-since-2015--un
[343] Kurzweil, R. (2005). *The singularity is near: When humans transcend biology*. Viking Press.

even perform creative tasks once thought to be uniquely human. Yet the rise of AGI – machines capable of learning and reasoning across a wide range of tasks at a human-like level – poses even greater challenges. AGI, while still largely theoretical, raises profound ethical and existential questions.[344] If realized, it could reshape industries, governance, and even the concept of work itself, making it imperative to ensure that such technologies understand the inherent value and dignity of every human person – and humanity's position in nature – in order to properly inform decisions.

Similarly, biotechnology, fueled by digital advancements, is transforming how we understand and manipulate life itself. From gene editing tools like CRISPR[345] to personalized medicine and synthetic biology, biotechnology holds immense promise for understanding genetic diseases, improving quality of life for the terminally ill, and even enhancing food security by sustaining international food supplies through efficient use of water and natural resources. However, these capabilities also carry risks, including bioethical dilemmas, potential misuse, and the exacerbation of inequalities in access to healthcare and technology. All of these questions must be addressed now in order to inform policy before such technologies are adopted by individual people.

Unlike previous eras, digital technology allows significant disruptions to occur without the need for traditional resources. A lone actor with access to digital tools can destabilize international norms, alter economic structures, or spread disinformation at unprecedented speed. These dynamics demand a reevaluation of how technological power is distributed and governed.

To harness digital technology responsibly, we must balance its potential for progress with ethical stewardship. Digital systems can democratize access to education, amplify marginalized voices, and solve complex global challenges. Yet they also carry risks, such as data privacy violations and the widening digital divide. Technologies like AGI and advanced AI must be developed with robust oversight, ensuring they serve humanity rather than foster conflict or inequality. Similarly, biotechnological innovations should align with principles of equity and sustainability, addressing the needs of the many rather than the interests of the few.

This moment in history offers us an unprecedented opportunity: to

---

[344] Russell, S., & Norvig, P. (2021). *Artificial intelligence: A modern approach* (4th ed.). Pearson.
[345] Doudna, J. A., & Sternberg, S. H. (2017). *A crack in creation: Gene editing and the unthinkable power to control evolution*. Houghton Mifflin Harcourt.

VIII. LEVERAGING TECHNOLOGY TO AID HUMAN DIGNITY

shape digital and biotechnological revolutions in ways that uphold human dignity, equity, and justice. How can we ensure these advancements contribute to a better, more equitable future? How do we prevent their misuse to sow division or perpetuate human-degrading conflict? Answering these questions will define how we navigate the digital era – not just as innovators, but as stewards of humanity's collective well-being.

VIII.iv HUMAN DIGNITY

The questions we face regarding technology are questions that we will continue to face for generations to come. They are complex, and often defy simple answers. However, history has provided a valuable framework for understanding how technology fits into the *Cycle of Conflict*. This framework allows us to anticipate the implications of technological advancements and identify the driving factors behind them. To ensure that technology supports stable political power structures and the ideologies we live by, we must anchor our approach in a fundamental principle: **the recognition of the inherent value and dignity of each human person.**

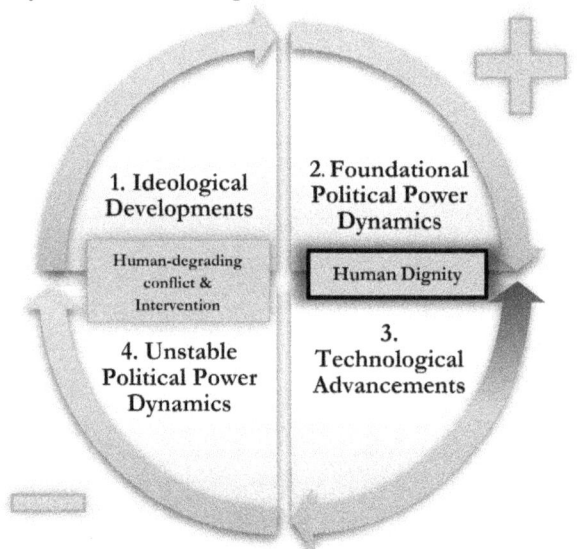

Reflecting once more on the *Cycle of Conflict*, and its associated factors, it is clear that human dignity does not limit us – it grounds us. It centers our potential to do good and prevents us from being drawn toward human-degrading conflict. While we often associate human dignity with ideological theories, throughout history, it has been deeply tied to belief systems as a means of understanding the value of the human person. Yet, unlike other ideological theories, human dignity is notoriously difficult to integrate into practice, particularly in political and technological initiatives. This difficulty arises from its perceived purity – a standard that feels nearly unattainable in a fractured and imperfect world.

VIII. LEVERAGING TECHNOLOGY TO AID HUMAN DIGNITY

However, human dignity, when genuinely embraced and implemented, possesses a unique ability to not only reorient political and economic systems, but to reorient individual relationships, too. It can guide technological advancements to prioritize the good of the individual rather than serving the interests of systems or ideologies alone. This shift in perspective allows technology to become a tool for empowerment, *not* power – a means to uplift humanity rather than perpetuate inequalities through various forms of human-degrading conflict.

In essence, human dignity offers an alternative to the in-group focus that has historically defined many ideologies. By placing the value of humanity as a whole at the center of our decisions, we create a framework that transcends divisions and seeks the good of all, regardless of group affiliation. This universal focus is not only necessary for addressing the challenges posed by modern technology but also fundamental to ensuring that technological advancements serve to uphold, rather than degrade, the shared dignity of all people.

CONCLUSION

We have traveled through the story of humanity, from its earliest origins to the present day, seeking a solution to end human-degrading conflict. Along the way, we have come to understand that our evolutionary instincts, combined with the weight of a bloodied history, have burdened us with a heavy backpack we must carry on the path to progress. Yet, the recognition of universal human dignity offers us a way to lighten this load – not by discarding our past, but by acknowledging it as a foundational reason for respecting our neighbors and moving forward together on the journey of life.

Humanity is a conflicted, complex species. What sets us apart is not the existence of degrading conflict, but our awareness of it – and our unique ability to evolve beyond it. Our capacity for growth, grounded in human dignity, is the key to building a future free of the divisions that degrade each other.

In this modern age, we are privileged to witness each other's perspectives on an unprecedented scale. Whether we approach truth from the vantage point of Group A or Group B, the global exchange of ideas through technology has provided an unparalleled opportunity for mutual understanding, if we remain open to it. Though the way we perceive truth may differ, the philosophies and logic laid down before us create a shared framework for seeking it as a unified humanity. By engaging with one another's perspectives and respecting the underlying logic of each worldview, we can foster healthy development and bridge divides.

CONCLUSION

Next time, when you look into the eyes of an unfamiliar face, recognize that their differences are secondary to the shared, inherent dignity within both of you. Their face should remind you – just as much as your very own face reminds you in the mirror – that regardless of cultural, physical, or ideological differences, every person carries the same fundamental worth on this world. By looking into the eyes of another and choosing to see dignity rather than division, we take a step closer to ending human-degrading conflict.

As we stand at the crossroads of our collective history and future, the journey continues. It always will, so long as we will it. Let it be one defined by the effort to live in harmony with one another, ensuring that human dignity is not an abstract ideal but a lived reality for all. In this endeavor, humanity's ability to reflect, evolve, and grow will be our greatest strength. Together, we can walk this path – lighter for having acknowledged our shared humanity – and create a world where dignity is not just recognized but universally upheld.

ABOUT THE AUTHOR

The Freedom and Responsibility Institute
seeks to advance an international culture of human dignity by
promoting the responsible use of freedom through education,
advocacy, and creating equitable opportunities.
To learn more, please visit
DignityThroughFreedom.org
Contact us at
info@dignitythroughfreedom.org
Or use the QR Code Below:

We appreciate your efforts
to help the world become a better place for all of humanity by
recognizing the inherent value and dignity of each person.

www.ingramcontent.com/pod-product-compliance
Lightning Source LLC
Chambersburg PA
CBHW020537030426
42337CB00013B/888